AESTHETIC LABOUR

Sara Miller McCune founded SAGE Publishing in 1965 to support the dissemination of usable knowledge and educate a global community. SAGE publishes more than 1000 journals and over 800 new books each year, spanning a wide range of subject areas. Our growing selection of library products includes archives, data, case studies and video. SAGE remains majority owned by our founder and after her lifetime will become owned by a charitable trust that secures the company's continued independence.

Los Angeles | London | New Delhi | Singapore | Washington DC | Melbourne

AESTHETIC LABOUR

Chris Warhurst &
Dennis Nickson

SAGE

Los Angeles | London | New Delhi
Singapore | Washington DC | Melbourne

Los Angeles | London | New Delhi
Singapore | Washington DC | Melbourne

SAGE Publications Ltd
1 Oliver's Yard
55 City Road
London EC1Y 1SP

SAGE Publications Inc.
2455 Teller Road
Thousand Oaks, California 91320

SAGE Publications India Pvt Ltd
B 1/I 1 Mohan Cooperative Industrial Area
Mathura Road
New Delhi 110 044

SAGE Publications Asia-Pacific Pte Ltd
3 Church Street
#10-04 Samsung Hub
Singapore 049483

Editor: Ruth Stitt
Assistant editor: Jessica Moran
Production editor: Sarah Cooke
Copyeditor: Aud Scriven
Proofreader: Katie Forsythe
Indexer: Judith Lavender
Marketing manager: Abigail Sparks
Cover design: Francis Kenney
Typeset by: C&M Digitals (P) Ltd, Chennai, India
Printed in the UK

© Chris Warhurst and Dennis Nickson 2020

First published 2020

Library of Congress Control Number: 2019956375

British Library Cataloguing in Publication data

A catalogue record for this book is available from the British Library

ISBN 978-1-8478-7084-1
ISBN 978-1-8478-7085-8 (pbk)

At SAGE we take sustainability seriously. Most of our products are printed in the UK using responsibly sourced papers and boards. When we print overseas we ensure sustainable papers are used as measured by the PREPS grading system. We undertake an annual audit to monitor our sustainability.

CONTENTS

LIST OF FIGURES
AND TABLES

FIGURES

TABLES

ABOUT THE AUTHORS

Chris Warhurst PhD FRSA is Professor and Director of the Warwick Institute for Employment Research at the University of Warwick in the UK. He is also a Trustee of the Tavistock Institute in London and an Associate Research Fellow of SKOPE at the University of Oxford. He is an internationally recognised expert on job quality and skills. He has published 16 books and more than 50 journal articles and 60 book chapters. He is or has been an expert advisor to the UK, Scottish and Australian Governments as well as to the OECD, Oxfam Scotland, Scottish Living Wage Campaign and Carnegie UK Trust.

Dennis Nickson is Professor of Service Work and Employment, University of Strathclyde. His primary research interests centre on work and employment issues in interactive service work, with a particular concentration on the retail and hospitality industries. His work has been published in journals such as *Work, Employment and Society*, the *Human Resource Management Journal, Human Resource Management* (US), the *International Journal of Human Resource Management, Industrial Relations Journal* and *Economic and Industrial Democracy*. Sole and co-authored books include *Human Resource Management for the Hospitality and Tourism Industries*, 2nd edition (Routledge, 2013). He is also Editor-in-Chief of *Employee Relations*.

ACKNOWLEDGEMENTS

Over the years what has become known as the 'Strathclyde Group' had a fluid complement. In alphabetical order, we would like to thank Anne Marie Cullen, Eli Dutton, Scott Hurrell, Eleanor Kirk and Johanna Macquarie (nee Commander) of the University of Strathclyde in Glasgow, Scotland for their fantastic research assistance and, in some cases, management of the projects that generated primary data for this book. Although she is no longer with us, dying tragically too young, we would also like to acknowledge the core participation of Anne Witz in the early stages of the projects that culminated in this book. We have also been lucky to have a number of excellent national and international research collaborators: Richard Hall and Diane van den Broek of the Universities of Monash and Sydney respectively in Australia, and Henrietta Huzell and Patrik Larsson of Karlstad University in Sweden.

There are a number of other people and organisations that have supported us as we sought to research aesthetic labour. The first were the Universities of Glasgow and Strathclyde. Other support, and in some cases funding, came from Allan Watt, Ken Mayhew, Ewart Keep, Caroline Stephenson, Lydia Rohmer, Jan Karlsson, the then Scottish Executive, Nuffield Foundation and Skillsmart. Finally, we acknowledge the UK's Economic and Social Research Council for funding the doctoral study of Anne Marie Cullen.

We would also like to acknowledge with profound thanks colleagues at SAGE for keeping faith with us over the years. Thanks to Kiren Shoman for initially working with us to develop the idea of the book, and to Ruth Stitt and Martha Cunneen for their infinite patience and much needed encouragement to bring the book to completion.

This book has been a genuine labour of love, taking far, far longer than we anticipated. For this reason, we also thank our families for their patience with our perseverance: Doris and Hannah; Susan, Christopher and Grace.

Last but not least, we would like to thank Whispers nightclub in Preston, England. There is an important story to be told about the sociology of small things from which big thinking is triggered. The job advertisement placed by Whispers in the *Lancashire Evening Post*, and that is the genesis of aesthetic labour, would be part of that story. A one-part Bench Punk Enterprise. The benches may have gone but the friendships remain – as do the aspirations for change.

1
APPEARANCES MATTER

Moira was an intelligent, well-dressed and attractive woman in her early 30s. She was the human resources manager of a boutique hotel, Hotel Elba, which counted amongst its guests minor rock stars and celebrities, well-heeled businesspeople and weekend holiday break yuppies. The hotel had an opulent style; all deep, dark colours and rich velvet drapes. Moira was reflecting on her hotel's hiring policies. She was staring at the company's recruitment advertisement and explaining that 'Nicole', the 'stylish', 'tasty', 'caring' and well-travelled young woman depicted in the advertisement, was meant to epitomise the type of workers that the hotel wanted: 'At Hotel Elba we didn't look for people with experience,' she said, 'they had to be pretty attractive looking people'. As Moira continued:

> The hotel owner is very sticky on the whole image thing ... attractive but friendly. There is probably a kind [of] look. It is this kind of not overly done up person but quite plain but neat and stylish. Someone who's got a nice smile, nice teeth, neat hair and [now laughing] in decent proportion. I wouldn't go for a fat person. It's that kind of pure, quite understated look.

Importantly, Moira noted how male employees were subject to similar criteria, with expectations of a 'neat appearance ... clean shaven... [making] an effort to look neat and tidy and presentable'. Using workers who look good and/or sound right is not confined to Hotel Elba; it is now mainstreamed in interactive service organisations in hospitality and retail and, as we discuss later in the book, increasingly beyond. These workers are hired because of the way they look and talk – or can be made to look and talk. Once employed, they are then instructed in how to dress and present themselves, and the use of body language and even speech to further enhance their appearance. For employers, such employees produce a desired style of service. It is what we term 'aesthetic labour' and its use is a deliberate managerial strategy perceived by employers to appeal to customers or clients and produce organisational benefit. This book examines this labour, placing it within the context of social and economic trends, how it is manifest in the workplace through the interactions of management, employees and customers or clients, and then, in turn, its social and economic effects.

DISCOVERING AESTHETIC LABOUR

The origins of our conceiving of aesthetic labour lay in a newspaper job advertisement that overtly stipulated the attractiveness of applicants. It was the early 1990s and we were both working at a university in Preston, in northern England. The town's history is long and illustrious but by the 1990s it was down on its luck. It had been an ancient market town made into a cotton mill boomtown in the industrial revolution of the nineteenth century. Serious worker unrest followed (Dutton and King, 1981) and Karl Marx and Charles Dickens visited the town to view the proletarian squalor. In the early twentieth century auto plants and engineering firms sprang up in the town. By mid-century, however, the mills had gone and the inland river port closed, and by the 1970s the auto plants and most of the other large employers had also left the town (Lambert, n.d.). De-industrialised, Preston suffered high levels of unemployment into the early 1990s, and unsung haunting melodies of better days gone by hung over the town.

In the midst of this economic gloom a job advertisement appeared in the local news-paper, the *Lancashire Evening Post* (see Figure 1.1 below). Some employers, it seemed, were still hiring. A local nightclub, Whispers, wanted new bar staff to start work immediately. Experience was not required but Whispers made it clear that it wanted very particular staff: applicants needed to be 'ATTRACTIVE' the advert stated in large, bold type.

Figure 1.1   Attractive bar staff wanted

Source: Reproduced with permission from the *Lancashire Evening Post* (1993), 1 September, p. 12.

The small and particular can have larger meaning and significance (Mills, 2000[1959]), and it was this advert that sparked our sociological imagination. It was a seemingly non-descript advertisement for a part-time, low-paid job tucked away in the back pages of a provincial newspaper, but the employer's stipulation for attractiveness as the sole hiring criterion opened up big questions about the nature of work and employment in economies increasingly dominated by interactive services such as hospitality and retail. We wanted to know the extent of aesthetic labour in these types of jobs and whether or not it extended beyond them. However, as Mills (2000[1959]: 364) stated, 'facts and figures are only the beginning of the proper study'. The main interest, he continued, should be 'making sense of the facts'. Beyond the level of demand for it, we also wanted to know how and why this labour is supplied, developed and deployed – and how it is experienced by workers and its consequences for those workers in an economy dominated by services and a society in which there is now greater emphasis on a person's looks. It is these questions that we seek to explore in this book. Questions that are crucial to understanding work and employment not just in Preston or even the rest of the UK, but in service-dominated economies throughout the world.

FOR APPEARANCES' SAKE

Whilst Preston has many claims to fame, we are not suggesting it is in this town that employers first became interested in and exploited the lure of their employees' appearance. The aesthetic appeal of workers has not gone unnoticed by employers in the past. As early as the sixteenth century the Society of Jesus – the Jesuits – were keen to recruit potential priests who, in appearance, deportment, conduct and style would not 'put the public off', according to Hopfl (2000: 204). The Society looked for candidates with 'a pleasing manner of speech and verbal facility, and also good appearance in the absence of any notable ugliness', because the priests' corporeality was 'part and parcel of the public face of the Society, its collective self-presentation' Hopfl states (pp. 204, 205). As the twentieth century unfolded and interactive customer services became more prevalent, private sector employers began to take commercial advantage of employee looks (see for example Belisle (2006) and Benson's (1983) discussion of the importance of the appearance of female employees in early Canadian and US department stores respectively). Indeed, Mills (1951) identified an emergent 'personality market' through which employers bought the personalities of service workers. This personality comprised the attitudes and appearance of these workers, who Mills referred to as 'the new little Machiavellians' (pp. xvii) for their manipulative capacities and their ability to 'sell' their personalities as part of their work. It is important to note, however, that these employers hired these physically attractive workers and then pretty much left them to get on with their job. It was the workers who first developed and then mobilised and deployed their looks in work – as Mills' flirtatious female department store worker illustrates in using money from her pay cheques to buy nice dresses that deliberately, 'focuse[d] the customer less upon her stock of goods than upon herself' and helped her 'attract the customer with modulated voice, artful attire and stance' (p. 175).

Unfortunately Mills' focus on 'personality' quickly narrowed to focus only on workers' attitudes, analytically ignoring their appearance. The reason might be a lack of employer intervention in employee appearance at that time, for example through training. It was, after all, the 1950s when customer service was still embryonic, as Mills recognised. This partial analysis, however, has continued more recently in Hochschild's (1983) seminal articulation of emotional labour. Hochschild draws on Mills' work and also notes the importance of flight attendants' attitudes and appearance in their interactions with customers for the airlines. 'Display is what is sold' (p. 90) Hochschild states, with airline companies seeking to standardise the appearance and transmute the feelings of flight attendants through recruitment and training. However, 30 years after Mills, she also quickly retired analysis of worker corporeality. We explore this important omission in more depth in Chapter 3. Here it is sufficient to note that much current research of interactive service work, framed by the emotional labour paradigm, has remained focused on attitudes rather than appearance – on employee feelings and not their bodies. As such it would be unfair though to single out Hochschild for this analytical myopia. Its cause may be the very shift to services. When it was dangerous and physically demanding, the impact of work on the labouring body was often immediate and visible. With the decline of primary and secondary sectors – coal mining and steel mill jobs for example – and the rise of the tertiary sector and service jobs, the centrality of the body to work and the impact of work on the body have become less visible, and much less analytical attention has been paid to the body at work according to Slavishak (2010).

Slipping under the academic radar in the late twentieth and early twenty-first centuries, aesthetic labour has become mainstreamed on the high street. During this time employers have shifted from simply recognising the commercial utility of employee appearance to now intervening to shape that appearance in order to lever that utility. For example, in 2009, whilst at the same time trying to shake off accusations of discriminating against employees on the basis of physical appearance (Malvern, 2009; Pidd, 2009), fashion retailer Abercrombie & Fitch (hereafter A&F) was still openly recruiting new store employees on the basis of their physical appearance. In 2010 and trading under the name of Hollister, the company opened a fashion retail outlet in Aberdeen in Scotland. At the opening, the company employed two 'well-toned' males to stand at the store door dressed in sunglasses, flip-flops and swimwear to welcome the 'good looking, cool' customers that it was hoping to attract (Allen, 2010; and see Chapter 7 for a fuller discussion of aesthetic labour in A&F). That these workers are there and made up in the way that they are is a strategy on the part of the employer intended to appeal to the senses of customers: these men are perceived, by their employers at least, to be attractive and their function is to attract customers. As such, standing at the store door, dressed as they are, is an explicit feature of these workers' waged labour.

THE LABOUR IN AESTHETIC LABOUR

This strategy highlights that employers not only need to ensure that workers' potential to labour is converted into actual labour but also want to determine the nature of that labour. An employment contract enables employers to have the right to direct, monitor, evaluate and even discipline employees – within reasonable limits of course and sometimes mediated by the state and trade unions (Kaufman, 2004) – and thereby set what work is to be done, how it is done and when it is done by workers in exchange for pay. In other words, for employers, it is not enough for workers to labour; how that labour occurs is also important to employers. Moreover, as labour process theory contends, to remain competitive there is a constant need for employers to revise or renew the production of services (and goods). Consequently the wage–effort bargain between employers and employees is dynamic and how labour is expended changes over time.

Drawing on the contributions to Thompson and Smith (2010) we discuss the importance of labour process theory for understanding aesthetic labour in Chapter 3. For Harry Braverman (1974), who is credited with reinvigorating theory of the labour process post-Marx, the analytical starting point was Taylorism or scientific management. In the first decades of the twentieth century and focused on manufacturing, F.W. Taylor was advocating scientific management, and through it encouraging employers to appropriate and transmute workers' knowledge of the production process in the drive for competitiveness. By mid-century as interactive services were expanding, and for the same reason, Mills (1951) was noting how employers were utilising worker attitudes in the production process, which they bought on the personality market. By the end of the twentieth century employers were intervening to appropriate and transmute these attitudes through feeling rules, and emotional labour was identified by Hochschild (1983) as an important feature of interactive service work. Aesthetic labour represents the attempt by employers to appropriate and transmute workers' corporeality and again for the same reasons. Put bluntly, employers once sought to control the heads and then hearts of workers; now with aesthetic labour, they seek to do likewise with the bodies of workers. As Wolkowitz (2006: 175) has noted, bodies are not just used in the capitalist labour process, this labour process determines which bodily capacities are recognised and recompensed. Aesthetic labour is therefore borne out in the wage–effort bargain, as employers need to secure competitiveness in the market and the service interaction between employee and customer. With employers aiming to create an appealing service encounter for customers, workers are hired because of the way they look and talk; once employed, they are told what to wear and how to wear it, and instructed how to stand whilst working and even what to say to customers. An important point to note here is that aesthetic labour includes but extends beyond the 'look' of employees, even if that 'look' has attained primacy in Western culture because of the emphasis on the visual senses, a point we discuss further in Chapter 2.

To understand how these bodies are made up, and appreciating that labour power is reproduced within and outside the workplace, we draw on Bourdieu's (1990, 1992, 2004) theory of practice. In this theory, and grossly simplifying at this stage, Bourdieu argued that each social class teaches or socialises its offspring how to think and be in the world in its own image. These 'meaning-giving perceptions' and 'meaningful practices' (or 'doxa' and 'hexus' respectively) are what Bourdieu calls 'habitus', and are character-ised by embodied dispositions, including body language, dress and speech (2004: 170). These dispositions are transposable in that they can be active in different fields, e.g. the home and workplace. In this sense workers bring their habitus to the workplace where it is mobilised, deployed and commodified by employers as part of the wage–effort bargain. Whilst Bourdieu's theory is focused on class reproduction, we use it to explain how employers want employees to inhabit that organisational context – though later in the book, in Chapter 7, we also reveal how many interactive service organisations are choosing, or discriminating in favour of, workers with middle-class habitus. Employers, not just families, can develop and mobilise and deploy dispositions. As we first defined aesthetic labour in Warhurst et al. (2000), it thus not only involves employees selling their corporeality to the employer, it also refers to that corporeality being 'made up' by the employer to embody the desired aesthetic of the organisation and is intended to provide commercial benefit. These embodied dispositions are, to some extent, possessed by workers at the point of entry into employment. However, and a key point, employ-ers then mobilise, develop, deploy and commodify these dispositions through processes of recruitment, selection, training and management, transforming them into a 'style' of service encounter that appeals to the senses of the customer. As explained in Chapter 3, however, this definition has been modified in light of subsequent research.

FROM SHIPPING TO SHOPPING, FROM MILLS TO MALLS

Whilst a beauty premium exists that rewards good looking employees in jobs across manufacturing and services (e.g. Hamermesh, 2011; Harper, 2000; Sierminska, 2015), the emergence and mainstreaming of aesthetic labour as a managerial strategy cannot be disentangled from the increase in and increased importance of interactive service jobs. The service sector now accounts for over 80 per cent of all jobs in the UK (House of Commons Library, 2019), with hospitality and retail providing around six million jobs (Rhodes, 2018; UK Hospitality, 2018).

Within this context of the growing importance of service sector employment, aesthetic labour's existence became more obvious to us when we both moved for new jobs to Glasgow in the mid-1990s. Glasgow is now a city with a vibrant services economy, which in large part contributes to it being ranked in 2019 by *Time Out* magazine as one of the world's top ten cities to visit (Harrison, 2019). The service sector accounts for 84 per cent of jobs in Glasgow, with retail, hospitality and tourism designated as key sectors in the city economy (Glasgow City Council, 2016; Invest Glasgow, 2018a, 2018b). However, when we started to develop research on aesthetic labour in the Glasgow of the late 1990s, the city – as with other de-industrialised cities in northern Britain such as Manchester, Newcastle, Sheffield and Leeds – was still undergoing a process of urban regeneration, with shopping replacing shipping, and malls replacing the mills. Indeed, as we were to discover it was increasingly seen as an exemplar of services-driven economic regeneration. The isolated advert in Preston was commonplace in Glasgow: local newspapers, such as the *Glasgow Herald*, *Sunday Herald* and *Evening Times*, frequently featured job advertisements that included reference to employee appearance. In retail for example, one stipulated that applicants had to have 'high standards of personal presentation'; in hospitality, another listed the need for an 'immaculate appearance'. Indeed, these local evening and daily newspapers were replete with 'upmarket' retail and hospitality employers' job advertisements signalling the importance of applicant appearance. Many advertisements also stipulated the need to provide recent personal photographs with applications – a practice, whilst common in countries such as France, is not common in the UK; indeed employers are cautioned against soliciting applicants' photographs by the UK Government's employment agency.

This economic repositioning masks the changes that have marked Glasgow's history. From the eighteenth century onwards, with a flourishing trans-Atlantic trade in tobacco and then cotton and sugar, Glasgow boomed from a small town to a bustling city, becoming the second city of the British Empire. Its wealthy, strutting 'tobacco Lords' commissioned grand buildings and public spaces, some of which aped parts of Paris (Johnston, 2008). It was, Daniel Defoe said at the time, 'one of the ... most beautiful and best built cities of Great Britain' (cited in Baxter, 2005: 10). By the nineteenth century light manufacturing spilled out across the city followed soon by heavy industry. The city became the shipbuilding capital of the world, producing two-thirds of all iron-built ships by the end of the century (Bruce-Gardyne, 2005). It spawned its own creative stars in Alexander 'Greek' Thomson and Charles Rennie Mackintosh, architects and designers who built innovative and influential public and private buildings in and around the city. As fashionably designed tearooms became the vogue, Mackintosh (and his wife Margaret Macdonald) collaborated with Miss Cranston to create tearooms with 'new art' interior décor that both shocked and attracted Glasgow's affluent businessmen and ladies who lunched: 'The vibrant urban chic ... was all wildly overdone,' writes Kinchin (1998: 65, 59), 'but it was an experience, and it was very appealing – the people came, whatever they thought'. It was not just appealing but influential: at the turn of the twentieth century Mackintosh was invited to Vienna by the Secessionists because of their admiration for his attempts to stylise everyday life through design.

The industrial and creative city of the nineteenth century fared less well in the twentieth. Suffering economic booms and busts, Glasgow developed a reputation as a mean city; strong on violence, alcohol, poor health and poverty (Turok and Bailey, 2004; Turok et al., 2003). With the decline and eventual disappearance of heavy industry and the dispersal of light manufacturing out of the city to satellite towns from the 1960s onwards (before further displacement overseas), the city went into decline and became, according to Honey (1989: 62), 'an ugly sprawling conurbation'.

In the 1980s, the city council sought to address this decline with a public relations exercise to rebrand Glasgow as a friendly city with 'Mr Happy' as its mascot and it hosted a successful international garden festival on reclaimed industrial land. Despite the initial mocking, Glasgow was then named European City of Culture in 1990 and in 1999 UK City of Architecture and Design (Bruce-Gardyne, 2005). This city, the promotional blurb declared, was being revitalised: 'Glasgow's miles better' now it proclaimed. Unemployment was down and investment up as the city reinvented itself as a regional service hub. The growing importance of hospitality and retail to the Glasgow economy can be seen by the recognition that by the turn of the twenty-first century Glasgow was the UK's second-biggest shopping city, second only to London (Donald, 2008), a position it retains today (Experian, 2016). The city was now being portrayed as one brimming with 'free-spending, label-loving, high-fashion consumers' (Davison, 1998: 14). The smart shopping malls with designer retail were matched by a plethora of boutique hotels and style bars, restaurants and cafés. Many of these bars and cafés were built in converted industrial buildings and warehouses; the first, Bar Ten in 1991, was deliberately intended as a watering-hole for what would now be labelled the city's creative workers – designers and architects (Braiden, 2007).

Two decades after Mr Happy and the 'miles better' campaign, in 2004 the city's latest image makeover positioned Glasgow as 'Scotland with Style' (Crichton, 2004). In 2008, as a further development on this theme, a 'Style Mile' steering group was convened of retailers, event management consultants and city council representatives to further develop and promote the city as one of 'the most inspirational and stylish destinations in the UK and Europe' (*Scotsman*, 2008: 7). The outcome of this regeneration was:

> ... increased private investment in smart hotels, fashionable bars and restaurants, new shopping arcades, designer clothes stores, modern cinemas, nightclubs, fitness centres and stylish loft apartments, most in and around the revamped city centre. They have coincided with changes in lifestyle for sections of the population with increased eating out, spending on clothing and entertainment, weekend breaks and city centre living. Glasgow has acquired a trendy, exciting and even glamorous image in certain circles as a place to shop, visit, live and socialise. (Turok and Bailey, 2004: 35; for a more critical account of Glasgow's re-branding see Lennon, 2014)

In short, Glasgow has shed its grim, brutish reputation. The city has successfully repositioned itself, recovering from what Donald (2008: 11) called its 'post-industrial hangover'.[1] Not surprisingly, with many other British cities suffering a similar economic malaise in the 1980s, Glasgow is not the only city to want a 'Style Mile'. Indeed, there was a perception that if the former Second City of Empire can affect an economic turnaround to become the Second City of Shopping after London then any city can (Ross, 2009). These other cities also wanted to be, or at least be perceived as, buzzy, vibrant and cool. If Glasgow had its Italian Centre of designer shops, its neighbour and rival Edinburgh sought to create a 'Continental' retail quarter (Kemp, 2008). As they too sought to replace their lost textile mills and light manufacturing, 60 other towns and cities across the UK similarly sought to regenerate (Donald, 2008). This process has not been unique to the UK of course. It is occurring across the developed economies in many other cities that have lost their manufacturing bases.

As Glasgow started to reinvent itself to be a style capital we started to discover with our research on aesthetic labour that many of the retail, hospitality and tourism jobs were populated by young, stylish workers. Thus, the labour used in these style bars and restaurants, designer retailers and boutique hotels springing up in Glasgow increasingly had to fit with companies' market positioning branding. As Moira, the human resources managers of Hotel Elba had explained, the aim was to have 'people that look the part … fit in with the whole concept of the hotel'. As a 'style city', Henderson (1999: 4) remarked bluntly, Glasgow now also needed a 'designer workforce'. Not surprisingly, our initial research focus was on what we termed the 'style labour market' for these particular upmarket services in the private sector.

FROM SOCIOLOGICAL IMAGINATION TO EMPIRICAL RESEARCH

It was in the context of this rejuvenating Glasgow that we found ourselves in 1997 sitting in a room with a small number of retail workers. We were not sure what to expect or how to guide the discussion. It was our first exploratory focus group with service sector employees to discuss aesthetic labour, and there were a few surprises. One young woman, working for a designer fashion retail store, explained that the company would not employ 'large' applicants (meaning any female applicant size 16 or more but the average size for British women), even if those applicants had suitable work experience and good customer skills. Another said that her male boss had sent home a female supermarket check-out operator to shave her legs: 'Customers don't like to see hairy legs' she said, noting that the manager claimed, 'it puts them off'. What was interesting was how easy it was to align each focus group participant with the type of company for which they worked. The woman who worked for the designer fashion retailer was glamorous, wearing make-up and well-groomed clothes; the woman working in the supermarket was without make-up, and wearing jeans and a plain tee-shirt. Both, however, were clear that their physical appearance was important in their work. Thus, although we were drawn initially to the style labour market, it seemed that an emphasis on worker appearance existed more widely in interactive service jobs.

As our research developed, and other researchers (e.g. Pettinger, 2004, 2005) began to explore the concept, it was clear that employer demand for aesthetic labour was extending beyond style bars and restaurants, designer retailers and boutique hotels into more prosaic services, and also advancing into public sector services, as we discuss in Chapter 3. With the first extension, it was clear that the style bars and restaurants, designer retailers and boutique hotels were creating demonstration effects for other high street retailers and hospitality companies. With the second, perhaps surprising, extension into other sectors, it was not competition that was driving the use of aesthetic labour but organisational branding, similar to that of private sector companies. In both extensions, however, organisations were using their employees' corporeality to appeal to customers and clients. If our development and empirical exploration of the concept of aesthetic labour was sparked by a single job advertisement in mid-1990s Preston, by the early 2000s we realised that it was part of a wider phenomenon. Michele Jackson and her colleagues at Oxford University had noticed that the putative new economy of the UK was dividing in 'high tech' and 'high touch' jobs. In her analysis of recruitment adverts for these latter jobs, it was clear that these adverts referred less to what potential employees could do and more to what they were like – 'well-spoken' and 'good appearance' for example (Jackson et al., 2002). The need for employees to mobilise an aesthetically pleasing corporeality can therefore extend beyond the style bars and restaurants, designer retailers and boutique hotels that we first identified as using aesthetic labour.

Indeed, as the 2000s unfolded there were claims of an emergent 'aesthetic economy' in which aesthetics and styling were said by Postrel (2004) to be infusing all work, and within which aesthetic labour is cited as a feature. But whether cast as a feature of this putative aesthetic economy or not, the work/body nexus, Wolkowitz (2006: 1) states, is now 'crucial to the organization and the experience of work relations, and ... that people's experience of embodiment is deeply embedded in their experiences of paid employment'. As we outline in Chapter 3, this work/body nexus can take many forms. Aesthetic labour, however, is a form of waged labour, and is intended to generate a defined service encounter and provide organisational benefit for the employer. As service jobs have come to dominate the advanced economies, aesthetic labour has become a key feature of many workplaces. This labour both reflects and pushes forward wider emphases on the body not just in the workplace but beyond the workplace. Indeed, in this respect, the labour process in which aesthetic labour is exercised has only relative autonomy, and is shaped by and also shapes practices and developments in the wider society such as the use of cosmetic surgery – now ironically often relabelled aesthetic surgery (and see Chapter 2 for further discussion of the increasing global prominence of the beauty industry and aesthetic surgery).

If aesthetic labour was born in the sociological imagination, it was developed through empirical research. This book draws on that evidence, some of which is from primary sources based on our research, some from secondary sources and the research of others. This material helps contextualise, position and frame our arguments about aesthetic labour.

Initially there was the exploratory focus group of Glasgow retail employees that helped affirm the existence of what we had already termed 'aesthetic labour'. Funded by the Universities of Strathclyde and Glasgow, there then followed focus groups with employees in the retail and hospitality industries plus interviews with retail and hospitality managers and significant others for these industries, e.g. trade union officials. Those qualitative data allowed us to explore in depth the nature of aesthetic labour and how it is experienced by managers and employees. It was at this point that we came across the overtly style-driven Hotel Elba and realised that it was emblematic of many of the issues associated with, and much of the ideas that we were developing about, aesthetic labour.

A report from this initial research project on aesthetic labour generated a huge amount of media attention. From Banff to Bath in the UK, from the *Irish Times* to the Italian *Il Corriere della Sera* across Europe, the research featured in a large number of newspaper articles, many choosing some variant of the 'good looking staff pull in the punters' angle (e.g. Burkeman, 2000; White and Nugent, 1999). It also had an immediate impact on policy debates about vocational education and training, and careers guidance in the UK and abroad. The Industrial Society (now the Work Foundation) published a report on it (Warhurst and Nickson, 2001), which generated further media interest (e.g. Freeman, 2001; McRae, 2001). Furthermore, the concept became embedded in the Work Foundation's commentaries on the future of work and employment, and the development of successful cities (e.g. Westwood and Nathan, 2002). On the back of this publicity we began to be told anecdotal stories by employees of how looks mattered in their employment. Some gave us their company training or performance evaluation material, e.g. guidance from a UK high street bank that stated it wanted staff who were 'bright, verbal and attractive', and from an office staff recruitment company that assessed applicants' appearance and grooming on a scale from 1–5 or 'poor' to 'excellent'.

The publicity also attracted the interest of the Wise Group, an intermediate labour market organisation concerned to help the unemployed back into work in Scotland. With our participation, it ran a consultative workshop on aesthetic labour and then a pilot two-week training course on self-presentation skills for the unemployed. Along with the UK's Economic and Social Research Council (ESRC), the Wise Group also co-sponsored a doctoral student to examine employer skill demands and training provision in interactive services, again with the intention of helping the unemployed back into work by targeting job opportunities in the hospitality and retail industries (see Cullen, 2008, 2011). This course also attracted publicity, but this time unhelpful. The course was slated in the tabloid press, which falsely claimed that it pandered to the unemployed who were 'too grubby' to get a job and questioned the use of public funding for this type of training (Howarth, 2000; and see Figure 1.2). Journalists door-stepped the course co-ordinator, forcing her out of her home for a few days. Although the unemployed 'clients' who participated in this course stated that they had gained much from it, including enhanced employability (Cullen, 2008; Nickson et al., 2003), the course was dropped because of the negative publicity and fears of public funding cuts. It seems that politicians can have makeovers to help them get and keep their jobs (see Chapter 2) but not their working-class electorate – a discrepancy that has potentially discriminatory effects and to which we return in Chapter 7.

Figure 1.2   Too grubby to get a job?

Source: Reproduced with permission from the *Sun* newspaper

    That experience hammered home the need to establish the importance and prevalence of aesthetic labour. Two surveys followed that were jointly funded by the then Scottish Executive (now the Scottish Government) and the UK's ESRC research centre for Skills, Knowledge and Organisational Performance (SKOPE) at the Universities of Oxford and Warwick (then, later, Cardiff). One was an employer survey, the other an employee survey. Both surveys were undertaken in Glasgow: the employers' survey encompassed retailers, hotels, restaurants, bars and cafés, and the employee survey was drawn from students who worked in the hospitality and retail industries. Supplementary focus groups were also conducted with employees as part of this research project. Importantly, it enabled us not only to assess the extent of employer demand for aesthetic labour but also further explore employees' experience of it.

Following the publicity generated by our research on aesthetic labour, we were also contacted by the co-ordinator of a course at a Glasgow-based further education college which was running a self-presentation course for tourism students that drew on our research. The course focused mainly but not exclusively on providing training for aspiring flight attendants. The students were surveyed and some participated in focus groups. Interviews were also conducted with relevant teaching staff and management at the college. The project was then extended to include analysis of two similar courses run by private providers, using interviews, participant observation and content analysis of web-based material. This dataset enabled us to examine the training and trainability of aesthetic labour and if workers' corporeal aesthetic appeal is fixed or formable. If it is fixed, or no opportunity is available to form it, or at least form it in the way that it is desired by employers, as we discuss in Chapter 7, aesthetic labour can create a form of social exclusion from a key source of employment in contemporary service economies. The opportunity to explore this possibility presented itself when, along with colleagues in Australia, we were able to undertake an evaluation of the *Equal Opportunity Act 1995* for the Equal Opportunity Commission (Victoria) in Australia. This Act legislated against discrimination based on employees' physical features. Interviews were conducted with staff of the EOC and archival analysis was conducted on complaints and cases brought to the EOC during the first ten years of the Act (see Warhurst et al., 2012). This evaluation provided an opportunity to explore the issue of lookism, or employment discrimination based on employee appearance, and produced some surprising results, as we reveal in Chapter 7.

Finally, the Nuffield Foundation funded a survey of fashion retail employers in Manchester that also had the support of Skillsmart, the then sector skills council for the UK retail industry. This survey allowed us to undertake an international comparative project, with similar surveys administered by colleagues in Sweden and Australia. The Manchester survey enabled us to triangulate our Glasgow data with those from another 'post-industrial' city in the UK, as well as with data from other non-UK metropolitan areas that are strong regional service hubs – Stockholm and Sydney (see Huzell and Larsson, 2012, and Hall and van den Broek, 2012, respectively). It is material from this and the other projects which forms the primary data that feature across the chapters in this book. In the primary research that we report from Glasgow and elsewhere, the names of any individual participants and their organisations have been changed to pseudonyms to provide anonymity. More details of the various research projects are provided in the Appendix.

THE STRUCTURE OF THE BOOK

Starting with the wider social and economic context, Chapter 2 outlines and evaluates claims of an emergent 'aesthetic economy' in which style overshadows substance, with places, products and people giving pleasure and deriving meaning from how they are sensorily perceived – in other words, how they look and feel. The chapter then drills down to discuss the various forms of aesthetics and organisation, and how there can be aesthetics *of* organisation involving the 'hardware' of organisations, such as product design and the physical environment of workspaces/offices; and aesthetics *in* organisation comprising a range of worker behaviours, most obviously manifest in the idea of impression management. As workers now seek to redesign themselves as a feature of impression management, this chapter also considers the scale and influence of the beauty industry and cosmetic surgery as increasingly workers seek to mobilise and develop their personal aesthetic capital in an organisational context.

Chapter 3 examines the labouring body. It notes how that body was once a key focus of attention in studies of employment but became analytically retired as economies transformed to be dominated by services. It notes also, however, that if the body was no longer a central concern in the study of employment, it remained a key issue for employers and employees. As the chapter shows, the study of employment has now come full circle, again recognising the importance of the body within and for employment. We highlight the nature of aesthetic labour, the types of occupations, industries and sectors in which aesthetic labour is present and becoming mainstreamed, what it is about workers' corporeality that employers believe aesthetically appeals to customers and clients, and why and how employers seek to control and transmute this corporeality. We make an important distinction though between employees required to be good looking and those required to have the right look, and how different organisations can seek different looks through their employees. In other words there may be a beauty bias but beauty per se is not the basis of aesthetic labour.

Drawing on our primary quantitative and qualitative data mainly from the retail and hospitality industries, Chapters 4, 5 and 6 examine empirically the demand, supply, development and deployment of aesthetic labour in the workplace. In other words, respectively: what embodied dispositions employers want; how employers acquire these dispositions, e.g. train or hire them; how workers come to possess them; and how these dispositions are used in work (cf. James et al., 2013). The chapters show how employers construct 'ideal' workers based on corporeality, through recruitment and selection processes, and the training and monitoring and disciplining of workers to ensure that these ideals are enforced in the workplace. Consequently, these chapters explain how workwear, dress and appearance standards (Chapter 4), body language (Chapter 5) and speech (Chapter 6) are the points of intervention for employers, as they seek to mobilise, deploy and commodify workers' corporeality in support of the organisational brand image.

Chapter 7 shifts the analysis from the experience of aesthetic labour to its potentially damaging consequences. Although portrayed within the aesthetic economy literature as a benign alignment of employee and corporate look, there is a darker side to aesthetic labour and Chapter 7 explores these elements. It begins by recognising how, in certain. organisational environments, some employers overtly sexualise employees in support of their brand image, leading to deleterious outcomes for employees, such as sexual harassment by customers. Beyond the issue of sexualisation we consider the concept of lookism, in particular considering some of the legal debates about whether legislation can address concerns about appearance discrimination, evaluating attempts to regulate lookism, and considering the desirability and feasibility of that regulation. Finally, in this chapter we consider an issue that is largely overlooked in discussions of lookism, that of social class. In their judgement about what appeals to customer senses, employers often fall back on middle-class corporeality so that people from working-class backgrounds can be excluded from some jobs in retail and hospitality. The chapter examines this form of social exclusion from the labour market.

The final concluding chapter considers aesthetic labour as part of the dynamic employment relationship and if aesthetic labour is a fad or fixture of interactive services. It pulls together the key arguments of the book and assesses the future of aesthetic labour as an employer strategy, linking that strategy again to wider public and academic debates about aesthetics, organisation, sexuality, work and employment, and the economy. It revisits the link between labour strategies and the heterogeneity of service jobs, the labouring body and how work and employment are changed and shaped with aesthetic labour. It also revisits the wider public debate linking body fascism and employer labour demand, and the public policy issues that arise from aesthetic labour in terms of skill formation, vocational training, social exclusion and employment discrimination. In this sense, to return to and paraphrase Mills (2000[1959]), if aesthetic labour is now a public issue, it also creates new and compounds existing personal troubles for many workers. In the context of a services-dominated economy and a society increased concerned with looks, aesthetic labour has become a mainstream feature of work and employment. It is important, therefore, that it is acknowledged, analysed, and its impact and consequences assessed. This book undertakes those tasks and in doing so recognises how the origins, operations and outcomes of aesthetic labour increasingly create branded bodies not only in the interactive service workplace but also beyond it.

NOTE

1. We do not use this 'post-industrial' term, recognising instead that services can be industrialised (see for example Taylor and Bain, 1999) and that the decline or, more accurately, the loss of manufacturing occurred to these cities in the 1970s and 1980s.

2
THE AESTHETICISATION OF THE ECONOMY AND SOCIETY

This chapter sets the scene for the manner in which style is increasingly seen to over-shadow substance. It charts the development of an aesthetic economy in which society, economy, organisations and individuals are taking on board the importance of aesthetics. The chapter charts the increasing aestheticisation of everyday life, a process that first began as early as the end of the nineteenth century. In his seminal work *The Theory of the Leisure Class*, Thorstein Veblen (1994[1899]) identified a shallow, materialistic 'leisure class' obsessed with the 'conspicuous consumption' of clothes and consumer goods. This consumption had no need but through its social visibility helped define the consumers' better social status. In the words of Heilbroner it 'advertised its superiority' (1995: 229), i.e. that more expensive means better. It also provided a benchmark for the aspirations of others, Veblen believed, creating a virus of 'competitive emulation'. Veblen's theory challenged mainstream economics (then and now), arguing, with some later empirical support, that consumption was socially driven and relative. Depressingly, Veblen noted that this consumption blunted working-class anger with the capitalist (leisure) class (or, these days, disdain for vacuous celebrities) and instead converted it into aspiration and the desire to be like, or at least appear to be like, the capitalist class through similar patterns of consumption. This virus seems to continue without antidote. A century later, Juliet Schor (2000) asked the question why do Americans spend too much? She arrived at a similar conclusion: to keep up with the Joneses – or rather by now keeping up with our *Friends* – the characters of the long-running US television sit-com. Whilst Joneses tend to be our neighbours and so have similar income levels, the characters of *Friends* had income levels that were typically higher than those of the viewers. Echoing Veblen, Schror points out that a fashion now exists for unnecessary marble kitchen tops, for example. These tops have to be imported from overseas, and could easily be replaced with a material sourced more locally and with at least as good functionality – but it might not look as good or help us project a certain status. Her point is that more of us are consuming more, and in doing so are creating more personal debt that is ultimately unsustainable but a hard habit to break.

Without the concern about debt and addiction, this form-over-function in consumption argument is a key feature of what is termed the 'aesthetic economy'. As a proponent of the aesthetic economy, Böhme (2003: 72) notes how it 'starts out from the ubiquitous phenomenon of an aestheticisation of the real, and takes seriously the fact that this aestheticisation represents an important factor in the economy of advanced capitalist societies'. Aesthetics therefore becomes the major economic phenomenon of our times and the aesthetic imperative pervades all aspects of our lives. In this putative new economy, style is used consciously and unconsciously to effect sensory appeal in goods and services, and superordinately complements function in these goods and services. Critical of modernist utilitarianism, proponents of this economy return beauty to the centre of consumption and production: 'The prophets who forecast a sterile, uniform future were wrong ... We are now at a tipping point' into an aesthetic economy, claims Postrel, heralding 'the age of look and feel' (2004: 33, 39,178).

Recognising this process of aestheticisation, the chapter initially considers the genesis and development of the aesthetic economy and the rise of designification. Following this discussion it then considers the manner in which aesthetics have increasingly influenced organisations. Specifically the chapter considers aesthetics *of* and *in* organisations. The first is concerned with the aestheticising of organisational hardware through the use of material aspects, such as the design of the building or the manner in which the interior design of the organisational space is geared towards creating a particular style for organisational members or customers. The second, aesthetics in organisations, refers to the way in which employees use aesthetics to firstly get in and subsequently get on in organisations through the use of a range of impression management techniques. We then highlight how workers are redesigning themselves now as a feature of this impression management. Consideration of this latter point allows us to assess the scale and influence of the beauty industry and cosmetic surgery as workers now increasingly develop and deploy aesthetics to gain advantage in employment.

THE GENESIS AND DEVELOPMENT OF THE AESTHETIC ECONOMY

Derived from the Greek *aesthesis*, aesthetics entered common usage in the English language as a neologism through debates about art in the eighteenth century (Williams, 1990). It was intended by its creator, Alexander Baumgarten, to stress perception through the senses. As a concept it distinguishes the intangible from the tangible, with only the materiality of the latter perceptible to the senses, most usually through visual appearance. As medical advances were made in the nineteenth century, picking up on the popularisation of the concept, *anaesthetic* referred to the deprivation of the senses or the absence of sensation. The study of sensory and emotional experience became known as aesthetics.

Baumgarten emphasised the salience of beauty, though wider use of the word, such as that by Immanuel Kant and sitting more comfortable with the Greek original, soon referred to that which simply affects the senses, beautiful or otherwise. Both uses have subsequently been popular though the 'claim to meaning' is not just pedantry. In the art world, the recurring public outcries about 'is it art?', as well as professional critical judgements and consequential monetary valuations, are made on the basis of this distinction. Some art critics still favour art that is beautiful – usually that of the Old Masters; others accept as art that which is merely affective, and even negatively so – shock art for example (Freeland, 2001). Kant argued initially that beauty is subjective. Aesthetes were those people, such as Oscar Wilde, who were judged, or more usually judged themselves, to have a superior understanding of beauty.

Both uses – that which is beautiful and that which merely affects the senses – assume of course that the perceivers' senses can be affected – itself a debatable point, as Freeland explains. Art can be regarded as a language that conveys knowledge about how the world is to be perceived. For some, such as Kant (later in his life it should be noted), judgements about beauty are universal, with a short leap to regarding the ability to perceive as biological. This approach is one being explored today within cognitive science, as neuroscientists map the brain and identify neuronal activities upon exposure to visual stimuli for example. Others, such as David Hume, argued that the capacity to respond to aesthetics is socially constructed. What is regarded as tasteful can be subjective, with some perceivers having taste and others not, with Hume believing that taste could be acquired through education and experience if a consensus about standards is first reached by those with taste. A similar position is evident in Bourdieu (1984), who regarded taste as not only socially constructed, but also socially differentiated and differentiating. He identified differences in how classes both relate to and express preferences in art, theatre and movies for example. 'Taste', he states, 'classifies, and it classifies the classifier' (1984: 6). Those differences are constituent of *habitus*: durable dispositions acquired tacitly through childhood socialisation, with different quasi-bodily ways of engaging the world that are the outcome of this socialisation. Thus taste, and with it, concepts of beauty varying according to class, reflect and also reinforce not only social difference but also social inequality.

A good example of these differences is highlighted in Entwistle's (2002) research of fashion modelling. At the start of her research Entwistle assumed that modelling involved the commodification of beauty, the recognition of which she would share with her research subjects. But she was wrong. Instead what agents would describe to her as beautiful models appeared to Entwistle as either odd or unexceptional. Researching outside her own habitus, presumably that at least related to academia, made Entwistle 'realize [her] own lack of the requisite taste or disposition for recognizing the fashion model aesthetic' (2002: 318). More generally, Hamermesh and Biddle (1994: 1175) note how:

> ... it seems quite clear that there are few consistent standards of beauty across cultures. Hugely distended lower lips are considered attractive by Ungabi men as were women's bound feet by Manchu dynasty men; and other less extreme examples of differences in standards of beauty across cultures could easily be cited.

Thus, what is regarded as tasteful is culturally and socially ascribed and within frameworks of asymmetric power relations or inequitable possession or access to resources (Bourdieu, 2004). This point is important because some tastes are either dismissed – the derisive epithet 'low brow' – or to be educated. An example of the latter is to be found in the emblematic Hotel Elba, which we introduced in the previous chapter. In each of the hotels in the chain a chair was always strategically placed in the foyer. A chair, we have noted elsewhere, is 'an artefact which connotes functionality. A chair is something to sit on. But not this chair' (Witz et al., 2003: 46). Instead in Hotel Elba:

> This chair signifies the style of the organization in such a way as to educate the customer in the eye. It instructs customers in the unique manner, the distinctive aesthetic of Elba, the way in which Elba will be experienced – the way in which, literally, Elba is *designed* to be experienced aesthetically ... In short, the chair, as part of the material culture of Elba Hotels, functions as a key signifier of the aesthetic of the service organization. (p. 46; emphasis in original)

Similarly, in his discussion of the etymology of the word 'aesthetic', Williams (1990) notes that material objects that appeal to the senses can be contrasted to those that are practical or have utility, and a division is often posited between the two. This debate is not just a philosophical one of the eighteenth century but has profound implications for our current economy and society. In the latter half of the nineteenth century a new 'art for art's sake' challenged the established British art world. A group of young bohemian romantics were in search of a new beauty and triggered what became known as the Aesthetic Movement. Its chief protagonist was Dante Gabriel Rossetti, though the movement was a loose constellation of painters, poets, designers and writers such as Edward Burne-Jones, Albert Moore, Christopher Dresser and Oscar Wilde. Daringly for the time, they believed that beauty should be the guiding principle of life. Their pictures had to tell no stories (the convention of the time) but merely be beautiful, be sensorily affecting. They wanted viewers of their paintings to distinguish between the feelings evoked by the subject matter of the painting and what they regarded as the more important qualities imbued by the painting as a work of beauty – hence the 'cult of beauty' (Calloway and Federle Orr, 2011; Little, 2004). In time, their output shifted beyond pictures to household furniture, fixtures and fittings and then general goods. Drawing on the artists' ideas and templates, product designers made wallpaper, women's dresses, tiles and even teapots. It was, Calloway (2011: 12) argues, 'a new desire to make interiors expressively personal spaces': it was design for life. What the movement did was to translate its art into a lifestyle and significantly, by selling their goods commercially, it was a lifestyle intended not just for the artists themselves but for the masses. The idea of 'the house Beautiful' gripped the London upper classes, and in true competitive emulation spread to the fashionable middle classes in London, then throughout the UK and over the Atlantic to the US. All could aspire to be 'artistic', Calloway states. Whilst the aesthetic movement had faded by the start of the twentieth century as its protagonists aged and died, its legacy lives on:

> It has long lasting relevance because it ushered into the wider national consciousness a sociological concept that would not be named as such for at least another half century. In its harness of 'art' to the chariot of retail and publicity, its spawning of countless paper fans, blue-and-white ginger jars and Kate Greenaway-inspired pinafores to an appreciative suburban and provincial audience, the Aesthetic Movement anticipated and hastened the consumerist idea of the 'lifestyle'. (Breward, 2011: 195)

This legacy is still apparent in the twenty-first century. The shift from utility to aesthetic appeal is the starting point for the 'new age of aesthetics' (Postrel, 2004: 9). Whilst Postrel talks about being at the tipping point into a new age of aesthetics, Böhme (2003) argues in his outline of the aesthetic economy that it is not a new development but one that can be traced back to the work of Veblen, a point we noted in our introduction. In recognising the claims put for an aesthetic economy within a historical context, Böhme usefully reminds us that capitalism evolves to recognise the changing nature of consumption and thus creates new value categories. Consequently, he argues that there has been a shift from satisfying the material needs of society, such as the need for drink, sleep and shelter, to another type of need which he describes as people's desires. These desires can now be commercially exploited because 'there are no natural limits to presentation, glamour and visibility' (2003: 73). Indeed, Böhme goes on to argue that this shift from needs to desires was arguably reached in Europe and North America in the 1950s and 1960s, suggesting that 'it is the phase in which a large part of social production becomes aesthetic production, serving staging values instead of use values' (2003: 78).

Whilst Böhme offers a useful historical corrective to Postrel's newness claims, the latter would nevertheless suggest that the process of the aestheticisation of everyday life has significantly intensified in recent years. Thus, while functionality is still present in artefacts, form now follows emotion rather than follows function, she states. Postrel claims that 'aesthetics has become the deciding factor in almost every product that we once considered primarily functional' (2004: 36). Similarly, according to Weggeman et al. (2007: 348):

> We live in styled houses, drive our beautiful cars through our meticulously planned city, go to shops with a carefully designed 'total shop experience', wander through parks and forests with nice lingering lanes and let our noses made perfect by our plastic surgeon. In other words we are transforming our urban, industrial and natural environment *in toto* into a hyperaesthetic scenario.

Form following emotion is a 'major ideological shift' (Postrel, 2004: 11) that has two drivers according to Postrel. The first is the failure of modernism to deliver to, and even understand, the variety of consumer desires: 'Modernist design ideology promised efficiency, rationality, and truth, today's diverse aesthetics offers a different trifecta: freedom, beauty, and pleasure' (p. 9). The second is the realisation that price and performance are no longer sufficient product differentiators in highly competitive markets: 'In a crowded marketplace, aesthetics is often the only way to make a product stand out', she states (p. 2). The benefit of the shift, according to Postrel, is that consumers are no longer trapped in the iron cage of uniformity and dourness. Instead beauty infuses not just the design of products but also the lifestyles that these products help consumers pursue. In an Echoing art world debate, Postrel vacillates on the issue of beauty. She suggests that this beauty is not universal, part of an absolute standard of taste, but rather what is offered is 'beauty in its many forms' (p. 10); it is 'not *what* style is used but rather *that* style is used' (p. 5; emphasis in original). Nevertheless it is beautiful design that marks the age of look and feel. As a consequence, design has become mainstreamed – it might even be thought of as the public art of today – and consumer expectations have been raised, 'ratcheted up', so that yesterday's leading edge is only today's minimum standard.

This perception of a shift to an aesthetic economy is understandable when design features so prominently in accounts of product offerings. Aestheticisation of our world and the seemingly infinite variety of expressive form it creates means that nothing is now judged on functionality alone, it is also the way things look. For example, when once a refrigerator would have been seen simply in functional terms it is now a form of self-expression as a good-looking refrigerator makes a statement about our lives, values and aspirations. It is unsurprising, then, to see Bennett (1998: 2) arguing that a 'designification of the UK' has occurred in which it is 'now more common to sit on a puce Arne Jacobsen Ant chair when you go out than a beer-stained, ripped leatherette bar stool'. As this trend continues beyond the upper or niche market segments to become incorporated into more prosaic product offerings, even mid-range budget hotels are having a make-over. Emulating the pricing system of budget airlines but incorporating the product offerings of upper market segment hotels such as the Metropolitan and Claridges, the co-founder of Pret A Manger opened a hotel in London in 2006, the Hoxton, which had tariffs from as low as £1 per night. Despite the modest price for a night's stay at the hotel, guests received design-led interiors that were described as 'jaw-droppingly good' by one critic (Robbins, 2006: 5; see also Willis, 2011). Other similar 'chic and cheap hotels' opened in the UK at the same time, including the Apex City in Edinburgh, Nite Nite in Birmingham and Dakota in Nottingham, and were described as 'well designed', 'cool', 'hip' and 'sleek' (and see Box 2.1).

Box 2.1   citizenM – 'affordable luxury for the people'

Styling itself as a collection of innovative concepts, the Dutch hotel company citizenM aims to create 'affordable luxury for the people'. The company, which opened its first hotel in 2008, is now expanding with hotels in prime metropolitan locations, such as Paris, New York and Shanghai. The hotel has won numerous awards for its style and design, including twice being voted as the world's trendiest hotel by Trip Advisor travellers in 2010 and 2011. It is suggested that the company reflects the manner in which the Dutch are masters at delivering functionality with flair, leading the *Daily Telegraph* to describe their hotels as being like 'a space that feels more like an arty friend's apartment than a hotel'. As one review notes about the company's Amsterdam city hotel, 'its boxy grey building on a residential street deftly belies the den of design within. Swiss furniture company Vitra rainbows the lobby with comfy-chic lounge chairs, whimsical wall décor, and an open-plan sushi and cocktail canteen'. Within the hotel the rooms are described as transparent and light, and playing 'a pivotal role in the interior concept, which is inspired by accommodations on luxury yachts and private jets'. The review suggests that space is maximised in the rooms 'through bright colours and sleek materials such as Corian®, glass and steel. The themes of airiness and coolness are offset by dark Zebrano wood flooring and juicy red Vitra furniture to create a cosy atmosphere. A floor to ceiling window allows the room to be flooded with natural light. The super king size bed dressed with the finest pillows and Frette linen, guarantee a perfect night's rest. Magnificent to-the-point functionality and design eliminates the need for extra fixtures and furniture' (www.citizenm.com/global/company; www.hospitalitynet.org/news/4036321.html).

As Weggeman et al. (2007) note, this process of aestheticisation is also increasingly seen within an organisational setting and there is now a much greater awareness of how organisations market and sell themselves with regard to aesthetics – something that is especially prevalent, as we have already seen, in service industries where face-to-face and voice-to-voice interactions are now 'aesthetically styled by organizations' (p. 348). To further appreciate the process of aestheticisation within organisations, it is useful to distinguish between aesthetics *of* organisation and aesthetics *in* organisation. The former shows why and how organisations mobilise aesthetics through their hardware. The latter shows why and how individuals mobilise their personal aesthetic capital. This distinction is important because they come together to form aesthetic labour, a point we develop further in Chapter 3.

AESTHETICS AND ORGANISATION

The 'aesthetics *of* organisation' are manifest in the 'hardware' of organisations, such as product design and the physical environment of workspaces/offices (Olins, 1991; Ottensmeyer, 1996; Schmitt and Simonson, 1997). The importance of non-human arte-facts and the deployment of stylised objects often play a big part in the aestheticisation of organisational spaces. Organisational artefacts become an important way in which to perceive and feel the 'reality' that organisations wish to project, and have an equally important role in, drawing on Gagliardi's (1996) work, 'landscaping' workplaces. Aesthetics are a key element of the design of goods and services as AEG's electrical products, London Transport's buses and Coca-Cola's bottles illustrate. At the turn of the century, when UK banks were the largest in the world, their sense of importance was expressed in the physicality of their buildings that exuded 'strong' and 'rich' symbol-ism. A good example was Midland Bank's former London headquarters, a Grade I listed building with stone arches and blocks that exudes solidness. With a changing banking culture, this physicality has also changed to offer a sense of participation and interac-tion with open-plan workspaces (Olins, 1991).

Three points are worth noting with regard to the aesthetics of organisation. Firstly, they are symbols and artifacts which are intended to influence the senses of people as either customers or clients: organisations 'use these symbols in a vivid, dramatic and exciting way, because they know that symbols have the power to affect the way people feel' (Olins, 1991: 71). Secondly, they are intended to 'add value' to the organisation: 'Generally speaking, when companies use identity expressed through design, they use it as a commercial tool; their purpose is to make greater profit out of what they do in the short term' (1991: 53) – though we would now argue that 'adding value' should not be confined to commercial economic activity, a point upon which we elaborate in Chapter 3. Finally, in highly competitive markets with little to differentiate most goods and services, aesthetics contribute to organisational distinctiveness: 'intangible, emotional ... The name and visual style of an organization are sometimes the most important factors in making it appear unique' (1991: 75; and see Box 2.2).

Box 2.2   Styling the hairdressing salon

Chugh and Hancock (2009) note the aestheticising of organisational space in hairdressing, drawing on case studies of two salons in stylish quarters of London. They show how the aesthetic identity of the two salons is managed through human and non-human artefacts. Material artefacts, such as colour-schemed towels, gowns, hairdressing tools, coffee mugs and satchels all become important in the organisational landscape. They also note the importance of furniture, variously described as 'cool', 'quality', 'classy and professional', and the deployment of magazines and photographs providing the latest hair styles. As they recognise, 'these artefacts seemed to provide not only a source of inspiration for clients but, perhaps more importantly, through the use of up-market examples of this media (for example *Vogue*) contributed to the aesthetic of leading edge style and distinction which the company clearly wished each and every patron to associate with the [company]' (p. 471).

Alongside the aestheticisation of organisations, individuals are now increasingly aware of how they present themselves, especially within the workplace. The need for workers to look good has long been a feature of employment. For example, the so-called 'dress for success' pop management literature has exhorted workers 'to look the part' in the attempt to get in and get on in jobs, whatever the industry, and in doing so promoting the use of aesthetics *by* employees *for* employees. This 'aesthetics *in* organisation' thus comprises a range of behaviours in organisations as potential and existing employees present themselves through comportment – posture, gesture, use of personal space, facial characteristics and eye contact, for example – at interviews and during meetings for personal gain (Huczynski, 1996; and see Chapter 5). Such behaviour is usually cast as 'impression management'. Wellington and Bryson (2001: 234) note how 'impression management or image consultancy has become a specialist service profession whose principal role is the provision of advice and assistance to corporate employees and private clients with regard to projecting their most positive personal image'.

Wellington and Bryson usefully trace the history of the image consultancy industry, suggesting it was begun in 1972 in Los Angeles by Gene Pinckney who applied her knowledge acquired in the fashion industry to advise individuals on how best to present themselves to enhance their image. Thus, as they further note, 'image consultants advise private clients on ways in which they can improve their "body idiom" (dress, grooming, and body language) to fit in with current fashions and expectations' (2001: 236). They also note that by 1999 there were over 800 image consultancy companies in the UK. Importantly, according to Wellington and Bryson, these image consultants are advising a wide range of clients, including teachers, clerical/office staff, personal secretaries/assistants, managers, bankers, lawyers, accountants and medical professionals. In short:

It is … about individuals trying to develop the right image to conform to the client, employer, societal, and professional stereotypes … The pressure to develop a particular image comes not just from the employer, but from the wider society and can be imposed on the individual by the individual themselves in an attempt to conform to a particular set of expectations concerning their position in society. (p. 242)

As already noted, this increase in the importance of impression management exists alongside a burgeoning 'dress for success' movement (Solomon, 1986). A search of the Amazon website for books concerned with 'dress for success' yields hundreds of books offering prescriptions on how to be successful in the contemporary workplace. Books such as *The New Professional Image: From Corporate Casual to the Ultimate Power Look – How to Tailor Your Appearance for Success in Today's Workplace, Dress Smart for Women, Wardrobes that Win the New Workplace, Dress Casually for Success for Men…, The Art of Dressing Down in Today's Workplace*, and *Branding Yourself: How to Look, Sound and Behave Your Way to Success* reflect the increasing importance of this 'movement'. As Solomon (1986: 20) notes, clothing 'is laden with symbolism that provides information about social and occupational standing, sex-role identification, political orientation, ethnicity and aesthetic priorities. Clothing is a potent – and highly visible – means of communication'. For the proponents of 'dress for success', the message that organisational members should aim to communicate through their clothing is one of professional success and upward mobility. As Davies (1990: 75) suggests, 'in the way that manufacturers pay great attention to the packaging of products in order to get us to buy them, we need to attend to our "packaging" if we want to "sell" ourselves to others, and get them to take a closer look at what's inside'. We discuss workwear – and the related issue of how employers develop and maintain appearance standards – as a feature of aesthetic labour in Chapter 4. The dress-for-success literature focuses on employee-driven workwear, worn for personal benefit, even if much of that workwear is to conform to social or organisational norms. What is a significant development in how we sell ourselves today is the way that the body itself, and not just how it is clothed, has become a point of intervention on the part of employees in organisations.

In this respect some workers are now attempting to give themselves an aesthetic upgrade to enhance their employability. Thus, it is not just the hardware in organisations that is aestheticised, people are also 'effective surfaces' that can worked on and worked up aesthetically: 'We are not only aesthetic consumers', Postrel (2004: 72) states, 'We are also producers, subject to the critical eye of others'. For Postrel, the obvious producers overtly concerned with their appearance are politicians. Her main example is Hillary Clinton, though there are now numerous other examples of politicians having makeovers to affect aesthetically pleasing dispositions and responses (and see Poutvaara, 2017 for a discussion on how looks matter for politicians, such that good-looking politicians win more votes across the globe). The so-called 'Blair babes', the raft of new female MPs to the UK parliament following Labour's general election victory in 1997, were another alleged group of politicians that had an aesthetic upgrade, with Mary Spillane's Colour Me Beautiful image-consulting organisation openly advertising its services to British politicians (Spillane, 2000). Even non-Blairite female and avowedly feminist Labour MP, Diane Abbott admitted that 'what you wear matters ... Politics is a people game, and if you're hoping to influence people how you look counts,' (*Observer Magazine*, 2018: 9). Clothes, hair and body language are deemed important for and by politicians, and these politicians, with the aid of advisers, seek to mobilise, develop and deploy this aesthetic armoury to win the favour of political consumers – voters (and journalists) – and often, as in Clinton's case, learning to do so in the public gaze.

As we noted above, however, it is not just politicians who are increasingly seeking a make-over to improve their aesthetic appeal. Realising that as organisations and people 'we declare ourselves through look and feel', says Postrel (2004: 112), job applicants now attempt to match their aesthetic identities with that of the potential employer. In addition, employers also seek the same match from potential employees. The hiring process then becomes aesthetically geared:

> Sensory pleasure works to commercial and personal advantage because aesthetics has intrinsic value. People seek it out, they reward those who offer new-and-improved pleasures, and they identify with those that share their tastes. If a nice suit helps some-one win a job, that's because the interviewer finds it more enjoyable to talk with someone dressed that way. The aesthetic ratchet effect, whether it demands deodorant and clean hair or well-cut clothes and attractive shoes, rewards what we find pleasing to the senses. (pp. 75–6)

Having good looks or the right look therefore matters to potential employers. It is not just politicians seeking office but now even welfare recipients who are having make-overs, and cosmetic interventions, surgical or otherwise, are becoming more common, and for women and men. For example, as we noted in the previous chapter, we worked with a social enterprise based in Glasgow called the Wise Group. Their objective is to help long-term unemployed people find and keep jobs by offering train-ing with the aim of getting people back into work. In conjunction with Wise Group staff we developed an aesthetic labour training programme to help prepare unem-ployed people for working in hospitality and retail. Additionally, the research engaged with local employers to ensure that the type of skills with which the unemployed were being equipped were indeed appropriate for accessing jobs in hospitality and retail. The general objectives of the programme were: to build confidence to improve social skills; to improve motivation; to improve health and fitness; to widen perceptions of job opportunities in hospitality and retail; and to obtain feedback and generate discussion of the course. More specifically, the training programme aimed to educate and inform clients of the recruitment, selection and training criteria demanded by potential employers in hospitality and retail, thereby increasing their chances of being successful in securing a job (see also van den Berg and Arts (2019) for a discussion of how aesthetic considerations are impacting on welfare to work initiatives in the Netherlands).

In short, there has been 'an explosion of activity designed to produce better-looking, or more aesthetically pleasing people' states Postrel (2004: 27). Indeed, Corbett (2007: 157) notes how American society is now 'obsessed with physical appearance' and individuals looking good, such that 'it seems that appearance matters in our society today more than it ever has before'. Similarly Jeffes (1998: ix) argues that 'we [the US] are truly and dangerously becoming an appearance driven society'. The same author also recounts a story of how he travelled to his local magazine store to check how many titles were concerned with fashion, appearance, looks and make-up, and in just 15 minutes had counted nearly 50 titles. Jeffes also notes when these titles had come into existence, with over 90 per cent of them published after 1968. As he observes, 'our conclusion is that this media-driven beauty bombardment has increased significantly over the past 20–30 years' (1998: 129).

Unsurprisingly, then, the US is the country with the highest number of cosmetic procedures, undertaking nearly twice as many procedures than the next country, Brazil (International Society of Aesthetic Plastic Surgery, 2018). Consequently, in 2017 the US spent $16.7 billion on aesthetic surgery (American Society of Plastic Surgeons, 2018). It is not just America though that is obsessed with appearance. Overell (2006: 14, 15), writing in the UK context, firstly asks 'can there be another era when so many people were quite so interested in improving appearance?', before going on to suggest that 'the injunction of our times is that appearance is to be optimized. Everyday life in the twenty-first century has taken a highly aesthetic turn as we choose to invest ever-greater proportions of our affluence in personal presentation'. This investment has its returns. At its most basic the relatively unattractive (who Corbett, 2007, terms the 'aesthetically challenged') often lose out on opportunities and benefits that are generally bestowed on the attractive. In this sense, there exists both a beauty premium and beauty penalty (or 'plainness penalty') in which physically attractive people (both men and women) are more likely to be recruited and once recruited will earn more – typically between 10–15 per cent – than those who are less attractive (see for example, Anderson et al., 2010; Anýžová and Matějů, 2018; Borland and Leigh, 2014). Whilst research has found that a beauty premium exists in the US (Hamermesh, 2011; Hamermesh and Biddle, 1994) and UK (Harper, 2000), more recent work suggests that this phenomenon is universal and that perceived good looks lead to a wage premium in most countries with the highest beauty premiums in Germany and China (Sierminska, 2015). Conversely Sierminska reports that the largest penalties for those with 'below average' looks are in Britain and Australia.

FEELING GROOVY: THE BEAUTY INDUSTRY AND COSMETIC SURGERY

These premia and penalties make understandable the increasing obsession with personal appearance and the major growth of the so-called beauty industry and cosmetic surgery (or as we have noted above, now increasingly referred to as 'aesthetic surgery'). Resultantly, as Barth and Wagner (2017: 146) state 'whole industries feed off the hopes of their clients to improve their appearance: beauty salons and cosmetics of course, but also the media, tattoo parlours, beauty coaches, makeovers and plastic surgery, all promising to meet the present standards of beauty and attractiveness'. Thus, as Corbett (2007: 157–58) notes, the increasing obsession with appearance 'might be a result of advances in science and medicine that have made alterations of physical appearance possible and more accessible than at any other time – what was once thought immutable has now become mutable'. The mutability of our appearance means we are also increasingly aware of aspiring to be 'aesthetically pleasing people', leading to a rapid expansion in cosmetic surgery and the broader beauty industry. As Overell (2006: 15) has observed, 'we spend quite a portion of our time waxing, plucking, tweaking, pummelling, titivating, working out and applying unguents; such activities are no longer viewed as the luxuries of an idle leisured class, but as everyday necessities for the vast majority or women and a fair proportion of men, too'. Beauty – or at least trying to beautify ourselves – has become a major activity for women and, increasingly, men. The beauty industry is now big business, but is not new. Over time there has been a subtle change in the industry from a position in which it promotes beautification and enhanced sexual allure to one in which its consumers also emphasise its potential use to lever enhanced employability.

As Black (2004: 20) notes, throughout time women and men have sought to conform to the aesthetic standards of the day by the use of 'creams, lotions and preparations'. The use of cosmetics can be traced back at least as far as the Egyptians. Their crafts-like production changed dramatically with industrialisation in the eighteenth and nineteenth centuries, and the then-fledgling 'industry' really took off in the early twentieth century as more women gained spending power through increased labour market participation in the European and US labour markets. The centre of the industry also shifted from Europe to the US as it piggy-backed on the also fledging movie, television, magazine and advertising industries, and from the 1920s a fully commercialised mass industry began to emerge (Jones, 2010). In this period ardently feminist advertising executives such as Helen Landsdowne Resor sought to promote beauty products as 'self-transformation' (p. 83) for women, through new forms of body work that would make them more sexually desirable to men. The industry needed the increasingly economically independent Western woman to buy into the beauty myth: 'to take control of her appearance and be her beautiful, successful best' (p. 102).

There was nothing inevitable about this process, Jones stresses. Given that many of its products had little or no physical need and the industry had to invent problems such as body odour and greying hair as a source of social ignominy. In doing so, Jones acknowledges, the industry persuaded people to buy its products and defined and promoted a beauty ideal. This ideal centred on classical femininity in which the emphasis was, and still is, on being young, blue-eyed and blonde, and which has now standardised beauty. As Gold (2011) points out, so aligned had beauty become with slim young, blond, blue-eyed things that when Dove, a cosmetics brand of Unilever, used 'real women' in a 2000s marketing campaign, it became a global news story. Likewise in 2015, model Charli Howard triggered a social media storm when she posted on Facebook 'Here's a big F*CK YOU to my (now ex) model agency for saying that at 5ft 8in tall and a UK size 6-8, I'm "too big" and "out of shape" to work in the fashion industry' (cited in Wiseman, 2018: 14; and see Box 2.3).[1]

Box 2.3   Fit or fat? The importance of size in the leisure industry and beyond

Fitness First, a UK fitness and leisure company, was reported to be targeting 'larger employees' as they were deemed to not fit the company's image. A leaked e-mail from the company's then human resources director, reminded regional mangers that the company should not give uniforms to any staff over size 16 as the company was concerned about the impact of having larger employees in a company which amongst other things promoted weight loss.[2] Whilst this concern might not seem surprising within the fitness and leisure industry, there are much broader concerns about employees being overweight and its impact in society and the workplace. Within the UK around two-thirds of adults are either overweight or obese, with around a third obese, whilst in the US nearly 40 per cent of Americans are classified as obese. Within the US it is estimated that obesity costs the US economy $1.2 trillion a year in medical expenditure, worker absenteeism and lost productivity, a figure much greater than that for smoking and alcoholism. As well as the overall costs to the economy there are also costs to individuals who will often suffer discrimination due to being overweight from what is described as 'obesity bias' or more simply 'fattism'. For example, in the US weight discrimination has become one of the top three reported forms of discrimination in employment and obese people are less likely to be employed and earn, on average, between 6–12 per cent less than people of average weight with the same skill sets. Overweight people are also stereotypically seen as being lazy, slow, lower in competence, sloppy, unlikable, and lacking in self-control. Research has found that for customer-facing roles in the service sector overweight and obese people are likely to face discrimination, with one experimental study finding that this discrimination is highly gendered with women, even when within a healthy BMI, much more likely to face discrimination than overtly overweight men. There can be exceptions though, and reflecting our notion of the need with aesthetic labour

(Continued)

to ensure a fit between the brand and its employees' research into a plus-size clothing store, found that plus-sized women were preferred over standard-sized women for sales jobs in order to embody the brand image and for their ability to interact sensitively and empathetically with plus-sized customers.[3]

(*Sources*: Baker, 2018; BBC, 2003; Finkelstein et al., 2007; Gruys, 2012; Huggins, 2015; Nickson et al., 2016; Waters and Graf, 2018)

Non-adherents to the beauty ideal, e.g. people from other ethnic origins, failed to win the early beauty pageants, and those who did in later years tended to conform in their own way to the beauty ideal by, for example, straightening afro hair or having the body proportions of European-origin women. This standard was also promoted worldwide by the US-dominated movie and advertising industries: 'Feminine grooming was turned into a widely watched media spectacle which set expectations and defined aspirations', Jones (2010: 152) states. This exposure created new markets both in the US and Europe and beyond in the developing countries. With rising GDP and incomes, India and China are now emerging as important markets (Lee, 2015). As in the US and Europe, Jones (2010: 189) suggests that the beauty industry offers these new consumers the opportunity to have more self-confidence by feeling more beautiful, and that the perfumes, potions, creams and dyes that women and, increasingly, men buy to restore or preserve their looks, will make them 'more attractive and, as they age, to keep them looking young'.

Jones admits that the industry pushes 'warped aspirational values' (p. 314) but also argues that the industry simply democratises beauty, making it available to all classes and nations. The reality, as much of the evidence in Jones' own book illustrates, is that the industry also creates these aspirations. Where previously China forbade beauty contests, at the time of writing they have now hosted nine Miss World pageants (second only to the UK where the competition was hosted from its inception in 1951 to 1988), companies are employing beauty consultants, and cosmetic surgery is booming with eyelid trimming and nose straightening as Chinese consumers seek to emulate Western beauty norms (see also Lee, 2015). It is instructive to note that China is now also a big spender on aesthetic surgery, with suggestions that the market was worth as much as $116 billion in 2017 (He, 2018). Similarly, China's cosmetics market is second globally in sales, only behind the US (Otis, 2016). Likewise, whilst the beauty industry has responded recently to demographic changes by extending its market to older, mature consumers, it is also extending it to younger teenage and, more recently, pre-teen markets. If the beauty industry is premised on making people feel good about themselves, it can only do so if they are made to feel initially bad – or socially inferior – about themselves.

The beauty industry has also become more varied. It now encompasses a number of sub-sectors including hairdressing, barbering, nail technicians, beauty salons and consultants, mobile beauty therapists and spas. The range of treatments offered is wide-ranging including manicures, pedicures, facials, waxing, electrolysis, aromatherapy, massage, reflexology and reiki. Black (2004) notes how clients in accessing these different types of treatments also draw on different discourses to justify them, and in that sense she notes how clients are likely to see them as entailing pampering, concerned with health issues, about routine grooming, or corrective, such as electrolysis to remove facial hair.

Although the UK's spend on aesthetic surgery, which is around £3.6 billion (Rackham, 2018), is relatively small compared to that of the US, Brazil, India and China, looks still matter. The Hairdressing and Beauty Industry Authority (Habia), the UK government-approved standards setting body for hair, beauty, nails, barbering, spa therapy and African Caribbean hair, suggests that there are nearly 55,000 businesses in the beauty industry in the UK, employing around 277,000 employees,[4] with an annual turnover of £6.2 billion (Habia, 2017). However, it not simply the growth in economic and employment terms of the beauty industry per se that is important, it is also its cultural impact. Hairdressing (and other 'bodily improvers', such as beauticians, physical fitness trainers, masseurs and trichologists) have been identified as 'iconic jobs' by the UK's Work Foundation (Overell, 2006). According to Overell:

> What gives bodily improvement its status as a paradigm trade is that it speaks of a society transfixed by the pursuit of physical excellence. The rise of their craft is a reflection of the prioritization of appearance, of perception, of looking a certain way, of the power of identity, of the power of lifestyle. (2006: 14)

It is not just the aestheticisation of our homes, as the Aesthetic Movement wanted, or the aestheticisation of organisational hardware, people are increasingly aestheticising themselves. A key reason for this personal aestheticisation links back to the employment-related beauty premia and penalties which we discussed earlier. Drawing on her typology of why clients seek treatments, Black (2004) notes how grooming treatments are often justified in relation to the need to maintain an 'acceptable' standard of appearance in the workplace. Grooming treatments are then necessities, based on 'small regular maintenance functions' that aim to give 'an overall impression of care having been taken with the body, but without dramatic changes in appearance' (p. 132). The maintenance of a certain standard of appearance in the workplace is now facilitated through regular, incremental treatment, though increasingly for some people at least more radical measures are undertaken with the use of cosmetic surgery, which is now discussed.

As we have noted above, aesthetic surgery is now big business globally and individuals labour to improve their aesthetic appeal both in and outside the workplace (Lee, 2015). The popular press is filled with stories of people using their savings, taking out loans and re-mortgaging their homes to pay for cosmetic surgery to improve their employ-ability (see for example Nisbet, 2006). Elliott (2008: 34) thus recognises that 'in the new economy, nothing is more sexy than surgery. From Botox and lipo to tummy tuck and mini-facelifts, cosmetic surgery is today a massive global business'. Whilst the main focus remains on women,[5] the industry now overtly targets men, with more younger men and women in particular opting to undertake procedures (see Box 2.4; also Hawkes, 2016; Ricard-Wolf, 2005).

Box 2.4   The search for male body perfection?

Historically cosmetic surgery patients have been women, but audits undertaken by the American Society of Plastic Surgeons and the British Association of Aesthetic Plastic Surgeons highlight a significant increase in the number of men having cosmetic surgery. From less than 3 per cent of procedures being undertaken by men in the late 1990s, the figure now stands at around 10 per cent in both countries. Moreover, a BBC survey in 2019 found that 50 per cent of men aged between 18–30 would consider having a procedure in order to look good. The increase in men undertaking such surgery is attributed to the need to look good, a pressure that has been faced by women for many years. As US columnist Glenn Sacks notes, the pressure on men to look good reflects their evolving role within society and economy such that 'fifty years ago the average man in England or in America was working class. The work was often dirty, grimy and hard. There was the image of a strong man who did what he had to support his family. Now, there's less physical labour. It's more office based. There's more expectations to look good'. Recognising this increasing pressure on men Peter Baker, then chief executive of the Men's Health Forum, suggested that 'Since the late 1980s and 1990s, the message to men is that they have to look good. We constantly see images of men with six packs and toned bodies on the front of magazines and on TV. It is similar to what women have had to put up with for much longer'.

(*Sources*: https://baaps.org.uk/baaps_annual_audit_results_.aspx; BBC, 2007, 2019; Fleming, 2008; Gabbatt, 2011; www.plasticsurgery.org/news/plastic-surgery-statistics)

Although there has been a rapid expansion in the cosmetic surgery market in the UK, Key Note (2008) still point out that attitudes towards cosmetic surgery in the UK remain nowhere near as positive as those in the US, something which is reflected in the respec-tive worth of the industries in the two countries noted earlier. Indeed, as Lee (2015) notes of the ten countries that globally account for 68 per cent of plastic surgery, the US is the highest at 16 per cent, closely followed by Brazil (at 15 per cent). Reaffirming our earlier discussion of the growing importance of the beauty industry in developing economies, such as China, the next two countries are China and India (both at 6 per cent). The UK is not in the top ten countries. Regardless of national differences Elliott (2008: 34) states that 'more and more, middle class professionals are turning to plastic surgery in an effort to retain, or sometimes, acquire, youthful looks'. Similarly, Sulaiman (2005) notes the increase in cosmetic surgery for men working in the City in London. She suggests this surgery is often a response to ageism in the City where there will often be a feeling that at a certain age men can no longer cope with the pressurised environment, so looking youthful becomes important. Elliott (2008: 34) also suggests that for professionals, in particular, undertaking cosmetic surgery is important for advancing careers and financial standing and as such 'to be surgically "freshened up" provides an edge in the marketplace' (though see also Gimlin, 2000, 2006, whose research suggests that many women who have cosmetic surgery do so to look 'normal' rather than necessarily beautiful; and Lee, 2015, who highlights how the costs of plastic surgery often outweigh the additional earnings someone might enjoy having undertaken such a procedure).

The rise in importance of the beauty industry and cosmetic surgery would also seem to reflect the increasing recognition of the relationship between how we look and self-esteem, particularly in the workplace. Westwood (2004: 7) has argued that:

> How we look and how we, and others, think we look – appear to matter a great deal and this is an important component of our self-esteem. Women may be no more obsessed about the way they look than men. In this sense the increased value placed on appearance is becoming a more gender-neutral phenomenon, aided by an evolving economy more dependent on personal and 'high touch' services.

It is interesting that the importance of looking good is attributed such significance in more general accounts of how to improve self-esteem. Indeed, although Westwood acknowledges the somewhat amorphous notion of the 'self-esteem industry', he does nevertheless highlight the growth of businesses which are concerned with improving our looks as being symptomatic of the self-esteem industry.

Westwood cites research undertaken on the *Yellow Pages* business directories, which found that since the early 1990s there has been a huge increase in entries for various self-improvement services. The example he offers includes: aromatherapists up by 5,000 per cent; a 1,780 per cent increase in cosmetic surgery services; and a 1,445 per cent increase in dieting and weight control. Additionally, he also suggests that the growth in the cosmetics and beauty industries is also illustrative of the increasing importance of looking good for self-esteem, noting for example how in 2003 the UK spent £6 billion on cosmetics, toiletries and perfumery, a figure that had risen to nearly £10 billion by 2017 (CPTA, 2017). It is also noteworthy that Westwood also recognises how some of the biggest growth markets in cosmetics have been in products for men, with the male grooming market growing by 800 per cent in the period 1998 to 2004, such that by 2004 men were spending on average £84 per year on beauty products compared to the £138 per year spent by women. By 2018 around 30 per cent of men were spending at least £250 per year in the UK on grooming products, with some suggestions that men were spending even more than women on beauty products (Hudson, 2018). Globally the market for male grooming products is projected to reach $60.7 billion by 2020 (Weinswig, 2017), as men are encouraged to consume products that 'make them look and perform better' (Moshakis, 2019: 25), reflecting concerns that if they do not look young and fit it will harm their career.

CONCLUSION

This chapter has charted the rise of the aesthetic economy and the manner in which society, the economy, organisations and individuals have taken on board the importance of aesthetics in everyday life. Importantly, the chapter recognised how the genesis of the putative aesthetic economy can be traced back to the nineteenth century but has been expounded as a key development of the twentieth and twenty-first centuries. Consequently, in this 'age of look and feel', evangelical claims are made by the likes of Postrel about how beauty and style are increasingly become a source of competitive advantage in the aesthetic economy enveloping both organisations and individuals.

Thus, whilst functionality is still present in artefacts increasingly it is this beauty and style that make products stand out. Importantly, this shift is enveloping a range of products and different market niches, including becoming increasingly mainstreamed, has been incorporated into more prosaic product offerings. The focus on aesthetics by product designers is now being echoed by everyone from retailers to homebuilders, restaurants, hotels and in nearly every facet of our daily lives. Aesthetics are no longer a luxury; instead people are being encouraged through social norms to believe that they can pick and choose styles that appeal to them as individuals. More generally through the aesthetics *of* organisations, organisations are increasingly concerned with aestheticising organisational hardware through the use of material aspects, such as the design of a building or the interior design for an organisational space.

It is not just organisations though who are paying ever greater attention to how they style themselves – the same is also true for individuals, who are developing and mobilising their personal aesthetic capital *in* organisations. The significant growth in impression management and the dress for success movement indicate how we increasingly package and sell ourselves. These aesthetic upgrades to enhance our employability are now also facilitated through the ever-growing beauty industry and the rise in cosmetic surgery – a trend that is also strongly linked to self-esteem. Importantly, these services are now also consumed by men as the pressure to look good extends to encompass both men and women. Thus, the aestheticisation of life, expounded by the Aesthetic Movement (Breward, 2011) and outlined by Böhme (2003) and Postrel (2004) as underpinning the emergence of an aesthetic economy, has become an aestheticisation of working lives. However, there is an important distinction that needs to be made between aestheticisation for organisational and personal advantage. As we have argued in this chapter, the latter is driven by individual workers for their own benefit – it boosts their pay and employment prospects most obviously. When employers' appropriate worker aesthetics for organisational benefit, a labour of aesthetics becomes aesthetic labour, as we discuss in the next chapter.

NOTES

1. As noted earlier the average size for women in the UK is 16.
2. See also Butler and Harris (2015) for the experiences of a woman working as a slimming club consultant and the extremes, through taking weight loss pills and illegal drugs, that she went through in attempting to move from a size 16 to the size 12 expected by the slimming company.
3. Plus-size in this context indicates those who are US sizes 14–28 (UK equivalent sizes would be 16–30).
4. It is noteworthy that 90 per cent of employees in the UK beauty industry are women.
5. For example, the British Association of Aesthetic Plastic Surgeons (BAAPA) annual audit in 2018 found that women had 91 per cent of procedures, a similar breakdown to the US (92 per cent women, 8 per cent men) (American Society of Plastic Surgeons, 2018).

3
IF YOU LOOK THE PART, YOU'LL GET THE JOB

In Chapter 2 we outlined claims for the emergence of a new 'expressive age' (Böhme, 2010: 30) or an 'age of look and feel' (Postrel, 2004: 178). Whilst we have some reservations about the more grandiose claims made, especially that of Böhme for a new stage of capitalism, we do recognise that an emphasis on aesthetics is now more pervasive and that a consumption-driven beautification is underway of products and people in the wider economy and society. This shift contrasts with claims made for the workplace: 'Much of modern work lacks beauty', states Donkin, 'there is no place for beauty on a balance sheet' (2010: 241). Instead, jobs are said to be becoming more ugly and brutish. This angst about the quality of jobs reflects a concern with a polarisation – at least in the UK and US – of the labour market into good and bad jobs (Hurley et al., 2015; Kalleberg et al., 2020). Whilst we share concerns about job quality, we would disagree that beauty has left the workplace: aesthetic labour indicates that beauty contributes to the balance sheet of some firms and is currently more rather than less important to employers.

This chapter outlines the fluctuating fortunes of the body in analyses of work and explains the current (re)turn to analysing the body in work. The first section outlines the initial concern and then disregard for the body in analyses of work. The following section then points out how it remained important to some employers, particularly in those putatively glamourous industries, and made a brief re-appearance in some, now classic, studies of work but was quickly dropped either because of a lack of empirics or because of other conceptual concerns with emotional labour (i.e. Hochschild, 1983; Mills, 1951). The following three sections then define, theorise and attempt to locate aesthetic labour. They show the current centrality in employer strategies of worker corporeality in work and employment, and how aesthetic labour conceptually captures this development.

THE GREAT VANISHING TRICK

The body was once a key feature in analyses of work, and particularly in those analyses concerned with the harsh working conditions wrought by the industrial revolution (Brody, 1960; Engels, 1971[1845]). The body is, after all, the source of labour. As part of the industrial revolution, employers needed to take workers physically out of homes and fields and put them into the mines, mills and new factories in order to be able to exert greater control over the labour of these bodies (e.g. Thompson, 1983). Once there, with employer oversight enabled, those bodies could be made to work longer or harder to enable employers to be more competitive in the market.

The nineteenth-century workplace became pathological as the debilitating effects of industrial life took their toll on workers' bodies, which were becoming 'stunted, enfeebled, and depraved' according to one contemporary commentator (Turner Thakrah, quoted in Rule, 1991: 145). In his *The Condition of the Working Class in England*, Engels (1971[1845]) charted the death and disease wrought upon urban workers in Victorian northern England. In one town, Carlisle, death rates amongst adults under 40 years of age rose 20 per cent with the introduction of mills. In the US steel mills of the early twentieth century, exhausting work, heat fumes and danger were endemic. In one mill almost a quarter of immigrant workers were injured or killed each year (Brody, 1960). An end of shift stupor would descend on those workers not injured or killed. Brody quotes one investigator at the time who wrote that on the trolley journey home from work, 'Nobody was talking. … [Some] were asleep. The rest sat quiet, with legs and neck loose, with their eyes open, steady, dull, fixed upon nothing at all … No man who works twelve hours … has time or energy to do much outside of this work' (1960: 94).

Work in the developed countries can still be debilitating, even dangerous. In 2004 in Glasgow, the Stockline plastics factory exploded. Nine employees were killed and 40 injured (Taylor and Connelly, 2009). In the US states of Georgia and Alabama there were 12 amputations, most involving the loss of fingers, at Hyundai and Kia component parts makers over 2015–16 (Silverman, 2017). However, the worst ravages of work have been ameliorated through preventative interventions. With agitation by organised labour as well as religion-inspired moralists and enlightened politicians, working time and occupational health and safety regulations were gradually introduced from the nineteenth century, and the physical toll on workers' bodies was mitigated as the twentieth century progressed (see for example, Hofmann et al., 2017; Rule, 1991). Moreover by the late twentieth century, jobs in the mines and mills were disappearing, replaced by service jobs.[1] As the mills have been replaced by malls, and coalmines by call centres, any residual health and safety issues have become less obvious – psychological not physical, as research on job stress and burnout amongst workers illustrates (e.g. Schaubroeck and Jones, 2000; Taylor and Bain, 1999).[2] These injuries tend to be less visible and less immediate.

It is not just that injuries became centred on the mind, with the shift to services, work itself changed from manual to mental. This change was articulated in Bell's (1973) *The Coming of the Post-Industrial Society*, using the metaphor of the game to describe work under different forms of production. Before the industrial revolution the game in agriculture was between man and nature; in the industrial age the game in factories was between man and machine. In the services-led, so-called 'post-industrial' age the new game is between people he claimed. Thus, in service jobs such as retail, Korczynski and Ott (2004) claim that workers now 'enchant customers' with their sales patter. However for Bell and other, more recent writers, the real focus is those workers driving the new 'knowledge society' or 'knowledge economy' using embrained knowledge. With work now said to be driven by brains not brawn, the means of production is lodged inside these workers' heads – their ideas (Nordstrom and Ridderstrale, 2002). The task for capital now, through 'knowledge management', is to help create and then capture and capitalise on these ideas. This emphasis on the stuff inside workers' heads has compounded the lack of interest in workers' corporality. The outcome is that whilst the body continued to labour, it disappeared from or was downgraded in analyses of work (Muñoz de Bustillo et al., 2011; Slavishak, 2010). It then receded from analytical sight by the mid-to-late twentieth century with economic structuring and interventions to improve workplace health and safety (Muñoz de Bustillo et al., 2011).

Whilst interest declined in the body as a factor of production, it rose in analyses of consumption, particularly leisure and pleasure (Turner, 1996). There were a number of sometimes overlapping reasons for this interest. For example, the popularisation of discourse analysis and the focus on the disciplined and sexualised body (Foucault, 1979, 1981), as well as the new potentials to refashion the body as an expression of identity and sexual identity (Featherstone et al., 1991; Giddens, 1991), all of which suggest that the body has become less biological and more social, physically malleable if not plastic, subjectable to what Giddens calls the 'body projects' of entrepreneurial individuals undertaking the type of cosmetic (now labelled 'aesthetic') interventions that we outlined in Chapter 2. These projects received a technological boost with twenty-first century advances in medical science, and the possibility of having a 'blank screen' from which we can choose our bodies and those of our offspring (for a discussion see Shilling, 2007). Even feminism, which had argued for the gendered body (e.g. Grosz, 1994), lost ground to a new sexual politics in which the body was no longer the outcome of social conditioning but a matter of personal preference. As an ironic consequence, the physical body has 'slid from view', according to Shilling, becoming 'a mere metaphor' (2007: 10). At best, Wolkowitz (2002) notes, the concern in these accounts is individuals' work on their own bodies, not individuals' working bodies.

That the body is analytically important as a site of consumption rather than a factor of production resonates with erroneous, evidence-free claims such as those of Bauman

(1998) that work is dead and that we are now what we buy. Unfortunately for Bauman, the evidence suggests otherwise – that, if anything, the developed countries remain work centric, even as the clever robots are said to be coming to take the jobs. Governments of the advanced economies are concerned to encourage, even coerce, more people into work; a concern that only increased as the global financial crisis turned into a global economic crisis and unemployment rose to high levels, as both the OECD's (Scarpetta, 2014) and EU's (EC, 2010) drive for 'more and better' jobs illustrates, with the latter even setting specific targets for increasing employment participation rates. Production, and within it work, therefore remain important. Indeed it is indicative that countries are today often referred to as economies rather than societies (Carlisle and Hanlon, 2011).

In this context, Wolkowitz (2002) has rightly sought to bring work back into analysis of the body, focusing on what she terms 'body work'. Occupations involving this body work are multiple, from maids and care assistants to medical doctors and retail workers. However as Wolkowitz makes clear, body work has a specific and intentionally bounded focus. What workers in these occupations have in common, she states, is that they are employed to work on the 'care, adornment, pleasure, discipline and cure of others' bodies' (2002: 497). In other words, the work of these occupations centres on servicing the bodies of others, a trait found in many of the beauty industry occupations that we discussed in the previous chapter. Nevertheless, this directing of attention to body work by Wolkowitz, and in particular its link to the employment relationship, is important. It attunes to the blurring of reproductive and productive labour as the former increasingly becomes commodified as it is pushed and pulled out of the home and into the marketplace (Wolkowitz and Warhurst, 2010).

The problem is that it is also a narrow conceptualisation of work and the body in services. In only focusing on those workers who work on others' bodies, it ignores a whole range of other service workers whose work is not the production (and reproduction) of others' bodies but involves the management of their bodies by their employers for those employers' benefit – aesthetic labour. Whilst these workers serve food and drinks, sell dresses and jeans or respond to insurance claims and banking queries for example, their bodies – not those of clients and customers – are part of the product being sold to customers and clients.

THE BODY, GLAMOUR AND THE PERSONALITY MARKET

If the body disappeared from research agendas, it remained of interest to employers as economies began to restructure and the workforce began to (re)feminise from the mid-twentieth century. That interest was most obvious in what at the time were regarded as the 'glamorous' airline and television industries. By the 1960s, airline cabin crew had become feminised (see for example, Barry, 2007; Mills, 2006). Airlines operated strict appearance rules for these workers – rules that still exist in some cases (see Box 3.1 below). Crew were required to take make-up, hairstyling, workwear and comportment classes as part of their training. The aim of this prescription was to standardise their appearance as part of the service offering (Riegel, 2013). Over the years there has been a lingering ambivalence amongst air cabin crew about this requirement. On the one hand, as Riegel makes clear, they enjoyed the training, even found it exciting: 'I loved every minute of those lessons', she says, 'I felt like I was a student at some Swiss finishing school' (p. 96). Moreover it made her and her colleagues the centre of much-wanted male attention – 'the men surrounded us likes flies', she says (p. 97). On the other hand, female flights attendants had regular, company-imposed weight checks and some companies even imposed body shape ratios (Shilling, 1996). Not surprisingly, these demands on their corporeality ran up against claims of sexual objectification – the 1970s Singapore Girl, for example, who became the brand embodiment of Singapore Airlines – and attendants were sometimes cast as little more than 'trolley dollies' (Bolton and Boyd, 2003). In an information leaflet given to us in the late 1990s, the UK-based Monarch Airlines stated that its cabin crew were the company's 'shop window'. Advertising for new crew it stipulated their height and weight, 'with weight in proportion to height', and said that they had to possess a 'pleasing appearance'. Whilst such explicit aesthetic demands have receded in the UK and US, in many other countries they remain alive and well, as Box 3.1 below shows.

Box 3.1   Looks as a business card

In 2017, the Russian airline Aeroflot fought a court battle over claims that it favoured the employment of slim and attractive female cabin crew. The company, asserting that it had a right to stipulate the weight and size of the crew, argued that 'stewardesses are the face of any airline, and the national carrier's stewardesses are the country's business card'. In China similar attitudes prevail with evidence of airlines paying more attention to women's appearance and figure in recruiting cabin crew, rather than elements such as foreign language skills or education. In 2008, one Chinese airline even selected flights attendants using a reality TV show that followed a six-month audition to work for the airline, and included activities such as a swimsuit competition and a race involving luggage, make-up brushes and drink trays. In 2019, Norwegian Air was criticised for its 22-page dress code which, for women, stipulates that they should wear high heels, eye make-up and a light foundation, and only gold- or silver-coloured jewellery. A spokesperson for the airline said, 'Norwegian Air has a comprehensive set of uniform guidelines to ensure that our flying crew represent our brand'.

(*Sources*: BBC, 2017; Oppenheim, 2019; Ren, 2017)

Similar debates occurred around the introduction of female newsreaders such as Angela Rippon and Anna Ford on British television in the 1970s.[3] The debates also focused on these newsreaders' physical appearance and its relationship to their work, as Box 3.2 illustrates.

Box 3.2   The rise of 'autocuties'

The public worried that the introduction of female newsreaders would distract the viewers with their looks: 'Could I suggest that Miss Ford cuts out the frosty lipstick and shiny blush-on' wrote one irate writer in the *Daily Express* newspaper in 1978. What these female newsreaders were saying was subordinated to how they looked when they said it. Newsreaders' looks continue to be debated into the 2000s. Some field reporters, for example Kate Adie, criticised the BBC for hiring news presenters 'with cute faces, cute bottoms and nothing in between'. Significantly, the accusations now extended to include men. Male and female newsreaders were similarly being castigated as 'autocuties': 'pretty young women and handsome young men without a solid journalistic background', according to seasoned male TV journalist Mark Austin.

(*Sources*: Armstrong, 2008; Holland, 1987; Packer, 2002)

Despite the complaints from Adie and Austin, by the start of the 2000s attitudes were seemingly changing and a counter claim was made that appearance is not a distraction from the work of news-reading but instead an integral part of it. Thus, if there was an attempt to deride the focus on newsreaders' appearance in the 1970s, it is argued that appearance is not only part of the job but also an important feature of the job. As UK newsreader Katie Derham explained, 'I'm on screen most evenings, and if you have an on-screen job people are going to employ you partly for how you look. But it's not a case of "Do you look gorgeous?", it's more like "Do you look appropriate and will people take you seriously?" When you're a newsreader you have to look like you know what you're talking about' (quoted in Packer, 2002: 14). Overturning Holland's argument, Derham claimed that her corporeality was an integral feature of her work and helped her to be taken seriously as a newsreader – to look the part. How she looked would impact viewers' perceptions of her as being fit for her job, she believed (and for an interesting discussion of how television viewers respond to the physical appearance of male and female newsreaders, see Mitra et al., 2014).

This shift from disparaging any emphasis on looks at work to not only accepting it but also suggesting that looks help underpin that work has now extended beyond the putatively glamorous industries. Across services, in retail for example, there is recognition that workers' corporeality is part of the job. In this respect, if Bauman is wrong about the death of work, he is right to suggest that capitalism now attempts to commodify everything, including the body. However, in contrast to Bauman we would argue that this shift indicates that a commodification of the body has occurred in production, not just consumption. This point was first made by Mills (1951) in his classic text, *White Collar*. As the twentieth century was unfolding and services were becoming more prevalent, so a 'personality market' was emerging, he observed, in which workers sold their personalities on the labour market to employers. This 'personality' comprised the attitudes and appearance of workers and was important in the workplace because the shift to services, he argued 20 years before Bell (1973), was accompanied by another shift – 'from skills with things to skills with people' (1951: 182).

From Mills' account, it seems that employer attempts to capture and commodify worker corporality were generally under-developed in these service industries. In Mills' department store, for example, the employer seemingly limited its interventions to the hiring of workers with appropriate appearance. Once hired, the employer left its workers to self-determine the development and mobilisation of their appearance in work. Employers might sanction worker use of their appearance, for example, but not actively seek to mobilise and develop it – an important distinction. As we have pointed out elsewhere (Warhurst and Nickson, 2009), Mills recognised that his analysis was occurring at a time when a customer service orientation was only just emerging. As such it was still under-developed: employers had yet to fully grasp the opportunity afforded by more fully exploiting their workers' corporeality. Offering no evidence of employers trying to mobilise or develop this corporality, Mills quickly dropped analysis of appearance in a further discussion of the personality market.

Thirty years later, Hochschild (1983) picked up on Mills' point, also arguing in *The Managed Heart* that worker personality was bought and sold on the labour market. She also noticed, however, that employers were now trying to manage that personality in work in mainstream service industries. By the 1980s a worker's personality was thus not just a labour market but also a labour process issue – appearance was not just a criterion for getting the job, it was also a criterion of doing the job. It is this new focus that accounts for emotional labour according to Hochschild. With workers now recognised as part of the product on offer, they are required to manage their own feelings and the feelings of customers in order to affect a managerially prescribed service encounter. This prescription results in the imposition of 'feeling rules' to which workers must adhere. These feeling rules result in a performance, with 'acting' by the worker, and which 'in a commercial setting … 'take[s] on the property of a resource' for the employer, 'a resource to be used to make money' (p. 55). Different organisations have different feeling rules that produce different styles of service: neighbourly or sophisticated or sexy for example – though each style is a variant of 'outgoing middle-class sociability' according to Hochschild (p. 97) – a point to which we return in Chapter 7.

As with Mills before her, Hochschild initially flagged worker appearance as a feature of this service encounter. As her core definition highlights, emotional labour involves 'the management of emotion to create publicly observable facial and bodily display' (p. 7). In other words, the body is used 'to *show* feeling' (p. 247).[4] Body language is the outward indicator of feeling; it is the bodily expression – the smile to indicate friendliness for example (and see Chapter 5 for further discussion of this issue). In referring to this display work, Hochschild fully acknowledged the importance of worker corporeality in making manifest the required emotions. However, as with Mills before her, Hochschild dropped further analysis of worker appearance and, with it, the management of workers' corporeality. This discarding of the body is not surprising: Hochschild's explicit aim was to foreground emotion in work and emotion work as a feature of the employment relationship. What she wanted to emphasise was that, as part of their surplus generating strategies, employers required that emotional labour be 'sold for a wage and therefore has exchange value' (p. 7).

By the end of the twentieth century, emotional labour had become an important, and even dominant analytical paradigm for research on interactive service work. Within it workers' attitudes, not appearance, became the sole proxy for personality, even when corporeality is revealed as an important managerial concern (e.g. Callaghan and Thompson, 2002). When worker corporality was raised in analyses of service work – by Adkins (1995) for example – it was as part of wider debates about feminised service and the propensity of women to provide 'service' work, and even portrayed as a 'gift' from female service workers to male service consumers (Tyler and Taylor, 1998). Alternatively it was seen through the lens of sexual harassment, with men's bodies an arbiter and potential and actual threat to women's bodies in the workplace. This 'point of departure' reflected wider feminist arguments about the marginalisation if not oppression of women according to Morgan (2002: 419). Whilst these arguments had a legitimate basis, the body was not the core focus; it was used to illustrate a concern with gender relations rather than employment relations.

DEFINING AESTHETIC LABOUR

Whilst studies of the personality market have dropped their focus on worker appearance, as we noted in the previous chapter, other studies, although not using the concept of the personality market, have demonstrated that labour market pay premiums and penalties exist for workers as an outcome of their perceived physical attractiveness (e.g. Hamermesh, 2011; Sierminska, 2015). In this analysis, all labour is aestheticised to an extent – with positive and negative material outcomes for workers, as we discuss in more detail in Chapter 7. Moreover, employers also materially benefit from this perceived attractiveness, with Hamermesh speculating that having workers with good looks 'affect[s] the bottom line of companies' (2011: 7). However, studies that explore the link between worker perceived attractiveness and organisational performance, even in the private sector, are sparse, Hamermesh notes. It is a 'best guess' therefore 'that having better-looking workers helps the company chalk up greater sales', he concedes (p. 100). However, the lack of evidence does not stop him from recommending that organisations hire better-looking workers if they want better sales and performance. The general point, made succinctly by Mears (2012: 815), is that 'looks translate into outcomes'; material outcomes we would argue – producing both value for employers and remuneration for workers. Whilst Hamermesh argues that the the efficacy of this labour is based on its scarcity – few workers are good looking and those that are therefore command more positive attention – we would hold that its efficacy is based on its affectivity, an argument that is beyond economistic analysis Hamermesh concedes, and which also allows us to extend the focus beyond workers with good looks to include workers with the right looks from the employers' perspective.

However, not all aestheticised labour is aesthetic labour. Just as emotional labour is a 'form of labour to be sold' (Hochschild, 1983: 89), so too is aesthetic labour; and if, through the employment relationship, workers' feelings are captured and commodified as emotional labour, with aesthetic labour is it workers' corporeality that is captured and commodified. More specifically, we define aesthetic labour as the supply of embodied capacities and attributes possessed by workers at the point of entry into employment. Employers then mobilise, develop and commodify these capacities and attributes through processes of recruitment, selection, training, monitoring, management and reward, transforming them into competencies or 'skills' which are then aesthetically geared towards producing a style of service encounter. It is an obligation within the employment relationship between employer and worker. With aesthetic labour, organisations seek to control and transmute the corporality of workers' bodies to affect a prescribed performance by the worker in his or her interaction with customers or clients. This service encounter involves face-to-face or voice-to-voice interaction in which workers' corporality is managed to deliberately appeal to the senses of customers or clients. It is a form of labour that is intended to appeal to the senses of customers and enhance their perception of the service encounter. At a very basic level, aesthetic labour is used as a means of delineating and projecting an organisational image or identity. In this respect, aesthetic labour is a twist on the 'person–organisation fit' (Kristof, 1996) approach to human resources. With their aesthetic capital captured by employers, employees become human hardware – a new twist on the aesthetics of organisation, intended to be the embodiment of the organisation's image or identity and part of the product on offer (Witz et al., 2003). As Postrel (2004: 127) states, 'When style is strategy ... how employees look can be as much a part of the atmosphere [of companies] as the grain of the furniture or the beat of the background music'. In his study of Disney, Van Maanen (1990) refers to these transmuted workers as 'talking statues' (see Box 3.3 below).

Box 3.3   Disney's talking statues

Employees ... are also a well-screened bunch. ... Single, white males and females in their early twenties, without facial blemish, of above average height and below average weight, with straight teeth, conservative grooming standards, and a chin-up, shoulder-back posture radiating the sort of good health suggestive of a recent history in sports are typical of these social identifiers ... The Disneyland look [is] put forth in a handbook ... in which readers learn, for example, that facial hair or long hair is banned for men as are aviator glasses and earrings and that women must not tease their hair, wear fancy jewellery, or apply more than a modest dab of makeup. Both men and women are to look neat and prim, keep their uniforms fresh, polish their shoes ...

(*Source*: Van Maanen, 1990: 32–3)

Conceptualisation of aesthetic labour thus recoups and foregrounds employer exploitation of worker corporeality in analysis of work and employment in services-dominated economies. It captures an attempt by some organisations to make those organisations more competitive (in the private sector) and better perceived (in the public sector). What is important to note is that it is a deliberate managerial strategy intended to determine a form of labour centred on using worker corporeality for organisational benefit. In this respect, aesthetic labour is not a 'gift exchange' from women to men, a form of interpersonal offering, as Tyler and Taylor (1998) suggest. Instead, it is an explicit feature of the employment relationship between employer and worker in the service sector.

Making this point does not exclude the role of customers and clients. Worker corporeality is socially relational, part of a triadic relationship between employer, worker and customers/clients: employers want their workers' corporality to affect the senses of the customers and/or clients in order to deliver a favourably perceived service encounter, and employers often legitimise the use of aesthetic labour by reference to customers' and clients' preferences. Thus, employers typically impose aesthetic labour on workers by reference to customers/clients (Warhurst et al., 2000). Indeed, this was the reason Aeroflot said that it prescribed the weight and size of its cabin crew – because passengers preferred attractive flight attendants (BBC, 2017). In our research its seems that employers, or managers as employers in loco, map their own experiences onto customers and clients or make assumptions about those customers' and clients' preferences. For example, a manager of a style bar in Glasgow told us, 'If you've got nice looking staff then it brings in people'. Other research suggests that these intuitive hunches on the part of employers and managers have some substance. Studies of the hospitality and retail industries have found that the appearance of frontline service employees, especially if they are judged to be attractive, has a positive impact with regard to: attracting customers; facilitating customers' understanding of the brand concept; creating strong, positive emotions amongst customers, such as pleasure and excitement; and enhancing customer satisfaction (see for example Kim et al., 2009; Magnini et al., 2013; Quach et al., 2017; Soderlund and Julander, 2009; Tsaur et al., 2015; Wu et al., 2019; cf. Pounders et al., 2015).

Our initial and others' subsequent research of aesthetic labour has tended to focus on visual perceptions of workers, i.e. employee looks. This dominance is not surprising; since the Enlightenment, there has been a 'visual hegemony in the Western sensorium,' according to Gurney and Hines (1999: 5). Western society thinks visually, dominated by the eye. Hence the emphasis within aesthetic labour on worker appearance or 'looks'. The sound of workers, though, is gaining research attention, and with good reason: there are some employers who emphasise it – it is important, for example, in call centres. In Glasgow, a tele-banking clerk explained to us how good service could be delivered without face-to-face interaction with customers: 'People can hear the smile in your voice. You have to have the smile in your voice', she said. 'You have to always present the nice face of the bank, even though it's on a phone'. Even the manager of the style bar in Glasgow noted that her workers had to be 'well spoken', not just 'well presented'. It is because employers emphasise the sight and sound of their workers in the appeal to the visual and auditory senses of customers and clients, that aesthetic labour is most obviously manifest in the 'ideal' workers sought by companies and prescribed by the use of uniforms, the appearance standards and dress codes, the body language and speech of these workers (see Chapters 4, 5 and 6).

There are, however, five traditional senses: sight, hearing, taste, touch and smell (or respectively, the visual, auditory, gustatory, somatic and olfactory). These five senses are hierarchicalised, with the visual sense prioritised (Gurney and Hines, 1999). Fine (2009) suggests that hearing comes a close second because it involves intellect. Of the other three senses, touch occupies an intermediate position, and as with sight and sound, is measureable and easily shared. Taste and smell are less certain – attempts to create a measurement for both have failed. Historically because they were said not to involve intellect, they have long been regarded as lower order senses, by Kant for example. Of course, such claims are social constructs, Fine claims, as 'any sense can be a window to the world' (p. 204).

As such, even if the visual and auditory senses dominate research of aesthetic labour, the other senses, e.g. the olfactory, are not necessarily redundant in organisations. Through the major histocompatibility genes, individuals have what is, in effect, a smell fingerprint, giving off odours to which others can be receptive or repelled (Dunbar, 2012). Depending upon the odour, an individual's smell can make other people calm, alert, or even fearful for example. Some companies use this capacity to effect outcomes through smell in their organisational aesthetics to sensorily affect the physical environment and perceptions of customers and clients. For example, there is a significant amount of research that examines how retailers can use aromas to positively influence shopper behaviour (e.g. Helmefalk and Berdnt, 2018; Morrison et al., 2011). At one time, British Airways pumped the smell of freshly mowed grass into its waiting lounges to create a more perceptibly relaxed environment for its customers (Thornton, 1999). More recently, it was reported that the 'lifestyle brand' Marie-Stella-Maris were launching a new fragrance for spraying in the workplace, with the aim of inspiring workspaces and enhancing productivity through stimulating employees' sense of smell and inducing greater relaxation (*People Management*, 2019). Being part of the organisational aesthetics, some companies also manage the smell of employees. They can, for example, as one UK sushi bar did, and drawing on the fragrance, give their workers an 'Issey Miyake makeover' to make them more appealing to customers (Sweet, 1997). Other senses, such as the olfactory, can therefore also be important potential features of aesthetic labour but are, as yet, relatively unexplored in research, though Karlsson (2012) has suggestions about how such a research agenda could be developed (see Chapter 8).

As we have long argued (Warhurst et al., 2000), aesthetic labour is clearly a form of labour; the aesthetics being mobilised, developed and commodified are those of workers. We appreciate that others use the concept differently. In his outline of what he calls the 'aesthetic economy', Böhme (2003), for example, also refers to 'aesthetic labour'. This labour centres on the totality of those activities that produce aesthetics and sensory experience. Aesthetic labourers are the painters, artists and designers who produce these sensorily affecting products, imbuing the mundane and the material with 'staging value'. This staging value refers to the positioning of the product to be exchanged with an appearance that offers new value based on 'intensify[ing] life'. These products are not needed but are desired for their 'aura' (p. 72). This formulation of aesthetic labour as those workers who produce aestheticised products is also evident in Wengrow (2001). His focus is the transition from simple to complex societies in the Neolithic Near East (c.9–10,000 BC), and he shows how the spread of pottery decorated with particular patterns reflects particular social knowledge in those societies. Different patterns reflect different societies and their knowledge. Through aesthetic labour such material objects are imbued with a 'sensuous and psychological force' (p. 170) that has an 'affective dimension ... making up the fabric of everyday life' (p. 182). This affection transforms ways of seeing and knowing the world, Wengrow states; it is about societies' social reproduction. In a more current context, Fine's (2009) ethnographic study of restaurant kitchen work uses 'aesthetics' in the same way to focus on the product being manufactured – in his case the dishes prepared by chefs and cooks. Echoing Böhme's understanding of the aesthetic economy, these dishes are 'expressive forms of work' (2009: 197). The chefs and cooks desire to produce objects – food – that is pleasing to the senses of customers (and the producer): 'When I make soup … I try to make it look as nice as possible, and to taste. I feel I take a lot of pride in it', one cook explained (p. 197). Chocolate sauce is drizzled over fruit, and plain dishes are arranged to look more abstract. In this way, the cooks and chefs apply their labour to material products and invest those products with an aesthetic appeal that they hope will positively affect customers' senses. Our conceptualisation of aesthetic labour is obviously different, though there is an overlap in that, with our aesthetic labour, workers can become the human hardware of their employing organisations and part of the product on offer. Conceptually it is different from that suggested by Böhme, Wengrow and Fine, who see the product as distinct from its labour.

THEORISING AESTHETIC LABOUR

Understanding of our aesthetic labour draws on several theoretical sources. The first, labour process theory as it morphed from labour process analysis (Braverman, 1974), helps to understand why aesthetic labour has emerged as an employer strategy. The second, the theory of practice (Bourdieu, 1990), explains how aesthetic labour is socially constituted and situated, and able to be used by employers as a strategy.

With regard to the first, the labour process comprises: first, the act of work; second, a product to be worked upon; third, the instruments of production. The labour process is a surplus-producing process in which more value is produced by workers than they need to subsist. Its outcomes are goods and services that have use values (Marx, 1946[1887]). This labour process exists in all forms of political economy: capitalist and socialist, market-based and non-market, the latter including the public sector (Reid, 2003; Warhurst, 1998). Employers' control and organisation of the labour process ensures the material and ideological reproduction of the social relations of production within particular political economies (Warhurst, 1998).

In capitalism, labour process theory points out that use value attains an exchange value through the market. Competition in market economies compels employers to continually develop not just new goods and services but to also re-organise how those goods and services are produced in the workplace. Control of the labour process allows this renewal (Thompson and Smith, 2001). The employment contract partially establishes this control, giving employers the right to direct, monitor, evaluate and even discipline workers – within reasonable limits (Kaufman, 2004); limits that are often challenged or tested by workers in the workplace (Edwards, 1979). The outcome is a wage–effort bargain between employers and workers. Different employer strategies to control and organise the labour process exist over time, location, and industry (Nienhüser and Warhurst, 2018). What strategies are pursued by employers is open to empirical investigation. In his initial rekindling of labour process analysis, Braverman (1974) thought it was the use of scientific management, regardless of sector. However by the end of the twentieth and into the twenty-first centuries, labour process researchers were exploring the use of emotional labour by employers in services (e.g. Callaghan and Thompson, 2002; Taylor, 1998).

Beyond the damage wrought upon bodies in the labour process (e.g. Brody, 1960), bodies can be confined within the labour process (see the hotel worker's complaint in Terkel, 1972) and labour processes can be shaped around bodies (see the maleness of the print industry identified by Cockburn, 1983). It is surprising therefore that consideration of worker corporality has largely been absent from labour process theory. This omission has its roots in initial Braverman-inspired labour process analysis that accepted a crude, dismissive account of the body. With scientific management brain and body were separated, thinking detached from doing. The former, as conception, was to be the responsibility of managers; the latter, as execution, the task of workers: 'we do not ask for the initiative of our men. All we want of them is to obey the orders we give them, do what we say', F.W. Taylor (1947[1911]: 9), the father of scientific management, explained. As such workers came to be regarded as mindless bodies, 'empty vessels, stripped of thought and made to act like machines' (Wolkowitz and Warhurst, 2010: 225). Simply having 'able-bodied' workers seemingly now sufficed (Windolf and Wood, 1988). As a consequence, the body held little analytical interest for labour process theorists.

Aesthetic labour offers labour process theory one possibility to rectify this omission (see Warhurst et al., 2009a). In return, labour process theory offers a useful materialist account of the body in work in which aesthetic labour can be understood as a feature of the wage–effort bargain, intended by employers as a strategy to produce a style of service encounter within service organisations that generates (exchange) value for employers. Nevertheless whilst labour process theory can provide the analytical tools to explain why aesthetic labour occurs, it does not provide the analytical tools for explaining how aesthetic labour occurs.

These tools can be drawn from Bourdieu's (1990) theory of practice. In this theory, the body is regarded as a form of physical capital. It is both biological and social, and through the latter acquires symbolic value. Key to understanding physical capital is 'habitus'. Habitus is the typical condition or appearance of the body. Through familial socialisation, habitus is 'internalized as a second nature' (1990: 53). Habitus has two parts: doxa and hexis. Doxa produces ways of seeing/knowing. It is the taken-for-granted understanding of the world, the perceptions, attitudes and opinions that constitute 'a particular point of view' (Bourdieu, 1998: 57). The inculcation of mental habits disciplines corporeal ones, which become inscribed and expressed through regular and ordinary practice. It simply becomes akin to 'techniques of the body' (Bourdieu, 1990: 13). This embodiment is expressed as hexis or the way of being in the world. It is the condition or appearance of the body manifest through body language, speech and dress for example, and which are 'durable, transposable dispositions' (Bourdieu, 1990: 56; see also 1992: 93). Once socialised, the body represents a 'memory jogger' involving 'complexes of gestures, postures and words' (Bourdieu, 2004: 474).

In addition to seeking to understand how the individual is socialised, the theory of practice also seeks to understand how the social is individualised. If producing habitus requires individual bodily labour, acquiring it involves social reproduction. Habitus thus marks and provides for a social identity, and as a concept was intended by Bourdieu to help bridge, even transcend, the objectivist/subjectivist divide (Jenkins, 2002). As Hanks (2005: 69) similarly notes, 'Through habitus, society is impressed on the individual, not only in mental habits, but even more in corporeal ones'. In this respect, whilst individuals exhibit habitus, what these individuals embody is collective, pertaining to all those individuals who are within a particular 'field'. These fields are durable but not fixed networks of relations. The field conditions the habitus whilst the habitus constitutes the field (Ritzer, 2000). In this articulation, 'Social positions give rise to embodied dispositions. To sustain engagement in a field is to be shaped, at least potentially, by the position one occupies', states Hanks (2005: 73). For Bourdieu, the social becomes the personal and the personal is the social, with habitus the embodiment of the field. Habitus are thus not only socially constructed but also socially differentiated and differentiating, denoting a class. Dispositions and manner of body language, speech and dress vary according to class. Whilst individuals within a class can affect their own 'personal style', this individuation 'is never more than a deviation in relation to the style of a ... class' Bourdieu stated (1990: 60). Indeed, it might be said that this interest in class production and reproduction is at the heart of the theory of practice.

Although more focused on class relations rather than employment relations, the theory of practice is theoretically useful in conceiving aesthetic labour. Not only does Bourdieu's analysis reveal the materialised body, it also highlights the symbolic value attached to bodily forms as physical capital, and that, whilst a collective manifestation, physical capital is mobilised by individuals. Nonetheless, pitched at the societal level it overlooks how that physical capital is individually developed and mobilised – and exploited – at the organisational level. In the same way that there is a fit between social position and bodily dispositions in Bourdieu's theory of practice, aesthetic labour indicates how organisational positioning manifests in the dispositions – body language, speech and dress – of workers to deliver an embodied style of service, and is intended to provide for successful organisational production and reproduction as well as delivering value for the organisation.

For aesthetic labour, the utility of labour process theory and the theory of practice comes in their combined complementarity. Both are grounded in materialism and, taken together, provide a theoretical understanding of why and how aesthetic labour occurs. Labour process theory's focus is explicitly the workplace. It reveals why employers are compelled to control the labour process as the surplus producing process. Moreover it highlights why, with control as the means, the organisation of the labour process is dynamic, and why employers continually seek new strategies. Aesthetic labour is one strategy in this respect, and with it worker corporeality has become a feature of the wage–effort bargain intended to help produce surplus. The theory of practice focuses on class relations rather than employment relations. However it explains how aesthetic labour as a form of labour is socially constituted and situated, and how worker corporeality becomes a form of physical capital that acquires symbolic value that can be used as a source of value creation for employers either as use or exchange value. What we would term 'aesthetic capital', imbued of workers but used by employers. It also allows identification and analysis of how the habitus at the centre of specific styles of service are perceived and enacted as an embodied resource for employers within the wage–effort bargain.

LOCATING AESTHETIC LABOUR

Despite Mills (1951) dropping analysis of worker appearance in his 1950s study for a lack of empirics, there are early examples of employers intervening to mobilise, develop and commodify their workers' corporality in order to affect a particular and distinct style of service. There were some employers in the retail and hospitality industries who, even earlier – at the turn of the twentieth century – were recognising the commercial benefits of hiring good-looking staff. Department stores, though not yet called as such, had emerged in the mid-nineteenth century on both sides of the Atlantic, and by the turn of the twentieth century were gentrifying shopkeeping and providing employment opportunities for respectable young women (see for example, Belisle, 2006; Benson, 1983). These stores were a new shopping experience, promoting luxury. Many feared the 'moral dangers' of this desire-driven consumerism, according to Cox and Hobley (2014: 75). Certainly the 'shopgirls' were part of the display – 'objects of male fantasy', they state, 'often hired for their looks above all other considerations' (p. 76). And yet, with an absence of proper management, Cox and Hobley note, those workers' aesthetic capital was not then explicitly mobilised in work by employers. Historically therefore employer interest in employees' aesthetic labour is not new but, we argue, was 'under-exploited' from the employer perspective. Indicatively, it was not unusual for these shopgirls in Cox and Hobley's study to provide their own workwear. An historical example of a more developed employer approach to mobilising employees' aesthetic capital comes from Glasgow as Miss Cranston's tearoom illustrates (see Box 3.4 below).

Box 3.4   Room de Good Looks

At the end of the nineteenth century Glasgow was a boom town. Building work was everywhere: new warehouses, new banks and new shops. Amongst this bustle, what are now called 'third places', a mixture of public social and work space, were needed for businessmen to meet and ladies to lunch. Tearooms sprang up in response. One such tearoom was that of Miss Cranston. She hired fledgling artist and architect Charles Rennie Mackintosh to design the tearoom's interiors. It was 'wildly overdone, but it was an experience, and it was very appealing' Kinchin states. A popular column in *The Evening News* at the time reported the rooms to be beautiful, decked out in Mackintosh's own Vienna-influenced art nouveau style. 'Even the waitresses were pretty', Kinchin claims. They too had their uniforms designed by Mackintosh – 'white with chokers of pink beads'. When one of the waitresses comes to take his order, the enamoured character in the newspaper column remarks that the 'art tea room', is more like 'the Room de Good Looks'.

(*Source*: Kinchin, 1998: 59, 53, 60)

Miss Cranston not only hired attractive workers, she also developed and mobilised their aesthetic affectivity as part of her desired style of service for the tearoom. However, Miss Cranston's tearoom was notable because it was exceptional, providing an exotic service offering. What makes aesthetic labour more salient now is that it has shifted from the margins to the mainstream in the service sector, from the exotic to the everyday. Our initial research focused on what we termed the 'style labour market' of the 'new' Glasgow, with its designer fashion retailers, boutique hotels and style bars and restaurants – the modern-day equivalents of Miss Cranston's tearoom. A significant body of research now exists that extends the analysis beyond the style labour market into more prosaic retail and hospitality jobs, and into a range of other occupational, industry and sector contexts. It is interesting to reflect on some of this research, starting with how differing aesthetics are used by different organisations as part of their brand/image management and market positioning.

Aesthetic labour and product market strategies

As the context of the reinvention of Glasgow, it is not surprising that our initial research focused on the style labour market, and seemed to suggest that employers were interested in only hiring and deploying workers with perceived 'good looks', i.e. those possessing the socially ascribed type of looks that the beauty industry uses to benchmark consumption of its products – typically thin, blond and blue-eyed (Jones, 2010; and see Chapter 2).

As Ian, one of our focus group participants noted, style-driven bars and restaurants would often 'just hire pretty girls', with Laura, another focus group participant, further suggesting that those 'attractive staff' would often be 'blonde and blue eyed'. Beyond this idealised worker likely to be found in overtly stylish organisations, it is clear from our survey undertaken in Glasgow's retailers, hotels, restaurants, bars and cafés that employers strongly believed that employee appearance was important to their businesses' success. Over half (53 per cent) of the sample felt it was critical, 40 per cent felt it was important, and 6 per cent somewhat important. Thus, at least 93 per cent of employers attributed significant importance to the image of customer-facing staff. Furthermore it is not simply judgements of attractiveness per se that matter. Table 3.1 details aspects of broader aspects of self-presentation that the Glasgow employers considered important.

Table 3.1   Image and aesthetic labour proxies (%)

	Critical	Important	Somewhat important	Not important
Age	5	12	35	48
Size		7	22	71
Height	1	3	16	80
Weight		6	25	70
Dress sense/style	7	42	34	17
Voice/accent	8	36	33	22
Physical looks	2	20	48	30

Clearly, some proxies are considered more important than others, with age, dress sense/style, voice/accent and physical looks all attributed significantly greater importance, than size, height and weight. Eighty-three per cent attached some importance to dress sense/style, 78 per cent to voice/accent, and 70 per cent to physical looks. If aesthetic labour is conceptualised as a composite of a number of aspects of corporeality, certain of these aspects are clearly more important to employers than others – a point we return to in the conclusion of the book.

However, it is important to recognise that there is a body of literature which argues that firms' different business strategies, such those of competing on cost, quality and innovation (Porter, 1980), are accompanied by different human resources practices (Schuler and Jackson, 1987). Firms in the same industry but with different competitive strategies can therefore have different human resources practices. To take the example of 'cost' in this body of literature, cost typically refers to companies that compete on low-cost products. However, firms' business strategies can also be based on high-cost products. Depending upon their product market strategy, companies can have different ideal workers in terms of the desired aesthetic or look. Put prosaically by Windolf and

Wood (1988: 24), 'What constitutes a good worker in an upmarket store, aiming largely at middle class customers, is not the same as the store catering for a traditional working class clientele'. This labour differentiation is a potential source of employment discrimination – an issue that is discussed further in Chapter 7.

To return to our initial research, upmarket, high-cost product retailers and hospitality organisations deliberately hired good-looking workers that aligned with the desired aesthetic of those organisations and in pursuit of competitive advantage. For example, in Glasgow's upmarket Hotel Elba, famed for its rock star guests, workers were expected to be, as we noted earlier, 'pretty attractive looking people', 'with a nice smile, nice teeth, neat hair and in decent proportion'. In short, there were expectations that people would look the part in order to be able to fit in with the brand image Hotel Elba was seeking to present. Significantly, because of their brand attraction, such employers can be selective in who they hire, and the demand for good-looking workers in such organisations has created a style labour market not only in Glasgow but also elsewhere, as Box 3.5 below illustrates for Sydney in Australia.

Box 3.5   We don't give an F how good they are as long as they're good looking

Silver Service in Sydney is a temporary work agency that provides waiting and bar staff to high-end and fashionable clients' corporate and other events. These events can be private parties in private homes and government offices or in retail and fashion houses such as Chanel and Gucci. Although high-end clients, the work has remained basic. Nevertheless, concerned about their own company brand or organisational image, the clients were often very specific about which staff were to be used by Silver Service. As the general manager stated, 'We have some clients who basically said to us "We don't give an F how good they are as long as they're good looking".' As a consequence, Silver Service assessed and monitored employee appearance: 'We know if someone's got a nose ring or yellow hair ... we keep track of that' the general manager explained. Sometimes Silver Service even used a modelling/acting agency to undertake casting calls to select the right staff.

(*Source*: Knox, 2013)

However, in Glasgow it became clear that demonstration effects existed amongst more prosaic retail and hospitality employers in the city – a development noted in research beyond Glasgow (e.g. Pettinger, 2004, 2005). Though with less attractive brands, these mid-market employers still seek to appropriate and commercialise their workers' corporeality, seeking, if not workers with good looks, then workers with the right look.

Having the right look can extend from some employers wanting generic aesthetic compliance from their workers – wanting them to be 'neat' and tidy' most obviously – to other employers wanting corporeal alignment with the organisation's image or brand, such as the employment of plus-sized employees for a plus-sized clothing outlet (Gruys, 2012), or the home improvement retailer B&Q employing a large number of older workers, often retired ex-tradesmen, who in addition to having a high degree of technical knowledge, were also felt to 'look the part' (Foster, 2004; and see Nickson and Baum, 2017, for a discussion of aesthetic labour and age). A further example is Oasis, a mid-market fashion retail company with branches across towns and cities in the UK. It has a well-defined and stringently applied dress and grooming code as one of its staff handbooks reveals in Box 3.6 (and see Chapter 4). Oasis staff need to look 'attractive' but, as we noted earlier in discussing workers as walking billboards, Oasis offers a uniform allowance to its staff – with company product purchased, it should be noted, at a discount rate to staff rather than provided free by the company. Managers must authorise all staff clothing choices however, making their decisions 'based on a commercial view, i.e. key fashion pieces must be represented on the appropriate body shape [of the employee] in a flattering size'. Moreover, the handbook continues, 'All clothing must be of current season and must be an accurate representation of the looks and trends of that season'.

Box 3.6   Definitely maybe

This dress code outlines the minimum required standards of appearance from all Oasis staff. Oasis staff must be well groomed at all times. You are the representatives of Oasis and it is your responsibility to create a good impression.

Hair must be clean and well groomed.

Nails must be neatly manicured, nail varnish ... should complement [sic] the colours of the season.

Personal hygiene ... When wearing short-sleeved tops, please pay particular attention to regular depilation.

Hosiery should always be worn with skirts and dresses. If applied, self-tanning lotion must be of a natural appearance.

(*Source*: Oasis staff handbook)

As part of an international comparative research project that we organised, our Australian colleagues Richard Hall and Diane van den Broek (2012) explored these differences in fashion retail in Sydney. They identified three market segments: a *Boutique Style market* with customers that are typically style-conscious but not very cost-conscious; a *Mass Style market* with customers who are both style- and cost-conscious; and a *Value Fashion market* with customers who are typically cost-conscious but not very style-conscious. Hall and van den Broek found that across these segments 'employers in fashion retail routinely recruit and select customer service staff on the basis of their aesthetic attributes' (2012: 99). They also found that the majority of all stores included aesthetic skills and appearance in their worker appraisals. All stores also provided some training in these skills. However, examining the looks policies of these stores, Hall and van den Broek also found that what constitutes aesthetic labour varies according to the market segment and character of the store and brand. For example, they found that it was the boutique segment that had the most pronounced policies in terms of clothing and appearance standards, which were used 'to promote a specific style of appearance and presentation exemplifying the brand' (2012: 95). This approach in the boutique segment can be compared to the value fashion segment where the looks policy was more about workers being 'neat and presentable' – 'a fairly basic level of aesthetic presentation' (2012: 95).

Similar differences have been found in the wave of research that followed our initial research. This research, which considers the retail and hospitality industries in a variety of different national contexts, has found that the expectations of aesthetic labour are shaped by the required brand image and product market strategies of companies (e.g. Boyle and De Keere, 2019; Cutcher and Achtel, 2017; Foster and Resnick, 2013; Gruys, 2012; Johnston and Sandberg, 2008; Maitra and Maitra, 2018; McIntyre Petersson, 2014; Pettinger, 2004, 2005; Quinn, 2008; Walls, 2007; Walters, 2018; Williams and Connell, 2010; Wright, 2005).

Aesthetic labour in other occupations and industries

Another wave of research sought to extend analysis of aesthetic labour beyond occupations in the retail and hospitality industries to a range of different occupations. At a general level, and using self-presentation as a proxy for aesthetic labour, one employer survey found self-presentation to be a 'critical skill' not just for sales and personal service occupations in the UK, but also for 34 per cent, 29 per cent and 39 per cent of associate professionals, professionals and managers and senior officials respectively (Bunt et al., 2005). Unfortunately, there are no disaggregated data to enable analysis of the industry location of these types of occupations. Singling out specific occupations and industries for which there is still a strong emphasis on workers affecting the visual senses of customers and clients, Jeffes (1998) noted the ten occupations most likely to have a significant emphasis on worker appearance:

- Model, actor, actress
- Television anchor, weather presenter, etc.
- Public/customer relations representative
- Sales, e.g. retail, estate agents, marketing representatives
- Hospitality, e.g. waiter/waitress, flight attendant
- Chief executive officer
- Hair stylist, cosmetologist
- Health and fitness trainer/aerobics instructor
- Politician

An obvious point made by Jeffes about this list is that those occupations characterised as having a greater emphasis on appearance involve significant interaction with the public, and importantly also 'require the person to influence others to buy, watch, assist, return for another visit, etc.' (1998: 37).

Other research has (re-)turned to the putative glamorous visual/entertainment industries and the first set of occupations on Jeffes' list. These and other industries – whether visually or aurally driven – are obvious loci for commodification of worker corporality. Some of the accompanying employer prescriptions however can be strict, if not plain draconian, as the rule book for the cheerleaders of the Cincinnati Bengals National Football League team in the US illustrates (see Box 3.7 below).

Box 3.7   Not a lot to cheer about

'Glamour is a priority' it states. The cheerleaders cannot have '... slouching breasts. Support is needed'. Cheerleaders' make-up and hair can be changed 'as the director feels necessary'. Frosted lipstick and eye-shadow are banned. Cheerleaders' 'ideal weight' will also be determined by the director and they are weighed twice a week. Failure to follow these rules can mean not being used and so paid. Flouting the rules is also forbidden: 'Insubordination to even the slightest degree is ABSOLUTELY NOT TOLERATED.* You will be benched or dismissed'.

(*Source*: Mangan, 2014: 3; *upper case emphasis in the original)

Dean's (2005) research on actors and Entwistle and Wissinger's (2006), and Wissinger (2012) research on fashion models have also usefully adopted the concept of aesthetic labour. Entwistle and Wissinger suggest that analysis of aesthetic labour should extend beyond interactive service work and organisational aesthetics to take into account fashion modelling, with its emphasis on 'display' and 'performance' work and 'where the look and appearance of the body is critical to the labour' (2006: 776). Dean also suggests that aesthetic labour has 'direct resonance with the non-service occupation of performer' (2005: 762). Both research areas focus on female workers. However, extending Dean's analysis, male actors too need to conform to aesthetic ideals in order to be hired. This need was made very clear to British actor Rafe Spall as he auditioned for a film part as a romantic lead. As he explained, the studio told him:

> 'You need to work on maybe becoming more handsome.' After my second audition I started running every day and got my hair cut … So for 16 weeks I ate no wheat, dairy or sugar. It was an absolute nightmare. That's bonkers I say. 'Ridiculous. Absolutely fucking ridiculous' … But it's my job. It's a weird thing to have to worry about, looking handsome. (Quoted in Hattenstone, 2013: 19)

Dean and Entwistle and Wissinger usefully reveal that, in the visual/entertainment industries, actors' and models' corporality is also managed and commodified. This use of aesthetic labour is interesting and has the potential to conceptually develop aesthetic labour, given that research to date has centred on occupations and industries involving a direct service encounter. With these other occupations and industries, the 'encounter' is non-direct, intended to affect the senses of customers (as audiences) and clients (magazine editors) – although it should be noted that the first models, who displayed the stock of early department stores, did directly encounter potential customers through what became known as the catwalk (Cox and Hobley, 2014). Unfortunately, whilst this modern-day encounter/non-encounter difference is signalled, it is not explored further by Dean or Entwistle and Wissinger. Moreover, research on aesthetic labour to date has focused on *employees*. The workers – actors and models – in this new line of research are often self-employed, freelancing across the proto gig economy, or working across a portfolio of short-term employment contracts (Eikhof and Warhurst, 2013). It is therefore initially not clear who drives aesthetic labour strategies. However, as Haunschild and Eikhof (2009) have pointed out, it is helpful to understand these sorts of workers in the visual/entertainment industries as 'self-employed employees' whose mindset is focused on self-managing, self-monitoring and self-marketing their own labour, regardless of their actual employment relationship. In this context an interesting research question then becomes if and how these workers exercise aesthetic labour: either in direct compliance with employers' or contractors' requirements or, possibly, in indirect anticipation of these requirements. Entwistle and Wissinger (2006) note that models commodify themselves to reflect differing fashions (see also Parmentier et al., 2013). This work on their bodies aims to ensure that they continue to conform to a demanding industry aesthetic, though how far it goes beyond what some other workers now do (see Chapter 2) requires continuing comparative empirical investigation.

THE SECTORAL REACH OF AESTHETIC LABOUR

Though still limited in number, more recent research has extended the exploration of aesthetic labour into the public sector. For example, Dahl (2014) uses aesthetic labour to explain recent developments in a Danish municipality workforce. Wanting to reduce verbal and physical attacks arising from their interaction with an (often irate) public, the municipality's traffic warden department now explicitly hires better-looking applicants, trains these new staff in body language, and dresses them in restyled uniforms in order to positively change perceptions of the occupation. How these traffic wardens look and behave is thus formally prescribed by this public sector employer and is now an explicit part of their job. In China too, aesthetic labour is being applied to traffic warden jobs and again with the intention of improving the image of their work with the public (see Box 3.8 below).

Box 3.8   Chinese flower vases

In the Chinese province of Chengdu, the authorities advertised city warden jobs stipulating that applicants should be tall, female, young and attractive in order to present a 'soft side' to law enforcement. The human resources director of the law enforcement bureau said that 'Their main job is to present a good image so they have to be good looking'. A Chinese idiom for women who are employed for their looks and nothing else is 'flower vases'.

(*Source*: Branigan, 2010: 44)

As we have noted elsewhere (Warhurst et al., 2009b), the BBC (2006) reported that the Chinese government has also stipulated that anyone joining its navy must be 'good-looking, tall and polite'. The reason again is that navy personnel are regarded as representatives of China and are being used are part of the country's rebranding of itself to the outside world. These examples suggest that aesthetic labour exists not only in the private but also in the non-for-profit public sector.[5] That it does so should not be a surprise given that the labour process and employment relationships exist in a range of political economies. What these examples show is that aesthetic labour helps employers in their pursuit of delivering both exchange and also use value, and that developing, mobilising and commodifying (through wage-labour) worker corporality extends beyond the market sector. and is now within the non-market sector of public services.

Aesthetic labour here, there and everywhere?

The danger is that aesthetic labour, as with emotional labour before it (cf. Bolton, 2004), is suddenly found to be here, there and everywhere, and especially if it is recognised that most if not all labour is aestheticised to some extent (see for example, Bruton, 2015; Hamermesh, 2011). For example, research using the concept of aesthetic labour has been conducted in a range of differing organisational and occupational contexts, including hair salons (Barber, 2016), style bloggers (Brydges and Sjöhom, 2019), recruitment agency consultants (Craven et al., 2013), fitness industry personal trainers (Harvey et al., 2014), language interpreters (Cho, 2017), musicians (Hracs and Leslie, 2014), PhD students (Brown, 2017), public relations (PR) practitioners (Simonrangkir, 2013), DJs (Willment, 2019) and circus acrobats (Zhang, 2016). An important issue therefore is delineating the boundaries of aesthetic labour. In this endeavour, all of the current research by ourselves and others highlighted here provides a useful body of work that enables cross-occupation, cross-industry and cross-sector comparison to help identify what is essential and distinct (cf. Stinchcombe, 1959) about aesthetic labour.

The key point we think is the 'stipulation' expressed in the Chinese traffic wardens example. What all of the jobs across the various industries and sectors have in common is that aesthetic labour is an organisationally required feature of the employment relationship. Returning to our earlier discussion about definitions, we suggest that aesthetic labour requires an interaction with customers and/or clients, with workers using their corporality to induce a sensory affect in these customers and/or clients, and that the capture of this worker corporality by employers is intended for organisational benefit and for workers is part of the wage effort bargain – an explicit feature of the employment relationship with their employer.

Being part of the employment relationship, aesthetic labour is not confined to one set of industries or even the market sector but can exist in a range of service industries and any sector, market or non-market in which a formal employment relationship operates. Reflecting back on Dean's and Entwistle and Wissinger's research of actors and fashion models, it might be worth returning to Hochschild's delineation of emotion in work and emotion work as a feature of the employment relationship, sold for a wage and producing (exchange) value for the employer and thereby transmuting into emotional labour. Similarly, as we have noted before, there are aesthetics in work – the embodied impression management used by workers to get into organisations at the point of hire, and by workers to get on within organisations in terms of their personal pay and career progression (Witz et al., 2003). It is when such embodiment is transmuted into a form of aesthetics of organisation, and sold for a wage as a constituent part of the job and part of the surplus-producing process, that it transmutes into aesthetic labour – whether this labour is employed or self-employed or producing exchange value or use value.

In the meantime, attempting to assess the extent of aesthetic labour is a challenge. Ours and others' research still largely draws on jobs that involve affecting the visual and auditory senses of customers or clients. One way to guestimate the extent of aesthetic labour therefore is to aggregate the number of workers in all occupations in the service sector that involve interaction with customers or clients in this way. This analysis was first undertaken by Alan Felstead et al. (2007) using the 2007 UK Skills at Work survey.[6] In this survey Felstead et al. attempted to assess the extent of aesthetic labour across the UK labour market based on the job demands of workers. Focusing on the required appearance and speech of workers, the survey asked employees if they needed to 'look the part' or 'sound the part' in their jobs. The findings reveal that these 'aesthetic skills' are required in 52 per cent of jobs in the UK. At the time of the survey this figure translated into 16.3 million jobs. These aesthetic skills are required almost equally by full-time and part-time employees but, unsurprisingly, are more prevalent in the service industries, particularly sales occupations (p. 30–2). Demand for these skills is relatively high compared to even basic skills. Across all jobs, aesthetic skills are rated as more important than literacy and numeracy skills. Moreover they are not sex-specific, they are a requirement of female and male employees. On a ranking from '0' (not at all important/does not apply) to '4' (essential), men rated their need for these skills as 2.47, and women as 2.83 (compared to 'emotional skills' at 2.73 and 3.17 respectively) (p. 47). Thus, not only does aesthetic labour exist across different product markets, industries and sectors, it also exists as part of male and not just female employees' jobs. An example of this both-sex aesthetic labour is provided by Oasis, the mid-market fashion retail company mentioned earlier in this chapter. Whilst it is a fashion store targeting female customers that stipulates the appearance of its female workers (see Box 3.6), male employees of Oasis are also covered by the company's dress and grooming code. These employees must, for example, 'be clean shaven', with any facial hair 'neatly trimmed and well groomed'. There are also cross-sex rules: tattoos must be covered at all times, the handbook states; any form of body piercing 'is strictly forbidden'; and double-sets of earrings worn by either men or women are also forbidden (and see Chapter 4 for a further discussion of dress and appearance standards).

CONCLUSION

With significant physical injuries wrought by the industrial revolution, the body was of key analytical concern. This concern dissipated with workplace health and safety improvements and the shift from manufacturing to services across the advanced economies in the twentieth century. The body as a feature of employment relations disappeared, though some workers, in putatively glamorous industries, continued to have their bodies managed and commodified by employers – and scrutinised by the public.

At the same time (the mid-twentieth century) a 'personality market' was emerging involving the selling and buying of workers' attitudes and appearance. The outcome is that appearance was now being captured and commodified by employers in the context of a developing service sector. Although by the 1980s it was recognised that this corporality was a feature of doing and not just getting the job (cf. Hochschild, 1983; Mills, 1951), for different reasons both researchers dropped further analysis of this capture and commodification by employers. Conceptually, aesthetic labour foregrounds this corporality to reveal its capture and commodification by employers for organisational benefit. Labour process theory provides the tools for understanding why aesthetic labour has become an employer strategy, and a feature of the wage–effort bargain between employer and worker (Braverman, 1974). How aesthetic labour is constituted as habitus and can appeal to the senses of customers and clients can be understood by reference to the theory of practice (Bourdieu, 1990).

Beyond our initial work the majority of research which has followed has sought to extend the analysis of aesthetic labour in different organisational contexts – sometimes in the same industries as our initial research, sometimes in other industries but within the private sector, sometimes in occupations and industries with non-direct worker-customer/client interaction, and more recently, in non-market sector organisations in the public sector. All of this research shows it to be a feature of the wage–effort bargain between worker and employer that determines what work is done and how that work is to be done. With respect to the latter, with the current emphasis within aesthetic labour on the sight and sound of workers and the visual and aural senses of customers and clients, the three key corporeal components that comprise the aesthetic capital of workers – their dress, comportment (body language) and speech – are explored in detail in the next three chapters.

NOTES

1. It is indicative that it is the newly industrialising countries that now feature in the major manufacturing accidents, as the collapse of the Rana Plaza factory in Bangladesh, which killed over 1,100 workers, illustrates (Butler, 2014).
2. Of course such dichotomies can be too neat. Service workers too suffer physical injuries; hotel room cleaners can suffer back injuries (Dutton et al., 2008) and call centre workers can lose their voice through over-use (Jones, 2011). Similarly, there are psychological injuries in manufacturing, as Baldamus' (1961) classic 'traction and tedium' illustrates.
3. Angela Rippon appeared on the BBC from 1975, Anna Ford on UK commercial television from 1978.
4. Fn. 2, emphasis in the original.
5. At the time of writing, we are unaware of similar research for the voluntary sector.
6. We would like to thank Alan Felstead, Francis Green and Duncan Gallie for making this suggestion.

4
READY TO WORKWEAR

In Chapter 3 we noted that with aesthetic labour workers are initially recruited because of the way they look and talk. Once employed these employees are then further 'made up' within the organisation to ensure that they present the appropriate organisational style, with employers manipulating employees' clothing, body language and speech. As a consequence employees have become increasingly reconfigured and utilised as organisational 'hardware' intended to portray the image of the employing organisation, in the process becoming 'artefacts of the brand' (Harquail, 2005: 162). This chapter considers this process of 'making up' employees by focusing on employee clothing, or what we call 'workwear', examining the important role played by uniforms, appearance standards and dress codes in portraying the desired organisational image in interactive services.

We recognised in Chapter 2 how employees are increasingly aware of the need to project a positive personal image to both get and do a job. The focus in that chapter was employee-driven workwear, as exemplified by the ever-increasing awareness of impression management and the need to 'dress for success'. In this chapter we extend the analysis to focus on workwear that is organisationally prescribed and so a feature of aesthetic labour. As Rafaeli and Pratt (1993: 32) note, 'organizations spend billions of dollars each year defining, acquiring, maintaining and often monitoring employees' dress'. Similarly, the IRS (2000: 4) notes the importance of clothing in the workplace: 'Whether the way employees dress is part of the corporate image, the key to a successful career or simply the most practical outfit for the job, organizations across all industries are telling employees how they should look when they arrive to work each day'.

Through his theory of practice, Bourdieu (1990) argued that habitus is embodied. Thereafter he explained how the habitus of different social classes are marked by different dress and clothing. He noted for example that what might be called the petit bourgeoisie like their carpet slippers more than other classes and that the bourgeoisies like formal attire at home. Fox (2004) has provided similar insights into the dress codes of the social classes in the UK. She notes that it is not just what is worn but how it is worn that matters. Upper-middle or upper-class women wear clothing that is 'fairly simple and understated', she explains, and by contrast, 'flashy, over-elaborate dress is still an unmistakable lower class indicator' (2004: 287, 286). In a very short discussion, she makes the point that these rules generally transfer over into workwear: brash, garish-coloured and patterned ties are lower class; single solid colours are worn by the middle class; dark-coloured ties with discrete patterns are typical of the upper-middle and above classes. In this respect, anthropological Bourdieu without Bourdieu, the key point that weaves through Fox's analysis is that none of this attire is natural or necessary but socially determined; learning to know what to wear is an 'important "life skill"' she states (2004: 293). As with Fox, little of Bourdieu's analysis slips over into the workplace though he does note there are occupational dress codes, with senior executives tending to wear overcoats and lumber jackets worn more by agricultural and industrial workers. His analysis therefore is more focused on consumption than production; how dress and clothing style are used is part of class reproduction – even if that class is manifest through occupations – rather than the reproductive strategies of organisations. Labour process theory has even less to say about workwear. It has been more concerned with effort (Thompson and Smith, 2010) than with how the bodies making that effort are clothed. Nonetheless one of the bête noires of labour process analysts, Henry Ford, did prescribe his employees wearing different attire in order to mark social difference and hierarchy in the workplace. In order to distinguish his foremen from operatives – those giving instruction and those receiving it – the foremen were required to wear white coats rather than blue overalls. Wearing white enabled Ford to see if any of his foremen had been doing rather than overseeing work because dirt would be more visible (Ford, 1991).

There is no single reason driving employees' appearance through uniforms, appearance standards and dress codes (Byrne, 2018; Nath et al., 2016). To a large extent the type of organisation and the nature of work undertaken in that organisation, will determine the reasons and also the extent to which organisations seek to regulate their employees' appearance through workwear. Moreover, there may also be an element of self-regulation on the part of employees in certain organisational settings, especially where it is felt to be beneficial to individual careers, a point we noted in Chapter 2. Clearly, then, there may be a number of reasons why workwear will vary from organisation to organisation. Thus, this chapter initially outlines how workwear within organisations can be located within four broad areas, i.e. that regulated by government, the occupation, individuals and the organisation. Having considered these four broad areas the chapter then goes on to explore the fourth aspect – organisational workwear as a feature of aesthetic labour in interactive service work.

As we recognised in Chapter 1, a key aim of this book is to assess how aesthetic labour is experienced by employees and in that sense the imposition of uniforms, appearance standards and dress codes can be problematic for both employers and employees, presenting practical and legal problems (House of Commons, 2017a; Middlemiss, 2018). The chapter therefore also considers how employees within interactive services react to attempts to further mould their appearance through uniforms, appearance standards and dress codes. It acknowledges that this process may be experienced both positively and negatively by employees. Finally, the chapter considers the balance that is being struck with workwear between employer and employee rights.

THE DIFFERENT TYPES OF WORKWEAR

Although the primary focus of the chapter is the manner in which interactive service organisations seek to shape and regulate their employees' appearance through uniforms, appearance standards and dress codes, it is important to place this discussion within a broader context of workwear generally. In much the same way that which we noted earlier that the importance of appearance is not a new phenomenon, the same is true of uniforms. Uniforms emerged from the Middle Ages to demarcate one group from another and to signify different levels of authority. Initially colours were kept simple – in England for example the House of York favoured blue and mulberry, the House of Lancaster white and blue. Sumptuary law dictated the material and cut that could be worn by different people – ermine for earls, for example – and type of footwear was strictly regulated by social status. This livery was thereby a way to identify who was who, so that 'you were what you wore' in the Middle Ages according to Groom (2006: 24). As we have noted, more recently Bourdieu (2004) and Fox (2004) have also noted how clothing continues to provide a social marker.

Workwear can also provide a marker for organisations, though we would suggest that most reasons for workwear can be located within four broad areas, i.e. that regulated by government, the occupation, individuals and the organisation. These four areas of workwear are shown in Table 4.1. This table also highlights these types' derivation, purpose, methods of enforcement and forms, and offers illustrative examples of each of the four types.

Table 4.1 Understanding workwear

Derivation	Purpose	Method of enforcement	Form	Examples
Government	Health, safety and hygiene	Law Codes of practice	Formal	Hard hats on construction sites; hairnets in food retail

(Continued)

Table 4.1   (Continued)

Derivation	Purpose	Method of enforcement	Form	Examples
Occupation	Communication	Uniform	Formal	Insignia on uniforms; wigs and gowns in court
		Dress code	Informal	Academics' elbow-patch jackets; barristers' dark pinstripe suits
Individual	Communication	Dress code	Informal	'Impression management' and 'dress for success'
Organisation	Communication	Uniform	Formal	Literal company uniform; employees 'modelling' stock in retail
		Appearance Standards and dress code	Formal	Prescriptions on jewellery, make-up, hair style and length
			Formally Informal	'Dress down Friday'

We recognise that these categories are not mutually exclusive and an organisation could conceivably include two or more of the above aspects in their dress and appearance policies. For example, an organisation may have a corporate uniform that the staff wear for the majority of the time but also have 'dress down Friday' or a food retailer may combine hygiene and safety aspects with uniforms that need to communicate the desired corporate image. To consider this point further we now consider each of these categorisations in more detail, with a particular focus on organisationally driven appearance standards and dress codes in interactive services.

The first aspect of workwear is that usually dictated by government and typically intended to address health and safety or hygiene considerations. Here we might think of the use of hard hats on construction sites or the need to ensure that hair or beards are covered in food processing or the catering trade for example. These are requirements that are formally imposed by law or codes of conduct and intended to protect workers' and/or customers' health and well-being.

The second category relates to occupationally specific clothing or workwear. This workwear is sometimes very formal and rigidly applied. In the UK, barristers, for example, have the exclusive right to wear wigs and gowns in court. This 'court attire' brands the occupation and is regarded as 'probably the world's oldest trademark' (Lusher, 2001: 21). Solicitors, who are also qualified legal practitioners, are denied this right. In 1990 solicitors were given the right, as with barristers, to address courts higher than magistrates but were instructed to wear different court attire – shorter gowns – in order to differentiate them from barristers. Sometimes this workwear is informal, little more than a dress code based on the social norms of an occupation. Barristers for example also have an informal dress code when not in court, wearing dark, usually grey pinstripe suits, a practice adopted too by their legal secretaries in chambers. This point is further illustrated in Darr's (2004) analysis of sales work by software engineers. These engineers also had to make software sales and provide after-sales service to client's engineers. To do so the sellers had to present themselves to the clients' engineers as members of their occupational community, and so dressed and talked like an engineer rather than a salesperson in order to establish trust with the client's engineers. For example, during trade shows, unlike most salespeople, the sales engineers dressed casually, much like the engineers who visited the show, as if declaring they were members of their professional community, not regular salespersons. The same was the case during sales visits, when sales engineers dressed like design and test engineers, not salespeople.

In both of these cases, formal and informal, this workwear portrays the occupation visually. It should be noted that occupationally specific clothing can also have an aspect of health and safety incorporated into it and also be branded by organisations through badges and other insignia, which may also mean such uniforms add to the perceived status of the person wearing the uniform. For example, in occupations such as the police, armed forces and nursing, the wearing of a uniform will often signify aspects such as authority, power and professional standing (and see Nath et al., 2016).

The third aspect of workwear identified in our categorisation is 'impression management' and 'dress for success', which, as we discussed in Chapter 2, is concerned with the self-regulation of appearance and dress by individuals as potential or existing employees attempt to 'get in' or 'get on' in organisations respectively. 'Dress to impress' is the advice offered by James (1999) for example, listing the dos and don'ts of haircuts, suits, shirts and ties for men, and hairstyles, jackets, skirts, pantyhose and tops for women:

- Hair apparent: Always make sure your hair is well groomed and up-to-date, without being way out. Women in more traditional companies should avoid wild, flossing locks. Try to keep hair sleek and tie it back if it's long. Men working for the same firms should keep hair short and well-cut.
- Suits: For men, blue or grey. Plain fabric (no man-made fibres) or a light pinstripe. Charcoal or navy are always safe colours. For women, suits are fine and you can mix or match the jackets with other skirts.
- Ties: create the greatest area of self-expression for the businessman (sic) but make sure that the message you're giving is one you want to send out all day … always keep a drawerful of appropriate looks.
- Tights: At all time for formal business wear. Sheer texture and neutral colours or black with a black skirt or shoes.

Here, then, the pressure to conform to particular dress and appearance standards might be implicit, rather than explicitly articulated by organisations. Equally, there may be a strong element of self-regulation, both in terms of conforming to the employing organisation's expected image and of seeking to further enhance professional success.

The fourth category is clothing explicitly dictated by the organisation in the form of uniforms, dress codes and appearance standards. We would suggest that this category is potentially the most problematic as organisations attempt to brand themselves, and by extension their employees, with an organisational image. Indeed, a survey undertaken by XpertHR of nearly 500 UK employers highlighted that over 80 per cent use their dress and appearance policy to support their organisation's external image (Byrne, 2018). This attempt at branding can be made formally through the use of uniforms, appearance standards or dress codes (a point we develop below), though may also be ostensibly more informal through 'dress down Friday' (and see Box 4.1). As noted above, whilst much of the 'impression management' or 'dress for success' prescriptions for individuals are likely to be concerned with 'dressing up', there are counter tendencies as well as organisations also seek to encourage employees' to 'dress down'. What is often termed 'smart casual' as part 'dress down Friday' across a number of organisations often creates real dilemmas as to what is acceptable in an organisation which is seeking an ostensibly more informal dress and appearance policy. The IRS (2000) suggests that the interpretation of phrases such as 'business attire' or 'smart casual' is largely subjective, and can create real dilemmas as to what is acceptable in an organisation which is seeking an ostensibly more informal dress and appearance policy.

Box 4.1   Dress down Friday – just what is 'smart casual' exactly?

A number of organisations have sought to offer guidelines as to what is *not* acceptable under the rubric of 'smart casual' or 'dress down Friday'. The general rule of thumb for 'dress down Friday' tends to be 'casual, but not too casual'. For example, Lloyds TSB, a then British bank, had a smart casual policy which excluded the following clothes as unacceptable: jeans, combat trousers, cargo trousers, leggings, shorts, very short skirts, non-collar T-shirts for male staff only, vests, any item of clothing bearing a large slogan or logo, items of sportswear, football/rugby shirts, trainers or similar footwear. Other guidelines on what was and was not 'smart casual' included: leather not PVC, skirts but not sarongs, no beach or sports gear or wear or body piercing, no wrinkles except with linen for example. Prescriptions of this type may also mean that dressing down in what are largely corporately dictated 'smart casual' clothes has the effect of creating a new de facto 'uniform', for example employees often dressing in Gap khakis.

(*Source*: Barton, 2001; IRS, 2000; Laabs, 1995; Spillane, 2000)

Perhaps reflecting some of the difficulties of striking the right balance in relation to 'smart casual' and/or 'dress down Friday', a number of companies now make dressing down optional. That said, although IDS (2001: 3) suggest that 'it should be borne in mind that some people see the shift towards dress down policies as only a fad, which may itself go out of fashion in due course', that 'fad' shows no signs of going away with over 50 per cent of organisations in the XpertHR survey of appearance and dress policies still operating dress down Fridays (Byrne, 2018).

Arkin (1995) attributes a relaxing of dress codes in many organisations to the greater influence of international companies, suggesting that Continental European companies often have fewer prescriptions than British companies. When such companies locate in the UK they bring their more casual attitudes with them. Arkin also points to American examples, such as Microsoft, where the need to create an innovative and creative ethos within the company is encouraged in part by a lack of uniformity in dress and appearance codes. Being 'dressed down' projects an image of 'appear[ing] more approachable and, potentially, more creative', states Spillane (2000: 181). Florida (2004) makes this point explicitly when discussing how organisations can successfully attract, retain and manage creative workers. It is a mark of such workers, he claims, that they dress as they please. By way of illustration, in her discussion of the changing dress codes of the English (read British), Fox (2004: 290) states that 'The young man going to work in jeans and a t-shirt could be a construction site labourer, but he could equally be the managing director of an independent software company'. The new digital tech companies often aim for a more relaxed atmosphere to encourage creativity and innovation in an environment that allegedly merges work and play. In one Glasgow-based company that on the back of our research we were invited to visit, the company created and built websites for a range of clients, including a number of ultra-cool clubs. In order to create the websites with strong 'aesthetic appeal', in the words of the founder, they sought to provide a 'beautiful' workplace which would create a relaxed working environment and more productive employees. Interestingly, though, when we visited the company the digital workers who were creating the content sat in front of their computers in hoodies and cargo pants, clearly distinct from the 'suits' in the company, dressed usually in a sharp suit and stylish t-shirt, who sold the digital content of the 'creatives': 'If you put people out in front of clients they have to be presentable and present the company image', suggested the founder of the company. The same argument could also be made for other professional groups, such as academics, designers, architects and those working in the creative industries, all professions where it is much less likely that normative prescriptions on dress exist. Such norms often result in emergent, informal dress codes. For example, in his travels around Middle England, Maconie (2009: 295) observes that there is a summer 'uniform' amongst Oxford academics of crumpled cream jacket and Panama hat, 'smarter perhaps than hoodies and tracksuits and baseball caps, but just as unthinkingly de rigueur'.

To think then of this 'formal informality' as a shift away from organisational prescription would be wrong. Not only is the occasion for dressing down determined by the organisation – as we noted above, usually Fridays – so that when (and for how long as a policy) it is acceptable is imposed, but also what clothing constitutes dressing down is also prescribed. The reason for both – when and what – is because dressing down policies are still concerned with manufacturing and projecting a corporate image – perhaps creativity and approachability, but still an image.

Where there are expectations of a more formal dress code it is important that employers are cognizant of the potential for discrimination and addressing notions of fairness, issues that have received significant attention with the case of Nicola Thorp in the UK, which garnered widespread publicity in 2016. Arriving for her first day at work as a PA with PwC, having been sent by a temporary employment agency, she was told that she had to wear two to four inch heels; when she declined to do so she was sent home without pay (LRD, 2016; Odum, 2016). As noted, the case attracted a significant amount of publicity, culminating in a petition signed by over 150,000 people calling for it to be illegal for a company to require its employees to wear high heels at work; something which attracted the interest of a number of politicians.[1] Resultantly, the House of Commons produced a report in January 2017, *High Heels and Workplace Dress Codes* (House of Commons, 2017a), leading to a subsequent debate in the House of Commons, a government response to the original report (House of Commons, 2017b), and finally the publication by the UK Government of a new dress codes guidance in 2018 (Government Equalities Office, 2018). Although the Government ultimately stopped short of making the wearing of high heels illegal, the case served to highlight continuing concerns around the potential for appearance standards and dress codes to be discriminatory, particularly for women (Kenner, 2018).[2] Indeed, as we noted in the previous chapter, budget airline Norwegian Air ran into a storm of controversy when it emerged in 2019 that its female flight attendants are forced to wear high heels, with the only exception being if they have a doctor's note. This controversy arose despite Norway being one of the most gender-equal countries in the world (Ellen, 2019). It is, then, these more formal attempts at prescribing employees' appearance within interactive services that is the primary concern for this chapter. Many interactive service organisations now increasingly seek to create an organisational image, developing and imposing prescriptions for employee appearance in terms of uniforms, appearance standards and dress codes, and this issue is now discussed further below.

UNIFORMS, APPEARANCE STANDARDS AND DRESS CODES IN THE INTERACTIVE SERVICE SECTOR

A major study of uniforms, dress codes and appearance standards in the UK by Nath et al. (2016) noted that the imposition and management of such standards are especially resonant and potentially challenging in occupations in frontline interactive service work. Indeed, a number of authors have considered various aspects of corporate clothing within the interactive service sector (e.g. Daniel et al., 1996; Nelson and Bowen, 2000; Rafaeli, 1993; Solomon, 1985; Wang and Lang, 2019). Rafaeli (1993) highlights how the dress and behaviour of employees with customer interactions shape customer perceptions of service quality. As she suggests:

> ... the thrust of organizational management of employees' dress is that the appearance of employees communicates something about the organization. The assumption is that what employees wear while at work, and how they appear when interacting with customers, can influence customers' feelings about the organization and the service that it provides. (1993: 182)

This development – the increasing emphasis on the aesthetic appeal of employees as part of the branding of services organisations – makes understandable the increasing corporate attention given to uniforms, appearance standards and dress codes as they affect employee appearance and so the desired image to be created and maintained by these organisations. We would suggest that this process is often sophisticated and dynamic as organisations attempt to brand themselves with a corporate image, what Rafaeli (1993: 182) terms 'organisational impression management'.

With regard to uniforms, as IDS (2001: 11) report, 'companies expend considerable amounts of time, money and effort on developing uniforms for their staff. They often do this to project a positive brand image to customers'. As Bentley (1995) notes:

> ... the uniform organization is all around us, in the shape of banks, building societies, shops, airlines, travel agents, hotels, transport companies or utility suppliers. The first impression is often a good one. Neat, smart and well turned out people give a surface impression of an efficient organization. The places they work and the vehicles they drive all display the corporate image. (1995: 20)

Similarly, Solomon (1985) notes how corporate uniforms, or what he terms 'service apparel', are crucial in the 'packaging' of employees', and are a major part of what the company wishes to communicate to the marketplace. Unsurprisingly, then, over 80 per cent of employers in our Glasgow and Manchester surveys of hospitality and retail employers indicated that they operated a uniform policy, primarily for the purposes of maintaining a corporate image, but also to ensure that staff looked neat and presentable.

Work by Daniel et al. (1996) on flight attendants, and Nelson and Bowen (2000) on employees in themed casino resorts, found that organisationally prescribed workwear can affect employees' feelings about their work which in turn influences their behaviour and performance at work. For example, the work of Daniel et al. and Nelson and Brown found that a well-designed, aesthetically pleasing, practical and comfortable uniform has a positive impact on employee performance, self-esteem, satisfaction and identification with the company aims and the 'role' they are expected to play in the workplace, thus conferring the wearer with status, authority, legitimacy and group identification (see Box 4.2). In this respect the wearing of a uniform can often encourage frontline service employees to attune to their 'role' and exhibit the 'right' kind of role behaviours in their interaction with customers, often creating stronger connections with customers and enhancing customer identification with the brand and customer satisfaction (Harquail, 2005; Nath et al., 2016; Wang and Lang, 2019).

Box 4.2   Wearing it well – uniforms in hospitality

Many hospitality businesses either choose bespoke uniforms or ready-to-wear clothing ranges in an attempt to create a modern stylish image. This attempt to create a stylish image also needs to be balanced against the need for functionality. According to Nick Juber, managing director of Denny's, a clothing supplier for the industry, 'uniforms should be fit for purpose and comfortable'. Getting the uniform right can increase staff morale it is suggested. Equally though, Juber recognises that 'wearers are often expected to accept an unflattering solution that makes minimal concessions for shapes, sizes and even gender'. However, according to Debbie Leon, director of uniform designers Fashionizer, style does not have to be compromised with elements of durability and convenience. Leon notes how Mandarin-collared shirts and jackets are popular in the hospitality industry, offering a 'smart and contemporary look, which looks equally good on men and women and replaces the shirt, tie and waistcoat combination'. An example of Fashionizer's style is the use of bespoke uniforms at the modern five-star Monogram 'g' Hotel in Ireland. The uniforms are based on the movie glamour of the 1950s coming in striking fuchsia pink with black, reflecting the hotel's interiors. This meshing of the uniforms with hotel interiors exemplifies how employees are increasingly utilised as organisational 'hardware' and thus become artefacts of the brand.

(*Source:* White and Lane, 2008; and see also https://www.fashionizer.com/)

Box 4.2 highlights the different types of 'uniforms' used by organisations. Some are generic ready-to-wear outfits, others can be bespoke, designed especially for the organisation. In our emblematic Hotel Elba, as part of the general process of instilling the importance of grooming and presenting the right image, the company had what Moira, the hotel's human resources manager, described as 'mini fashion shows' for the new staff. The idea was to ensure that staff appreciated the 'before' and 'after' effect of the grooming tips offered by the image consultancy utilised by the hotel to ensure staff were fully aware of the importance of their image. As Moira explained:

... they got to dress up in their uniforms and then we took photographs of them all with their hair and their make-up and their uniforms on, and it was very much a before and after of Polaroids because we took photographs of them in the morning when they first came in and then last thing in the afternoon when they had their uniforms on and their hair and make-up all done.

The uniforms themselves varied depending on where employees worked, with staff in the hotel's café wearing what were described as 'little Chinese tunics with little stand up collars and buttons down the front' in either pink, pale blue or beige, with chino trousers, with the female staff wearing 'trendy little hipster ones. They were quite with it'. The tunics were made especially for the hotel, whilst the chinos were bought from Gap. Management and reception staff had a similar style which was described by Moira as having the 'same little Mandarin collar' but were instead styled as black trouser suits with fitted jackets. Consequently, as Moira acknowledged these suits were 'much more expensive', costing £300 from Hobbs, an up-market fashion retailer.

In addition to wearing company-bought uniforms, in fashion retail employees can often 'model' current company stock as a uniform. Our survey of Manchester fashion retailers found that around 50 per cent of employers expected staff to wear clothes that were from current stock, compared to around a third of employers who provided staff with a company uniform. Pettinger (2004, 2005) notes there is often a distinction between mass/mid-market fashion retailers, who will frequently have a corporate uniform, which the employee must wear and which clearly marks them out as employees; and high fashion retailers, where employees will often model current stock and consequently may be potentially indistinguishable from consumers. Pettinger describes this as the difference between 'uniform' and 'model' companies. She argues that the former often employs aestheticised labour, whilst the latter are more intent on overtly creating a particular organisational style with the use of the aesthetic labour and more reflective of our characterisation of the style labour market. As Pettinger (2005: 469) notes for aspirational brands, which are usually 'highly fashionable, designer intense and "cool"', an 'ideal' employee is described in the following manner:

The worker, wearing current stock and with appropriately fashionable hairstyle and make up, appears as a consumer as well as a worker, signalling what is fashionable to customers, and how they might look in the 'right' clothes. Workers at such stores are not only fashionably dressed, they are young, usually slim, with 'attractive' faces. (Pettinger, 2004: 179)

It is not just what is worn however, but how it is worn, hence the additional attention paid to appearance standards and dress codes: 'Emphasis is placed on projecting the right image and customer focus means that employee appearance in relation to clothes, hair, jewellery, make-up, hands and personal hygiene is still set out clearly in many dress and appearance policies' (IRS, 2000: 16). As IDS note (2001: 3), 'There is little mileage to be gained from introducing a smart new uniform if the general appearance of staff undermines the overall look'. Consequently, if companies are willing to spend money on uniforms to project a positive brand image to customers then they are equally keen to ensure that other aspects of employees' appearance do not undermine the overall 'look'. It is unsurprising then that the findings from our surveys of hospitality and retail employers in Glasgow and Manchester indicated that virtually all of the companies operated appearance standards and dress codes for employees. Aspects of these appearance standards and dress codes are further outlined in Table 4.2.

Table 4.2   Aspects of appearance standards and dress codes in hospitality and retail companies in Glasgow and Manchester

Element of appearance standards and dress codes	% of Glasgow employers	% of Manchester employers
Rules for general tidiness	99%	91%
Clothing style	74%	76%
Jewellery	66%	49%
Make-up and/or personal grooming	63%	55%
Hair style and length	45%	20%

It is equally noteworthy that 31 per cent of respondents in the Glasgow employer survey did not allow visible tattoos in their customer-facing staff, though there was significant differences between the sub-sectors, with hotels being far more prescriptive at 50 per cent, compared to restaurants/bars/cafés (27 per cent) and retail (30 per cent).[3] Similarly, for the Manchester survey 44 per cent of the respondents would not allow visible tattoos. One of our focus group respondents remembered how a colleague 'was told to wear long sleeved shirts to cover up his tattoos because it didn't portray the right image'. Another recalled how a colleague who had several piercings was deliberately placed in a backstage environment out of sight of customers (and see Box 4.3):

> ... there is one guy in the place where I worked, he had a piercing in his lip and his eyebrow and he had a few piercings in his ears as well, and they didn't really tell him to take them out but he was just shunted from doing bar work to kind of doing kitchen porter work ... so people wouldn't really see him out front ... he wasn't happy and left after that.

Box 4.3   Body art at work

Although in the UK and US around 30–40 per cent of adults has a tattoo, a body piercing or a combination of both, employer and customer attitudes towards employees' displaying body art in customer-facing roles in hospitality and retail remain surprisingly mixed. A number of studies have highlighted how visible body art can significantly decrease an individual's hireability for a frontline, customer-facing role. Managers and recruiters often hold negative perceptions about visible tattoos and piercings (including nose, tongue, eyebrows and single or multiple ear piercings) when interviewing potential employees for roles in hospitality and retail. That said, there is some evidence that customers are becoming more tolerant towards employees displaying body art due to its increased prevalence in society. In response to this greater tolerance there are examples of companies relaxing their attitudes to body art, including the citizenM hotel brand discussed in Chapter 2. In keeping with their innovative and fashionable style they welcome employees with inoffensive tattoos and body piercings. In 2014 Starbucks, having consulted with their employees, changed their previously hardline policy on visible tattoos to allow employees to show non-offensive visible tattoos, as long as they are not on the face or throat. Indeed, in certain organisational contexts body art can be used strategically to ensure an appropriate fit between the organisational brand image and individual employees. Organisations which primarily target a younger, 'edgier' customer demographic will often see employees' body art as an integral part of the branding and marketing of the organisation. For example, a study of a 'hip' and 'rebellious' skateboard and apparel shop and 'edgy' chain of craft beer pubs found that these organisations actively encourage 'creativity' and self-expression in the appearance of their staff through their body art, and so these elements are seen as an integral part of their employees' aesthetic labouring.

(*Source*: Ozanne et al., 2019; Swanger, 2006; Timming, 2015, 2017a; Timming et al., 2017)

Allowing managers greater judgement rather than adhering to blanket policies would, therefore, seem a sensible way to address the issue of body art. Pyrillis (2010: 24) cites Professor Myrna Armstrong who has studied body art for two decades and suggests that 'I'm seeing more waiters and waitresses, salespeople, bank tellers, people dealing with customers every day who have tattoos and piercings'. Consequently Armstrong suggests that the role of HR and managers should be to develop policies that talk about the tastefulness, non-offensiveness and neatness of tattoos and piercings rather than banning them outright.

In seeking to make clear these appearance standards, many service organisations have sometimes developed extensive policies which outline in great detail what is acceptable and appropriate for employees. For example, as we noted in the previous chapter Disney has an extensive list of what is expected of cast members' in terms of their appearance, detailing expectations around length and style of hair and the colour and quantity of cosmetics (Disney, 2016). Walmart too, until recently, had a dress code stipulating no nose or facial jewellery, dangly earrings or blue jeans – except on Fridays when employees have to pay $1 for the 'privilege' of wearing them (Ehrenreich, 2001).[4] There can, however, be cross-cultural difficulties in the imposition of dress and appearance standards. Whilst Disney has an extensive appearance guide which was rigorously enforced within the US, it is noteworthy that when the company first located in France to open Euro Disney, it failed in their attempts to transfer 'The Disney Look' (Laabs, 1995). Employees in France refused to sign the 10-page addendum to their employment contracts agreeing to the specified dress and appearance code, which prohibited men from wearing moustaches, required women to wear modest hemlines and regulated use of perfume. Resultantly, and despite a legal battle, Disney was forced to introduce a much less stringent code in France (and see Box 4.4).

Box 4.4   UBS a prescription too far?

The Swiss banking giant UBS was widely mocked when it introduced a 44-page dress code at the end of 2010. The dress code, which was developed by senior executives in the company as a means to improve its image, suggested that female employees should wear skin-coloured underwear and offered advice to male employees on how to knot a tie. Female staff were given tips on what kind of perfume to wear and were told to avoid black nail varnish. Similarly, men were told to have their hair cut every month and to avoid unruly beards. All customer-facing staff were also advised to avoid garlic or onion breath. Other pieces of advice in the document included 'You can extend the life of your knee socks and stockings by keeping your toenails trimmed and filed'. Staff were further advised that 'Glasses should always be kept clean ... dirty glasses create an appearance of negligence'. The dress code was subsequently revised in 2011 following widespread derision.

(*Source*: BBC, 2010, 2011a)

THE EMPLOYEE EXPERIENCE OF WORKWEAR

As the examples above illustrate, some organisations in interactive services are becoming ever more prescriptive in seeking to 'make up' their employees in support of the 'right' corporate look. The imposition of uniforms, appearance standards and dress codes can be experienced very differently by employees. As with other industries and occupations, frontline employees in retail and hospitality may passively accept, actively embrace or reject the management of their appearance.

An obvious reason why employees accept prescriptions on their appearance is because organisations monitor appearance standards through performance management and other mechanisms (Byrne, 2018; Nath et al., 2016). Certainly employers monitor employee workwear, as our research of interactive service organisations across the retail, hospitality and airline industries highlighted. One focus group participant talked about her up-market fashion retail company's prescription of 'model' employees: 'The Leviathan Girl', 'The Leviathan Boy'. This initiative involved the company circumscribing the appearance of their employees such that, for example, 'If I was to have my hair done or anything ... if you're going to cut you hair in any way, well drastically or highlights, you've got to discuss it with the manager first'. In a supermarket, as we noted in Chapter 1, an employee was sent home to shave her legs because the manager believed that the employee's hairy legs were off-putting to customers. In another focus group, a participant working in the hospitality industry recalled an incident at a major sports event in which employees, who had been sent by an agency, were lined up to be checked by a supervisor before they could start serving customers in the food court outlets:

> ... we had to go through a grooming check before we went to work. They checked your shoes, they checked your hair, it had to be tied back with a dark haired bobble and boys were sent away with disposable razors before they were allowed to go to work ... one guy ... got sent back because he didn't pass the grooming check.

In a similar vein, Moira (the human resources manager of Hotel Elba) noted how supervisors would check that staff uniforms were pressed and shoes were clean, and if not they would be sent back to the staffroom to rectify any concerns. The regulation of appearance and adherence to company standards was, in the airline industry, overseen by the 'grooming standards committee' or, in the words of one focus group respondent who had worked in the airline industry, the 'uniform police'.

Our surveys of hospitality and retail employers in Glasgow and fashion retail employers in Manchester found evidence that having an appropriate personal appearance and adherence to dress codes was often shaped by training and also part of the formal appraisal process. For example, over 60 per cent of employers in Glasgow offered training in dress sense and style, with the figures being just under half in Manchester. Moreover, around a third of employers in both surveys offered training in make-up and personal grooming. For example, in Hotel Elba the induction process for new waiting staff included extensive grooming and deportment training, which was done by external consultants. Such training encompassed haircuts/styling, 'acceptable' make-up, individual make-overs, how men should shave and the standards expected in relation to appearance. In a similar vein, for the Manchester survey aesthetic elements (self-presentation/appearance and adherence to clothing standards) were reported as part of the appraisal process by around 60 per cent of establishments. Although product knowledge was the area of appraisal highlighted as the 'most useful' by the greatest number of respondents (44 per cent), followed by social and interpersonal skills (36 per cent), 17 per cent reported that self-presentation was the most useful element of appraisal and 14 per cent that adherence to company clothing standards was the most useful.

Many employees in our research seemed to accept the need for employers to dictate how they looked, with the majority of our focus group participants being generally happy to support prescriptions on their appearance, with one noting that 'I think it looks good when you come in somewhere that everyone wears more or less the same uniform'. It is noteworthy that the employee who talked about her company's 'uniform police' did so unproblematically: 'I think it's necessary for someone who is in uniform … What's the point in giving somebody a corporate image and then having big bits of hair everywhere'. The 'uniform police are constantly out and about' monitoring employees' image and 'it was a good thing' the employee insisted. This acceptance of, even agreement with, the business case for organisations prescribing the 'look' of employees was common. In answer to the question of whether they ever resented organisational prescriptions around appearance, a typical response from the focus groups was bar worker Elizabeth, who suggested 'No, because it's perfectly acceptable that your appearance is very important'. It was also the case amongst some of our focus groups participants that they liked what they had to wear, believing that it offered social status and brought self-confidence. Amongst the focus groups with potential airline industry employees, most respondents supported the often stringent requirements. One suggested that 'when you're in uniform you feel good about yourself like you think people look up to you'. Indeed, one of the trainers on the one of the airline preparation courses suggested that:

> I think in a way they've got to earn that, like when getting a uniform on a cabin crew course with an airline – getting the uniform is like a reward because you get it at a certain stage in your course, you have to have passed so many exams and assessments prior to getting a uniform. We would never put them in a uniform right away, plus they've got to have the uniform standards training before you put them in a uniform, and that would not be the first thing you would do.

Indeed, within a number of our employee focus groups there was recognition that often it would be self and peer pressure that would ensure conformity to company uniform and appearance standards (see also Cutcher and Achtel, 2017). Failure by employees to observe these aspects would be considered as letting their colleagues (and customers) down. As Marcella, an employee in an upmarket fashion retailers noted, 'You've got to be presentable. Like a customer wouldn't trust someone if you're standing there looking awful'. Similarly, Rhona, who worked for a different fashion retailer noted, 'You're sort of PR for the shop. Before you start … you actually think: "Right, I'll do a once over. Do I look the part?"'.

Nevertheless, some employees may attempt to resist or at least mediate organisational prescriptions of workwear, though in our research we found surprisingly few examples of such resistance. One of the few examples occurred in Hotel Elba, Moira, the human resources manager, noted how their female reception staff would seek to customise their uniforms by wearing scarves and broaches on their jackets. Such embellishments though were not allowed because it was suggested by Moira that 'the point of having uniforms is that everybody looks the same'. Failure by employees to adhere to appearance requirements was likely to lead to disciplinary action by employers. Evidence from our own and other research (Byrne, 2018; IDS, 2001; IRS, 2003, 2005; Nath et al., 2016) suggests that organisations are prepared to take disciplinary action against their staff for contravening appearance standards and dress codes. For example, over 80 per cent of the employers in our Glasgow and Manchester surveys indicated that they would take disciplinary action against employees if they contravened employer expectations for their dress and appearance.

In taking disciplinary action, employers in our research would typically first attempt to deal informally with appearance transgressions by simply talking to employees. Employers emphasised, however, that failure thereafter to comply with organisational prescriptions would lead to formal action. Such actions, one employer explained in an open-ended question in one of our surveys, might involve employees not being allowed to work, being sent home to change if their dress or appearance was deemed inappropriate, loss of staff discounts, loss of shifts and counselling/training. Other examples from our survey of employees of how dress codes were enforced in a punitive manner included employees being sent home to wash, to change their clothes or appearance and not being paid for the loss of hours; tips being withheld; facing disciplinary procedures such as receiving verbal and written warnings; and not being allowed to work. One focus group participant who worked at a prominent golf course recalled how, before a major golf championship, one of her colleagues was told to take a week's holiday, 'because they didn't think she was what they were looking for for such a prestigious event'. Employers indicated that repeat offenders would in the first instance be given a verbal warning, followed by a written warning and ultimately dismissal. Employees also confirmed that dress codes were rigidly applied and that they had seen or even experienced instances of being disciplined for not conforming to the company dress code, including the ultimate sanction of being dismissed for repeated infringements. As one recalled, 'they had one girl in the restaurant and she came in with sort of highlighted strips [in her hair]. There wasn't anything wrong with it but she was told to get it changed or lose her job basically'.

Over and above employee acceptance of organisational prescriptions on uniforms, appearance standards and dress codes as simply being part of their employment contract, in some circumstances employees may positively embrace organisational intervention in their appearance and dress. For example, Nath et al. (2016) recognise how employees in interactive service work may see dress and appearance standards in a positive vein in terms of enhancing self-esteem and work performance. Pettinger's research (2002, 2004, 2005) on retail assistants exemplifies this point. She highlights the manner in which employees modelling current stock in prestigious high quality fashion retailers would often feel this clothing enhanced their status. Thus, although she notes how shop work is often seen as a low-status occupation, 'the image of French Connection workers may enhance their status in an environment where looking fashionable is important and where people are judged on appearance' (2002: 12). Similarly we found that the £300 designer uniforms from Hobbs supplied by the emblematic Hotel Elba, and worn by the management and reception staff, were appreciated and worn both in and out of work by employees. Indeed, this notion of display as work and the opportunity for employees to wear 'designer' uniforms appears to be particularly apparent in style-driven, 'high-end' services, such as designer fashion retailers, style bars, cafés and restaurants, and boutique or 'lifestyle' hotels:

> Take a look at the jet set's favourite hotels ... Staff wear all-black Versace with specially designed gold-printed ties or scarves ... It might not be your style, but the staff sure do look good – so good that they are dangerously close to inverting the rules of status. These days, the people you are paying to serve might just show you up. (Forte, 2002: x).

Examples of designer-clad staff include: Armani at Nobu, Rebecca Moses and Calvin Klein at Spoon+ in the Sanderson Hotel, Asia de Cuba in St Martins Lane Hotel, and Hussein Chalalyan at Hakkasan. As Forte (2002: x) notes, 'such uniforms don't just pass the test with the most aesthetically conscious crowd; those wearing them also up the fashion ante, oh so casually, while setting down that second bottle of brouilly'.

The discussion above points to the manner in which employees may not simply accept but actively embrace corporate uniforms, appearance standards and dress codes, viewing them in a positive or even an aspirational manner (see also Boyle and De Keere, 2019; Cutcher and Achtel, 2017). Consequently, in undertaking such aesthetic labouring employees are willing to accede to the demands of the employer in embodying the required 'look'.

IS IT LEGAL? BALANCING EMPLOYER AND EMPLOYEE RIGHTS

Alongside these positive aspects of corporate clothing for frontline service employees, as we alluded to above, there is also potential for uniforms, dress codes and appearance standards to be experienced more negatively. In this manner and following Hochschild's (1983) notion of 'emotional dissonance' – whereby service employees do not necessarily feel the positive emotions they are expected to portray in the service encounter, thereby creating a sense of dissonance between their felt and publicly portrayed emotions – there may well be 'aesthetic dissonance'. Such 'aesthetic dissonance', can create a situation where an employee's self-image is at odds with the organisational 'look'. For example, some of our focus group respondents noted how some uniform and dress code prescriptions can impact negatively on employees or potential employees. One employee working for a high-end fashion designer retailer tried to get her best friend a job and was told that the friend wore too much make-up and so would not be considered (and see Box 4.5). The focus group participant who had recalled being lined up for a 'grooming check' recognised that 'I'd have been devastated if I'd been turned away, imagine failing a grooming check'.

Box 4.5   Too much or too little make-up? The case of Harrods and Virgin Atlantic

In 2011 Melanie Stark resigned from her job in top people's London department store Harrods. She said that she couldn't face more battles with management over her appearance. She had been commended for her customer service and scored highly in a 'mystery shopper' assessment, and yet management were still unhappy that she didn't look right for the job. The reason was that Melanie was refusing to wear make-up. Harrods has a prescriptive two-page dress code for its staff – female and male. Female staff were told to have 'full make-up at all time: base, blusher, full eyes (not too heavy, lipstick, lip liner and gloss'. They must also style their hair to flatter their features. Hair can have highlights or colour but regrowth is not allowed. They cannot have visible tattoos, mismatched jewellery or large hoop earrings. Earrings must be pearls or diamond studs. Male staff likewise must have well-groomed hair and also be clean shaven. Beards are allowed but no goatees or moustaches of 'contemporary style'. Sideburns must be no longer than mid-ear and no wider than one inch. Their fingernails must be well-manicured. After a floor walk by senior managers, during which Melanie was, as usual, not wearing make-up, she was asked to comply with the code. She had been sent home twice previously from not complying; 'Surely', she says, 'I had the choice to wear none'. A spokesperson for Harrods said that 'All staff are subject to a dress code which they sign up to on joining the company, which relates to overall polish'. After five years working for Harrods, Melanie said that she was happy working for the company 'but I've been driven out'. Whilst some companies become ever more prescriptive about their employees' appearance others are taking a more relaxed view. For example, Virgin Atlantic announced in 2019 that female cabin crew can now work without wearing make-up if they so wish.

(*Sources*: Davies, 2011; Topham, 2019)

Workwear and the related aspects of managing employee appearance, then, raises a number of ethical, legal, employee engagement and human resource management issues in terms of the extent to which organisations can legitimately involve themselves in policing an individual's appearance in the organisational setting. At the heart of this sensitivity lies recognition that imposing uniforms, dress codes and appearance standards may often mean that employees' have to subvert their own identity and style for the organisational good. As Rafaeli (1993: 204) notes, 'dress is a very personal matter in all other settings. It is an unspoken assumption in modern society that individuals are allowed to choose what to wear. Individuals do so in ways that respond to their personal orientation as a means of individuation'. Uniforms, appearance standards and dress codes clearly cut across such assumptions, and for many employees' wearing a corporate uniform could be seen as a process of 'deindividuation'. As one supermarket cashier plaintively notes in Rafaeli (1993: 175), 'They tell me what to wear. They tell me what to say. They tell me how to say it. Am I a real person?'. Moreover, the 'deindividuation' that the imposition of uniforms, appearance standards and dress codes might denote can be seen alongside organisations' attempts to also control other parts of their employees' behaviour, most obviously requiring employees to have or at least display the 'right' type of emotions in their interactions with customers (Hochschild, 1983). The danger lies in the sense of invasiveness that the imposition of standards of behaviour and appearance may create, and whether employees are likely to resist or even reject such attempts at control. When employees do fail to adhere to standards with regard to appearance, uniforms or dress codes, then they may, as we have recognised, find themselves disciplined by the organisation and ultimately dismissed. There is clearly the potential for tension between organisational prescription and individual expression, and the business case versus human rights (Middlemiss, 2018; Nath et al., 2016; see also Box 4.6 and Chapter 7 for a further discussion of how some prescriptions on appearance lead to the potential for sexual harassment from customers).

Box 4.6   When being 'easy on the eye' becomes discriminatory and harassing

Employment Tribunal cases in the UK highlight how women in the hospitality industry often face pressure to conform to discriminatory and harassing dress codes. One such case saw a Muslim cocktail waitress winning nearly £3,000 in compensation from her employer for hurt feelings and loss of earnings. The case centred on the attempt by the employer, the Rocket Bar in London's Mayfair, to make the employee wear a red sleeveless dress. The employee felt that the dress made her look like a prostitute and resulted in customers pestering her for sex, which ultimately led her to resign. The Employment Tribunal panel rejected the claim from the employee that her only choice was to resign but did conclude that her employer's insistence that she wear the dress amounted to sexual harassment and violated her dignity. Another, more recent, case saw a teenage waitress being awarded over £3,500 after refusing to wear a skirt and make-up in an attempt to make her 'easy on the eye' for customers. The restaurant's dress code specified that staff should wear all black, and in response the waitress wore trousers to be comfortable, as well as using minimal make-up and keeping her hair up. The restaurant owner requested that she wear her hair down, apply a 'full face of make-up', and wear a skirt to she would be 'easy on eye'.

(*Sources*: Calnan, 2016; *The Caterer*, 2009.)

Despite these concerns about the invasiveness of appearance standards, it is important to recognise that employers do have a legal right to regulate their employees' dress and appearance (Hay and Middlemiss, 2003). Indeed, Middlemiss (2018) and Nath et al. (2016) state that the managerial prerogative is very strong in relation to the issue of corporate image, and that employers have the right to stipulate employees' appearance, dress and grooming, except in cases where these are blatantly discriminatory. It is also important to note that such codes are often unilaterally enforced by the employer. It is less common for the imposition of regulations covering clothing and appearance standards to be mutually agreed with trade unions or employees prior to their introduction. How organisations introduce new uniforms, appearance standards and dress codes or modifying existing requirements can be significant. Indeed, flagging the need for consultation and engagement with employees is an integral aspect of the more policy-oriented writing on this topic – for example, conducting wearer trials on new uniforms before they are 'rolled out' (IDS, 2002; IRS, 2003, 2005; Nelson and Bowen, 2000).

Thus, as long as employers can make a case that clothing and appearance standards are in the company's business interests and non-discriminatory, then they can develop the often stringent codes we have noted above (and see Chapter 7 for a further discussion of how this issue impacts on broader debates around appearance discrimination or 'lookism'). Consequently, as long as employers proceed on the basis of 'mutual trust and confidence' – namely not imposing unreasonable dress and appearance standards, e.g. introducing a dress or appearance requirement which is deeply embarrassing to the employee and wholly unnecessary – then employees must, in turn, 'obey reasonable instructions' (IRLB, 1993). The balance then between employers' and employees' views on matters of style, taste and expression clearly falls on the side of the employer. That said, the interpretation of what denotes 'acceptable business interests' and 'discriminatory' can sometimes be challenged. Within both the UK and US discrimination largely refers to so-called protected characteristics, such as sex, race, disability, age, religion or belief and sexual orientation, where the imposition of certain dress and appearance standards could be thought to be sexist or racist, for example (for a review of key UK and US employment tribunal decisions in this area, see Hay and Middlemiss, 2003; King et al., 2006; Middlemiss, 2018; Nath et al., 2016).

CONCLUSION

Despite the proliferation of discussion on workwear, it has barely featured, if at all, in the theory of practice and labour process theory. This chapter has sought to address this gap. Focusing on how organisations seek to maintain their 'look' through workwear it has considered the role of corporate clothing in the contemporary workplace. It recognised that the impetus for regulating employees' appearance through uniforms, appearance standards and dress codes can come from a number of sources including the government and occupation as well the organisation. However, the primary focus of the chapter was on the interactive service sector and how organisations are seeking ever more congruence between their corporate image and the employees who embody this image. In particular, the chapter considered the role of uniforms, appearance standards and dress codes, and how these aspects can impact both positively and negatively on employees' experiences of aesthetic labour, creating the potential for both 'aesthetic congruence' between the organisation and individual, wherein the corporate image of the organisation is compatible with the self-ascribed image of workers, and 'aesthetic dissonance', wherein an employee's self-image is at odds with the organisational 'look'.

The study of workwear is an important feature of aesthetic labour and allows us to appreciate how organisations seek to mould their employees beyond the point of recruitment and selection into the embodiment of the required corporate image through dress and appearance standards – creating Harquail's (2005) artefacts of the brand. The chapter outlined how and why the manner in which organisations develop uniforms, appearance standards and dress codes varies. For example, the use of generic ready-to-wear outfits to bespoke uniforms to staff modelling current stock will often reflect the degree to which an organisation is style-driven. It is not only the use of workwear, though, that is important. As the chapter also noted, organisations will also often develop prescriptions through appearance standards and dress codes, which seek to further reinforce the desired corporate image. It is noteworthy that this process of making up employees through uniforms, appearance standards and dress codes was one which was felt to be largely unproblematic by a number of the employees that we spoke to during the course of our research. Generally the weight of evidence suggested that employees accepted or even sometimes actively embraced these attempts to manage their appearance in the workplace. There was much less evidence of resistance or resentment from employees, though we did note that employers were also willing to take disciplinary action if necessary to reinforce the need for employees to conform to appearance expectations. Having considered the manner in which organisations make up employees through appearance standards and dress codes the following chapter assesses the increasing importance of body language in organisations. In particular it focuses on how service organisations seek to create the 'right' kind of body language in their employees as they interact with customers.

NOTES

1. A similar petition was launched in Japan in 2019, protesting against the expectation that female staff are required to wear high heels at work (Weaver and France-Presse, 2019).
2. See also pp. 36–44 of *High Heels and Workplace Dress Codes* to see how the PR company in the Thorp case amended its dress and appearance guidelines after May 2016.
3. More generally across the economy, attitudes towards tattoos and piercings seem to be relaxing. For example, a survey of nearly 500 UK employers across a broad range of sectors found that around 60 per cent of organisations allowed tattoos and piercings without restrictions, though it is noteworthy that restrictions were much more likely to be imposed in customer-facing roles (Byrne, 2018; see also Wolff, 2015).
4. Walmart has recently relaxed its dress code to allow employees to wear what they feel comfortable in and demonstrate their own personal style, though employees will still be expected to wear the company's 'iconic' vest and name badge (Sprague, 2018).

5
BODY TALK

As we noted in Chapter 2, potential and existing employees present themselves through comportment – posture, gesture, touch, use of personal space, facial characteristics, and eye contact. These aspects are largely concerned with our non-verbal communication or what is more usually described as body language. Ectoff (2000: 246) suggests that in using body language we are 'signalling with more than looks'. Although describing this phenomenon within the context of discussing how women attract men, the notion of 'signalling with more than looks' is one that has also been enthusiastically taken up within an organisational context. This chapter considers the importance of body language within organisational settings, recognising how either consciously or unconsciously non-verbal communications have a significant impact in interacting with others. Before considering this issue, though, the chapter outlines the genesis of body language, noting how it is a relatively recent term dating from the 1960s.

Having considered the genesis of body language, the chapter then discusses in more detail how posture, gesture, touch, use of personal space, facial characteristics and eye contact can be important in an organisational context, e.g. during selection interviewing. This general consideration of body language serves as the background to consider the specific nature of how these issues play out within interactive services generally, and through the use of aesthetic labour specifically. Drawing on our own and others' research we consider the importance of body language in recruitment and selection, training, interactions with customers and the manner in which hospitality and retail organisations monitor and control body language, including how it may be included in performance reviews.

THE GENESIS AND DEVELOPMENT OF BODY LANGUAGE

Apparently a translation of the French '*langage corporel*', Ayto (1999: 392) states that the term 'body language' was first coined in 1966 and is defined as 'the gestures and movements by which a person unconsciously or indirectly conveys meaning'. Although the term emerged in 1966, it was popularised by the publication in 1971 of *Body Language* by Julius Fast. As Fast notes on the opening page of his book, 'Within the last few years a new and exciting science has been uncovered and explored. It is called body language' (1971: 11). Blackman (2008), whilst recognising the importance of Fast's work, also acknowledges the precursors in the sociological literature, most obviously in the work of Erving Goffman (1959, 1963). In his recognition of a dramaturgical analysis of how individuals manage the impression they give to others, Goffman (1959) amongst other things noted the signals 'leaking' out through bodies such that we create impressions both intentionally and unintentionally through the notion of 'body idiom' (Goffman 1963: 35). This body idiom encompasses 'dress, bearing, movement and position, sound level, physical gestures such as waving or saluting, facial decorations, and broad emotional expression' (Goffman, p. 33). Clearly, then, a number of elements of body idiom, such as physical gestures and facial decorations, are similar to what could be considered body language. Fast's (1971: 12) definition of body language suggests it is 'any reflexive or non-reflexive movement of a part, or all of the body, used by a person to communicate an emotional message to the outside world'. Thus, as he later notes:

> ... we all in one way or another, send our little messages out to the world ... We act out our state of being with non-verbal body language. We lift one eyebrow for disbelief. We rub our noses for puzzlement. We clasp our arms to isolate ourselves or to protect ourselves ... The gestures are numerous, and while some are deliberate and others are almost deliberate, there are some that are mostly unconscious. (1971: 17–18)

Following Fast's groundbreaking book, this sense of body language being in some cases deliberate has led many populist and academic authors to offer a range of prescriptions as to how individuals can utilise their body language to get in and get ahead in an organisational setting (e.g. Bonaccio et al., 2016; Everett, 2008; Huczynski, 2004; Michael, 2000; Spillane, 2000), and it is this area to which the chapter now turns.

BODY LANGUAGE IN AN ORGANISATIONAL CONTEXT

The starting point of much of the work about how body language can be used to get in and get ahead in an organisational context is the adage that 'you don't get a second chance to make a first impression'. For example, Huczynski (2004) recognises that within ten seconds of meeting a person for the first time we make judgements about them. Lyle (1990: 58) thus suggests that 'the importance of body language during the first four or five minutes of an encounter cannot be over-emphasized'. To further consider this point we will now briefly discuss the key elements of body language – posture, gesture, touch, use of personal space, facial characteristics and eye contact.

Posture

It is suggested that having an appropriate posture is important in making clear you are ready for business and conveying a visual impression of self-assurance. As Lyle (1990: 6) notes, 'As any actor will tell you, your posture – that is how you hold your body while sitting, standing and lying down – is the first clue to your character and personality'. Good posture, then, identifies you instantly as someone with something to contribute, suggest Bixler and Nix-Rice (1997). Accordingly, good posture – when you are erect and walk tall – enhances confidence, projects youthfulness, improves self-esteem, and ensures that you look slimmer, taller, and more toned (Everett, 2008). The flip side, as Everett (p. 131) baldly states, is that 'bad posture is not only bad for you, it makes you look older and fatter, too'. It sends all the wrong messages, indicating a lack of strength and conviction (Huczynski, 2004). However, as with many other aspects of our non-verbal communication, there are means by which we can improve our posture. Everett (2008), for example, notes how posture can be improved through the use of the Alexander Technique and Pilates (and see Box 5.1).

Box 5.1   Learning to bow correctly in Japan

A number of companies run training courses for new employees at Japanese companies to ensure that they have appropriate 'business manners'. These seminars encompass the use of language, tone of voice, gestures, movement, facial expressions, grooming, and use of space. This business etiquette training in Japan has a long history and recognises the need to pay attention to ensure appropriate aesthetics for everyday activity within an organisational context. Situated within the prevailing culture of Japan, a key element of the course is to ensure new employees are appropriately trained in bowing correctly. Bowing is a ubiquitous form of greeting in Japan, and the students are taught how to maintain the correct form and three degrees of bowing (the 15-degree bow, the 30-degree bow, and the 45-degree bow). Each of these bows should be held for the requisite number of seconds. Learning to bow correctly ensures that undesirable features such as speaking to the floor, repeatedly bobbing up and down, or bowing with a curved back are eliminated. The aim of the training is to ensure that students, who at the start of the course may have a variety of stances and timing in their bows, have, by the end of the course, eliminated these 'imperfections' to ensure standardised bows. Standardising how employees bow thus ensures conformance with societal norms and creates a positive corporate image on behalf of their companies.

(*Source*: Dunn, 2018)

Gesture

Whilst Spillane (2000) suggests that often too much may be read into gestures, especially by body language gurus, she nevertheless suggests that certain gestures may be inappropriate or irritating to others. Often these may be unconscious and some examples highlighted by Huczysnksi (2004) and Spillane (2000) include: pen doodling; picking off imaginary fluff from clothes; scratching the chin, ear, nose; collar/tie fiddling; nervous cough; lip licking; wringing hands; picking at cuticles; nail biting; ring twiddling; pen tapping; pointing; and mouth covering. These gestures suggest that a person feels nervous and tense, can be very off-putting to the person observing, and ultimately suggest they are not in control. In addition to these potentially inappropriate gestures, it is also suggested that how open or closed our gestures are sends a powerful message. Michael (2000), for example, recognises how someone who sits with their arms and legs in an open manner sends a signal of being receptive to new ideas and suggestions. In *Hard Sell*, Jamie Reidy (2010) gives an autobiographical account of his time as a pharmaceutical sales rep. During his training, his manager encouraged him to think about his body language during sales interactions with medical doctors. As part of monitoring and modifying Reidy's sales behaviour, his manager exhorted him to uncross his arms to make himself seem less distant and defensive.

It is also important to recognise the culturally bound nature of gestures. For example, HSBC, the British multinational banking and financial services company, ran a series of adverts in the early 2000s which sought to convey the manner in which the bank operated as a global financial organisation, whilst also highlighting its ability to operate as a truly local organisation in each of the markets that it served (Koller, 2007). Trading on the tagline of 'We never underestimate the importance of local knowledge', the adverts were a series of clever vignettes to appreciate the importance of how non-verbal communication differed across the world. For example, one of their adverts illustrated how the 'A-Okay' gesture can mean very different things depending on the cultural context. A biker travelling across South America uses it happily in all of his travels, but when in Brazil, in using this gesture to signal his appreciation of a meal in a café, the 'A-Okay' sign causes consternation. This is because in Brazil the 'o' sign has less to do with okay and more to do with orifice.

Use of personal space

The importance of recognising the culturally bound nature of non-verbal communication has a particular resonance in considering the need to respect the personal space of others. Huczynski (2004) notes the importance of being aware of avoiding people's space unintentionally, particularly their 'intimate zone'. In general the so-called intimate zone is 0–18 inches, the casual or person zone is from 18 inches to four-and-a-half foot, the social zone four foot to 12 foot and the public zone over 12 foot (Lyle, 1990), though it is important to point out that this may vary across cultures. Huczynski exemplifies this point by noting how there are preferred personal zone distances which vary across cultures: close includes Arabs, Japanese, South American, French, Italians and Spanish; medium includes British, Swedish, Swiss, Germans and Austrians; and far includes White North American, Australian and New Zealanders.

Facial characteristics

It is widely acknowledged that the smile is probably the most powerful of all the facial expressions. Indeed, it is suggested that smiling is one of the most universal expressions of pleasure, delight and self-esteem readily recognised all over the world (Huczynski, 2004). Consequently Lyle (1990: 48) suggests that 'smiling is probably one of the most important components of body language we possess'. For example, a smile, or the lack of a smile, is likely to give an indication to the other person of how you are feeling. According to Bixler and Nix-Rice (1997) the smile is an under-used business tool and in the right context can project warmth, convey confidence, increase self-esteem, and can be useful in establishing rapport. As we discuss later in the chapter, the smile is particularly important within the context of interactive service work, and especially the vexed issue of whether a smile is 'genuine' when employees are interacting with customers. Lyle (1990) cites research by Ekman who identified three different types of smile with each denoting a different emotion: the felt smile, the miserable smile, and the false smile. The felt smile 'is the genuine article, expressing spontaneous pleasure, amusement and joy' (p. 52). On the other hand, the miserable smile is employed when somebody is acknowledging defeat or unhappiness. Lastly, the false smile is more asymmetrical than a genuine smile, lasts longer and is slower to spread across the face, and is most likely to be found in the fixed professional smile or insincere smile of the salesman, for example. According to Lyle, 'a false smile rarely deceives anyone for long, for it produces an uncomfortable sensation in the onlooker – who may not be able to analyse his or her reaction to it, but instinctively knows something is not quite right' (p. 54). Not surprisingly, Everett (2008: 138) advocates that people who are not good at smiling should work on their smile by practising in front of the mirror. Seemingly the best way to practise smiling is 'to raise the cheekbone rather than moving the lips' (see also Box 5.6 later in the chapter).

Eye contact

It is suggested that eye contact is probably the single most researched aspect of body language (Huczynski, 2004). Indeed, we learn from an early age the importance of eye contact in social interaction (Everett, 2008) such that our eyes can convey a range of emotions. For example, whilst wide eyes suggest we are attentive, questioning, interested and attracted, narrow eyes suggest suspicion and anger (Spillane, 2000). Unsurprisingly, within the self-help literature we are entreated to fully recognise the importance of eye contact: 'if you want your interactions to be congenial and productive, always start by looking the other person in the eye', suggests Michael (2000: 117). Failure by the person we are talking to establish eye contact is likely to make us feel uncomfortable, irritated and invisible, and suggests they are uninterested, ill mannered, unattractive and 'shifty' (Everett, 2008). That said, there may be differences in the amount of eye contact that we receive or is appropriate, driven by nationality, race and sex for example. Thus, Spillane (2000: 111) recognises that 'you may "win" eye contact more quickly and for longer periods because of your sex, colouring, age and attractiveness'. Similarly there will be certain cultures where prolonged eye contact may or may not be appropriate. For example, in an Anglo-Saxon context prolonged eye contact can be disturbing, whereas in Japan people tend to avoid eye contact, considering it impolite and intimidating, and will instead look at each other's necks during conversation, using the direct mutual gaze infrequently (Lyle, 1990; Michael, 2000). In other cultural contexts, however, there will be an expectation of direct and prolonged eye contact, with people in Arab cultures habitually using a far greater level of eye contact and Mediterranean people more likely to stare at strangers in public places (Lyle, 1990).

Touch

There are different types of touches, such as the professional touch, as used by GPs or beauty therapists; the social touch; the friendly touch; the loving touch; and the sexual touch (Lyle, 1990). Of course within a business context the social touch is the most likely aspect of touching, most obviously exemplified by the use of the handshake.

Huczynski (2004: 26) recognises that 'In Anglo-Saxon cultures, the single most important, and often only touch, is the handshake. It is usually the only physical contact that you will have with another person'. For example, a handshake can often be an invaluable opportunity to set a cordial tone for interaction within a business setting. Despite the potential importance of the handshake, Everett (2008) suggests it is 'bizarre' that we rarely receive feedback on our handshake given its importance when we are meeting somebody for the first time in particular. Michael (2000: 145), for example, argues that 'your appearance and your words will be confirmed by the way you shake hands'. It is also highlighted by various authors that it is important for men and women in a business situation to use the handshake to demonstrate confidence and professionalism. An appropriate handshake should normally last for three or four shakes: 'any more and you will appear overly friendly; any less, and you will appear dismissive', according to Everett (2008; and see Box 5.2).

Box 5.2   Avoiding the 'dead fish'

Whilst there is plenty of advice as to what denotes a 'good' handshake, there is equally a recognition of ineffectual handshakes such as: 'the limp loser' who has a limp handshake and suggests a 'bit of a pushover'; 'the dead fish', where having a sweaty palm leads to a limp, clammy handshake; 'the bone cruncher' which denotes arrogance and a 'tough guy' impression; the 'double handed' or 'sandwich' which despite its use by politicians to suggest a sincere and trustworthy impression, often gives the opposite impression, suggesting a condescending attitude; and a fingers-only handshake which suggests a lack of involvement and that a person is uncomfortable shaking hands.

(*Sources*: Bixler and Nix-Rice, 1997; Everett, 2008; Huczynski, 2004)

The importance of body language in the employment interview

Whilst the importance of non-verbal communication in our day-to-day workplace interactions is widely recognised, the management of non-verbal signals has a particular resonance in employment interviews (Bonnaccio et al., 2016; and see Box 5.3). In many respects this is unsurprising as much of the above discussion has highlighted the importance of a range of non-verbal cues, especially when we meet someone for the first time in a business or organisational context. In considering the non-verbal aspects of the employment interview Huczynski (2004) cites the work of Raffler-Engel (1983), who recognises which aspects job interviewers paid particular attention. According to Raffler-Engel, interviewers would focus on a candidate's appearance, what they are wearing, whether they look neat, are appropriately groomed and their personal hygiene. As well as these obvious aspects interviewers would also assess a candidate's posture to gauge how interested they were in the job and how attentive they were towards the interviewer. In addition to posture, eye contact and mutual gaze are also important non-verbal behaviours to which interviewers paid particular attention. Eye contact was used by interviewers as an indication of a candidate's honesty, confidence, self-pride and determination for example. Reflecting our discussion above, a lack of eye contact is likely to adversely affect a candidate's chances as it conveys shyness, insecurity, nervousness, a lack of general motivation, drive, interest in the job applied for, and shiftiness or untruthfulness.

Box 5.3   The 3 Ps of interview preparation and how to avoid sweaty palms

In the BBC TV series *Who Would Hire You?*, business psychologist Rob Yeung worked with eight job seekers throughout the recruitment process. Yeung's role was to hone their interview skills and point out their mistakes. It was suggested that he was able to transform the candidates from no-hopers to model potential employees in a matter of days. His 'masterclass' for successful job interviews was premised on the idea of the three Ps: preparation, practice and performance. The latter two aspects of practice and performance have significant non-verbal elements. Yeung advocates that candidates should practise in front of a mirror in order to watch their facial expressions and body movements. He suggests that candidates should ask themselves whether their face is inexpressive, whether they have an appropriate posture and can they use their hands appropriately to illustrate points, which in turn makes them visually more interesting. In performing at the interview candidates were told to think of themselves as an actor seeking to present a professional front, e.g. dressing in a way that fits with the company dress code. Candidates were also entreated to learn how to shake hands properly. Having first highlighted the need for candidates to avoid sweaty palms – 'Before the interview, go to the loo and run your wrists under the cold tap to cool your hands down' – Yeung suggests that you should not just proffer your hand but give two or three pumps, whilst not overdoing it to give the impression that you're overcompensating for an insecurity. Lastly he advised candidates to adopt a posture which mirrors, but doesn't mimic the posture of the interviewer: 'If they're very stiff and upright, so should you be. If they're relaxed, look relaxed'.

(*Source*: Freeman, 2005)

The discussion above outlines the significant evidence of the importance of body language within an organisational context. Awareness of how we present ourselves both consciously and unconsciously is likely to impact on both getting in and getting on in organisations. As we similarly noted, though, in the previous chapter on organisational dress, whilst there may be a range of prescriptions that seek to improve the manner in which we use our body language for individual benefit, interactive service organisations have also recognised the importance of employees' non-verbal communication for organisational benefit and this is considered in the following section. Specifically, our focus shifts from employees using body language as a means to personally benefit their organisational selves to organisations, through aesthetic labour, seeking to create appropriate body language for their benefit. Resultantly, this form of embodiment is transmuted into aesthetic labour as organisations seek to utilise body language within the service encounter to create positive interactions with customers.

BODY LANGUAGE IN INTERACTIVE SERVICE WORK

This section of the chapter draws on our own and others' research to consider the elements of body language – posture, gesture, touch, use of personal space, facial characteristics and eye contact – within the interactive service sector. These elements are considered within four headings: recruitment and selection, training, customer interactions, and finally the manner in which organisations seek to monitor and control these aspects, including through the use of performance reviews.

Recruitment and selection

Recruitment and selection processes are an ideal opportunity for service organisations to assess the aesthetic capacities of potential employees, including their non-verbal communication. For example, Chugh and Hancock (2009) note that their study of work in hairdressing salons supports others' research in terms of confirming the importance of body language as a selection criteria in order that employees can become human artefacts contributing to the aesthetic landscape of the workplace. Indeed, this need for candidates to be cognizant of the importance of body language in the recruitment and selection process is highlighted in Hochschild (1983), who recognises how the inculcation of required behaviours starts even before cabin crew are employed. Noting a 1980 publication called *Airline Guide to Stewardess and Steward Career*, she recognises how under a section called 'The Interview' there are guidelines as to how prospective employees should present themselves. Advice includes having a 'modest but friendly smile' and a reminder to maintain eye contact with the interviewer, whilst not overdoing such eye contact by avoiding 'cold or continuous staring' (1983: 96). This type of advice is still being offered and was a strong feature of the research we conducted on the training programmes for aspiring cabin crew with our colleague Johanna Macquarie. For example, during the participant observation undertaken by Johanna with one of the private providers the course leader explained that body language is monitored at a recruitment day from the moment applicants enter the room at the start of the day. During the training day all the applicants were gathered together in a room and allowed time for mingling/chatting, before everyone was then asked to stand and introduce themselves to the rest of the group. It was later explained by the course leader that the body language used by applicants during the mingling time was often more telling than at the interview, as applicants were often unaware they were being watched and thus act more naturally than when at interview.

Several of the trainers from both the public and private sector providers who were offering training to aspirant airline cabin crew also highlighted the importance of body language during the interview process and why trainees needed to be fully aware of its importance – 'Well obviously we're watching their body language from the moment they walk through the door at an interview and yes that is important, that's extremely important', noted one public sector trainer. Similarly a private sector trainer noted that inappropriate body language could scupper an applicant's chances, even if, for example, they had good qualifications:

> Also the whole thing about body language, negative body language, positive body language, what their looking for, what qualities. You can be bright as a button, you could have a Master's degree in aviation studies or whatever but if you haven't got the personal qualities they're looking for you're never going to get in, and the main quality, and I know it sounds ridiculous, is if you walk into that room and don't smile, it's over.

In addition to the need to smile, other aspects of body language were noted as being important, such as posture, and particularly the need to maintain an open posture:

> Say, for example, if they're sat with their arms folded we can say 'well look if you did do that at an airline interview then your chances of getting through are going to be very slim'. So it's encouraging them and helping them throughout the day and preparing them for what's out there ... (Private sector trainer)

Thus, trainees were encouraged to think about how they could 'sparkle' at interviews and how their body language played an important role in this process.

> I do quite a lot of body language, you know their facial expressions, how they walk, how they sit, everything should be geared towards looking enthusiastic and professional and it's all kind of summed up by [company name] in that you must sparkle at interviews. You know if they can get that in their heads they've got to sparkle that should immediately make them stand up straight or sit up straight, and their eyes bright and their smile over their face. (Private sector trainer)

Our findings on the importance of applicants' and trainees' body language during recruitment and section confirmed by other examples from the airline industry, as Box 5.4 illustrates.

Box 5.4   Virgin's 'ideal' candidate for cabin crew

It was reported in 2007 that the characteristics that Virgin were seeking in their 'ideal' candidates to work as cabin crew encompassed a range of attributes related to service attitude, physicality and creativity. For example, with regard to service attitude Virgin was seeking employees with a desire to please, a friendly demeanour, an ability to appropriately use humour, listen to customers, remain calm under pressure, and have an understated air of self-confidence. In assessing creativity the company sought people who had a passion for new ideas and could smell new business opportunities. With regard to physicality it was suggested that candidates should, amongst other things, have a nice bum, attentive eyes, a friendly smile, and a reassuring voice.

(*Source*: Weller, 2007)

The importance of non-verbal communication is equally apparent in other parts of the interactive service sector, such as hotels and banks. For example, Michael (2000) notes how one large hotel chain, when faced with selecting employees from a large number of applicants, would exclude candidates who smiled fewer than four times during the interview. In answer to the question of whether she was watching a potential employee's body language in the interview, Moira (the human resources manager at Hotel Elba in Glasgow) replied, 'Yeah, very much. Whether there is eye contact, whether there is a smile, you know their gestures, just to see what kind of person they are ... if somebody is sitting there and frightened to look at you, you're a bit wary of that'. Thus, the hotel was seeking applicants who were 'smiley' and maintained eye contact: 'That's quite important. If they're going to be dealing with people on a regular basis I think they have to have that', said Moira.

Training

As well as the pre-work training described above in the specific context of the airline industry, there is also evidence that organisations continue to encourage employees to adopt appropriate non-verbal behaviours through in-work training. In our survey of

Glasgow's retail and hospitality employers 77 per cent offered training in employee body language. Similarly, our survey of Glasgow employees found that 60 per cent of respondents answered that they had received training in body language. Training in aspects of body language encompassed elements such as posture and facial characteristics, most obviously encouraging employees to offer 'genuine' smiles. Our research found that with regard to posture the training was concerned with the intent of portraying the correct and welcoming 'image' to initially attract potential customers, and then training in how best to approach customers by 'reading' their body language and responding accordingly. Molly, a retail worker, who worked for a stylish, luxurious fashion retailer, noted how:

> ... the supervisors do a wee act kind of thing and pretend they are a customer and say 'this is a bad example and this is a good example', and the good example is when you smile at them as soon as they walk in and you acknowledge that they [the customer] are there.

Another retail worker, Jacinta, described this role playing, reflecting Goffman's (1959) dramaturgical analysis, as 'like being in drama school', with employees instructed in how to present themselves to customers. As Jacinta described it during the training the employees were instructed in 'the way you stand, the way you look at them [customers]'. Another focus group participant recalled training to encourage 'heads up', wherein 'whatever you're doing you're always to have your head up so that customers are aware of you' (and see Box 5.5).

Box 5.5   Providing service with a side of poise and grace

Marriott hotels offer a training programme called Poise and Grace, which was developed in conjunction with the Joffrey Ballet company in Chicago. The training aims to ensure that employees interact with guests with, as the title of the programme suggests, poise and grace. Employees are taught by dancers from the ballet company to improve their body language to further enhance customer satisfaction. The initial success of the programme locally at the Marriott Hotel in Chicago saw it rolled out across the company. Employees in high guest-contact positions perform up to 15 minutes of exercises covering aspects such as breathing, posture, eye contact, and flow of movement. It is suggested the frontline employees now hold their heads higher, make more eye contact, have a warmer smile and carry themselves with greater poise and grace, leading to enhanced confidence in the staff and a better first impression and stronger connection with the guests.

(*Source*: Gallo, 2016; and see also www.youtube.com/watch?v=Mbr902Hkqgc for a description of the programme)

As we noted above, the smile is probably the most powerful of all the facial expressions and unsurprisingly smiling, and encouraging the 'right' kind of smile, has often played a prominent role in the training of frontline service employees. Hochschild's (1983) work makes several references to the expectations of the airlines about how smiling is an integral, though often resented, aspect of the job (and see the next section which discusses the manner in which frontline employees interact with customers). For example, she reports how, at a training session for newly employed staff at Delta Airlines, a pilot talking to the trainees entreated them to smile: 'Now girls, I want you to go out there and really *smile*. Your smile is your biggest *asset*. I want you to go out there and use it. *Really* smile. Really *lay it on*' (cited on p. 4, emphasis in original). Similarly in our research on the airline preparation courses there was a great deal of emphasis on the importance of practising smiling (and see Box 5.6). As one of the public sector trainers in our study of airline cabin crew training noted:

> I tell them why I think they need to improve their skills and for [one of the students] I told her she really, really had to practise smiling. I said 'when you're talking to your friends don't you smile?', you know, 'when you greet a friend don't you smile?' – 'no I don't think I do'. I said 'well you have to practise this every morning when you get up and go in your bathroom, you practise smiling because if you don't you won't get a job, that's for sure, if you really, really want this you have to practise the smile'.

Box 5.6   Learning to smile for the Beijing Olympics

Reflecting the rise of consumer services in China, women who aspired to be hostesses for the 2008 Beijing Olympics were expected to be of uniform height and bone structure with 'neat' buttocks. The hostesses were selected to carry the trays which had the medals and flowers for medal winners at the medal ceremonies. Whilst it would seem that holding trays whilst smiling would be a straightforward task, in reality all of the hostesses went through months of intensive training which allowed them to 'endlessly rehearse' every smile. Training entailed the hostesses working with each other to ensure that their smiles were 'warm' and 'sincere', including manipulating each other's faces to produce the required smile, with the secret to what was described as the 'perfect' smile being that the hostesses were to show between six and eight teeth and be capable of unflinchingly holding their grin for up to 10 minutes at a time. To train for these requirements some hostesses would spend hours with a chopstick clamped between their teeth to build up their facial muscles.

(*Sources*: Otis, 2012; Rayner, 2008)

Interactions with customers

Much of the manner in which the employees in our focus groups talked about aspects of body language was in terms of how they presented themselves to the customer. Organisations though do not rely solely on their employees to hone their intuition with regard to how best to present their body language to customers, and would often offer prescriptions to employees about appropriate body language. Lowe and Crewe (1996: 200) note, for example, that as customer care initiatives became increasingly important in the late 1980s and early 1990s, a whole host of consultants sought to 'educate retailers in the nuances of the hard sell'. An example of this development is provided by one consultant lecturing for the British Shops and Stores Association, who suggested that 'arm folding, nose-scratching and slouching posture are all vital body language signs now being squashed' (cited in Lowe and Crewe, 1996: 200). Echoing our earlier noting of Van Maanen's (1990) comment about employees as 'talking statues', in one retail outlet that we studied, employees when not serving or replenishing stock were required to stand near to the entrance, smiling invitingly at prospective customers. Jacinta, an employee of the store, described how 'we are told to stand 45 degrees toward the door so that we're actually visible at the door … if they [customers] glance at you, as people do, then you have to smile'. Posture at this outlet was also prescribed: 'You're not allowed to stand with your arms crossed, because that's closed,' said Jacinta.

This sense of being open with customers was also noted by Eleanor, who had extensive experience as a supervisor and manager in hospitality. She suggested that employees in interactive service jobs should be proactive whilst recognising that this was often not the case: 'a lot of people try and avoid you when you walk into a restaurant … their head goes that way instead of looking at you. They just don't look at you. I mean that's their job, they are there to serve you'. Eleanor further noted that staff:

> … have to look genuinely interested, good at eye contact and quite sort of confident when they're talking to these people. And not turning round and chewing gum and that sort of thing. I don't know if you've been into TGI Friday's, staff have to go down on one knee when they serve customers … if they're there on one knee you are below the customer. You are their puppy dog.

In further explaining this point Eleanor elaborated on the 'puppy dog theory', which suggests to customers that employees are 'like a little lap dog'.

Sue, a manager in women's fashion retail outlet in Glasgow, also highlighted how she was now able to 'read' body language and suggested that employees may unconsciously give out the wrong type of body language:

In their body language you can tell a lot. For someone to actually be serving the public and their body language is all wrong. I mean they may not realise the body language is all wrong ... Many a time I've had someone being nice to a customer but I can tell there is something irritating her. She doesn't realise maybe that her eye contact is wrong ... she may be shrugging her shoulders. Or the hair may be [flicks hair and all focus group participants laugh]. Body language can tell you a lot ... I've been into stores and didn't think the body language of the assistant was appropriate – maybe she'd had an argument with another member of staff and didn't realise she was still giving out these vibes.

Employees giving out the 'wrong' vibes will often be most acute when they were constantly being entreated to smile at customers. Hochschild notes how the cabin crew she spoke to had smiles that looked 'as being *on* them but not *of* them' (1983: 8, emphasis in original). This is most memorably illustrated in her recounting an example of how one flight attendant responded to a customer's request to smile during a long-haul flight:

The smile war has its veterans and its lore. I was told repeatedly, and with great relish, the story of one smile-fighter's victory, which goes like this. A young businessman said to a flight attendant, 'Why aren't you smiling?'. She put her tray back on the food cart, looked him in the eye and said, 'I'll tell you what. You smile first, then, I'll smile'. The businessman smiled at her: 'Good', she replied. 'Now freeze, and hold that for fifteen hours'. Then she walked away. (1983: 127)

Unsurprisingly, given much of the above discussion – and echoing Goffman (1959) – many of our focus group participants drew on the oft-used metaphor of being on stage when working in a frontline service position, and how there would often be a transformation as they moved from front to back of house in presenting the right kind of body language. As Jacinta described it, 'You try and stand upright at all times, then you get like downstairs [away from customers] and you're [gestures slump, others laugh]'.

Monitoring body language

Following Hochschild (1983) clearly there is a need to appreciate how organisations seek to control not only employees' emotions, but also the bodily displays that go with these emotions, such as gestures, smiles, furrowed brows, grimaces and so on. Key to this process would often be monitoring by managers to ensure that employees would present appropriate body language. For example, Otis (2012: 85–6) describes how at the beginning of each shift in one of the luxury hotels she studied in China:

... female workers line up in military fashion in their respective departments, standing at attention as middle managers inspect their appearance, scrutinizing their fingernails and make up. This is a routine occasion for manager to incite staff to smile, to make eye contact with customers, and to enact a feminine comportment, sometimes pointing out particular workers who 'walk like men' (i.e. rocking back and forth).

Ogbonna (1992) similarly reports the example of one supermarket that as part of a culture change programme encouraged employees to smile more when engaging with customers. However, the company went one step further in introducing de-facto 'smile supervisors' who were tasked to assess whether employee smiles were 'genuine'. As one such smile supervisor noted, 'we are able to detect when a checkout operator is not smiling or even when she is putting on a false smile' (1992: 85). If smiles were felt not to be genuine employees were invited for a chat by the 'smile supervisors'. Needless to say this approach created a good deal of employee resentment.

Beyond the obvious aspects of body language, such as smiling, Otis (2012) describes the prescriptions in the hotel's employee handbook about how employees were to greet customers. For example, employees were required to initiate non-verbal acknowledgement at ten feet and verbal acknowledgement at five feet. The handbook also highlighted how employees should use their bodies in public areas of service: 'Do not lean or squat, do not place hands in your pocket, do not pick your nose, do not talk loudly or shout, do not hold hands, do not clear your throat, do not scratch any part of your body' (2012: 86).

If employees do not adopt appropriate body language then managers are likely to intervene to encourage them to do so. Sometimes this intervention can be relatively benign. For example, in answer to the question in one of our focus groups of how managers corrected the wrong body language, Jenny, a fashion retail manager, noted that:

> I tend to make a joke of it. 'Do you realise what you were doing'. 'Tell me if I do that'. 'If you see me doing the same thing let me know'. I tend to use that type of humour. I think it keeps everything on a nicer level rather than use your authority.

Rather more punitively, Otis (2012) reports performance reviews undertaken with employees in which managers would routinely highlight an employee's weaknesses. She points to how one manager in evaluating a hostess who worked in the hotel's restaurant suggested that 'You are the hostess because you are pretty. But it won't do you much good if you don't smile. Patrons won't want to come in if they see you like that from the outside … A beautiful smile is a good start' (2012: 88). Similarly, a waitress was scolded by her manager for not maintaining a 'good image' (p. 88):

> I've seen you talking to guests without any facial expression. It's a habitual problem. You can't even feel it when you frown. When guests ask for something, you just frown when we don't have the item … You should [also] be aware of the way you stand and the impression that you give. (2012: 88)

Some managers in Otis's research would parody workers' gestures to prompt reflection on the employees' part of how they presented themselves through non-verbal means. One manager, for example, accused a waitress of 'swaggering back and forth like a man' and 'personally demonstrated how to walk like a "lady", pointing out the slight sway of his hips, his upright neck and shoulder, and his tightrope-treading gait' (2012: 89).

As well as managers reminding employees of the importance of prescribed body language, Molly also described her experience in an upmarket Glasgow retail store where employees would be monitored via the security cameras in the store:

> Well in [name of organisation] they've got a video camera in the shop, and we thought it was just for security but apparently they sometimes even sit and play it back. Like on a Sunday when there's a manager in they sit and watch the staff, and see how you behave and that kind of stuff ... to see how they're approaching customers, if they're standing chatting or whatever.

Jacinta, picking up on the point above, noted how managers would do a 'circuit' of the store to closely monitor employees to see how they were behaving, but also to ensure, as we noted earlier, that they were facing 45 degrees to the door and adopting an appropriate posture as prescribed by the organisation.[1] In sum, through the use of body language employees have increasingly become human artefacts contributing to the aesthetic landscape of the workplace as organisations seek, through aesthetic labour, to instil the 'right' kind of body language to create positive interactions with customers.

CONCLUSION

This chapter considered the importance of body language within organisational settings. Having outlined the emergence of the term 'body language', the chapter considered how potential and existing employees present themselves in an organisational context through aspects such as posture, gesture, touch, use of personal space, facial characteristics and eye contact. Specifically, in noting the importance of body language within organisational settings the chapter recognised how either consciously or unconsciously non-verbal communications have a significant impact in interacting with others. Having established the importance generally of body language in an organisational context the chapter considered this issue within the specific context of the hospitality and retail industries.

From both our own and others' research it is clear that in attempting to create human artefacts who contribute to the aesthetic landscape of the workplace, many service organisations pay great attention to their employees' body language. At the point of entry to organisations we found significant evidence of employers assessing potential employees' body language during employment interviews, e.g. evaluating their posture, gestures, eye contact, and whether they maintained a 'smiley' appearance. As we discussed in the previous chapter though it is not only at the point of recruitment and selection that employers pay attention to employees' body language. Once in the organisation, through processes of training, employees were further encouraged to adopt appropriate body language, especially with regard to encouraging them to offer 'genuine' smiles. These prescriptions around presenting appropriate body language were driven by organisations' desire to encourage positive interactions with customers. The use of body language within customer interactions is also a source of management intervention and monitoring, again highlighting the use of often detailed prescriptions to shape employees' non-verbal behaviours. It is not though only non-verbal behaviours that many service organisations attempt to shape customer interactions, and the following chapter considers the importance of those verbal behaviours, assessing how workers' speech features as a key element of aesthetic labour.

NOTE

1. The same respondent noted how the circuit of the store was actually based on a drawing that was on the back of one of the doors: 'They've got a big drawing. It was sent in actually by head office, the footpath they actually take'.

6

IRRITABLE VOWEL SYNDROME

In Chapter 3 we noted that the most obvious manifestations of aesthetic labour centre on two of the five senses – the visual and aural; the sight and sound of employees. These two senses translate into three particular features of employees' work and employment: dress sense or what we call 'workwear', comportment or body language, and speech. With the visual senses dominating Western society, and workwear and body language affecting the visual senses, it is these two features of aesthetic labour that tend to be emphasised most by employers and the focus of most research. As a consequence the aural senses and employee speech have received less attention, which is an oversight that needs to be addressed.

It is, however, an oversight that is not confined to research on aesthetic labour. Early labour process theory, with its focus on the stuff inside employees' heads – knowledge – and employers' attempts to extract that knowledge through scientific management, had nothing to say about workers' speech. (Interestingly though F.W. Taylor did mimic Schmidt's heavy Dutch accent in his account of how he tried, repeatedly, to teach and bribe Schmidt to load more pig iron into rail wagons; see Taylor, 1947 [1911]). As we noted in Chapter 3, labour process theory is, however, useful in highlighting capitalism's need to generate surplus value, and how the means to do so in the production of goods and services necessarily changes over time because of competition. With its incorporation of emotional labour, labour process theory became aware of employers being interested in the hearts, not just the heads, of workers, seeking to mobilise, control and transmute employee feelings (Bolton, 2010). Within this shift the study of call centres, and workers' speech (what they said and how they said it) became of interest (e.g. Taylor, 1998). However this interest was never developed empirically or conceptually within labour process theory, though there are studies of the call centre labour process that attempt to more comprehensively incorporate speech into their analyses, as this chapter highlights.

It is Bourdieu's (1992) theory of practice that most explicitly signals the importance of speech in social interaction. Habitus generates bodily dispositions, and with those dispositions ways of speaking. Speech, in turn, is not just constituent of habitus; it reinforces and helps reproduce it. Language therefore defines and assigns value. Those individuals with positional power in a field seek to impose their style of language. In this respect Bourdieu's analysis of language is not particularly novel. Bernstein (2003) also noted that the working and middle classes have different linguistic codes, even when speaking the same language, and that those codes are shaped by power relations. What Bourdieu adds is recognition that this power can be obscured by the normality of language and the unconscious incorporation of the disempowered into the code's reproduction (Hanks, 2005). What becomes the standard does so because of asymmetries of (economic) power, at least initially. Speakers of non-standard language are inculcated, or worse, excluded. To be accepted means speaking acceptably.

Bourdieu's focus was social reproduction, i.e. class. However organisations also proscribe and prescribe employee speech. Workplace language can create symbolic capital for organisations, help constitute customer and client perceptions, and so contribute to the generation of surplus value and profit for private sector companies and affect more favourable opinions about their use value for not-for-profit organisations. Thus, what workers say and how they say it matters to employers. Verbal interactions between workers and customers are an important part of the service encounter and can negatively and positively affect customers' perceptions of the organisation. Workers knowing what to say and how to say it – or being told by management what to say and how to say it – is assumed by employers to generate a positive service interaction. To this end, Eustace (2012) believes that language is becoming commodified, recast as a 'skill' by employers to be deployed in the service encounter.

This chapter analyses workers' speech as a feature of aesthetic labour. The first half of the chapter outlines the social construction of speech, the emergence and importance of different linguistic codes, and how those codes socially differentiate and affect employment generally. The second half analyses how employers attempt to mobilise, control and transmute this speech in interactive services so that, as a feature of aesthetic labour, it has become one of the points of intervention by employers as they seek to shape the labour process in the pursuit of profit or otherwise. The latter part of the chapter also highlights how these managerial interventions are experienced both positively and negatively by workers.

SOCIAL DIFFERENTIATION THROUGH SPEECH

Speech encompasses what we say and how we say it. Within this speech dialect usually refers to terminology – or *what* we say; our vocabulary, grammar and idiom. Accent by contrast is about pronunciation – or *how* we enunciate words with their vowels and consonants.

Even using the same language, there are different ways to speak. How we speak is a feature of habitus, affected primarily by familial socialisation but also education, both of which relate to social class and locality. Learnt in childhood, speech becomes habitual and is literally embodied: speaking in different ways requires different bodily uses – jaw, lips and throat movements (Honey, 1989). The British working class drops its consonants, the upper class drops its vowels for example. In the mouths of the working class the word 'handkerchief' becomes 'ankerchief' and in those of the upper class 'hnkrchf'' (Fox, 2004).

Speech helps us navigate the world socially. It is our aural guide, our classifier. In her anthropological study *Watching the English* (which is really about the British), Fox (2004) uncovers the hidden rules of behaviour. She quotes Ben Johnson's benign 'Language most shows a man. Speak so that I may see thee' (2004: 73). She also highlights the seven deadly word sins in Britain that starkly and finely differentiate the social classes (see Box 6.1).

Box 6.1   The seven deadly word sins

Pardon: the middle-middle classes say 'pardon' if something is not heard, the upper middle 'sorry', and the upper and working classes 'what?'

Toilet: the working class and lower- and middle-middle classes use the word 'toilet', whilst the upper-middle and upper classes use 'loo'. Pretentious social climbers opt for 'the gents' or 'the ladies'.

Serviette: the working class use this word, the inhabitants of 'Pardonia' (see above) call it a 'napkin', as do the upper class.

Dinner: only the working class call their midday meal their 'dinner', all others refer to it as 'lunch', though things become more complicated in the evening when the working class eat their 'tea' whilst the upper-middle and upper classes have 'supper', with the upper class having 'tea' slightly earlier in late afternoon and actually consisting of a cup of tea accompanied by cake or scones.

Settee: is the upholstered multi-seat of the working and middle classes but is the 'sofa' for the upper-middle and upper classes, unless they are absorbing Americanisms in which case it becomes the 'couch'.

Lounge: in working and middle-class homes the settee can be found in the 'lounge' or 'living room', whilst the sofa can be found in the 'drawing room' or, more frequently these days, the 'sitting room' of the upper-middle and upper classes.

Sweet: the final course of a meal consists of 'pudding' for the upper-middle and upper classes; a 'sweet' is served amongst middle-middle and lower classes. 'Dessert' is different, served by the upper classes after the meal and consists of fruit and is eaten with knife and fork.

(*Source*: Fox, 2004)

Speech does not just create habitus, it is an indicator of it. Knowing what to say and how to say it establishes both membership of and position in a field, to use Bourdieu's term. What we say and how we say it contributes to our identity and sorts us into types of people. Speech helps constitute an 'us' and a 'them' through its representation of class, education and geography.

SOCIAL HIERARCHY, STIGMA AND SPEECH

Linguistic codes do not just socially differentiate and classify, they also hierachicalise. Speech is evaluable and evaluated. In the UK, Standard English derives from what used to be referred to as Received Pronunciation (or RP). From the early Middle Ages RP was indicative of the ruling class; spoken by the court, the landed gentry, their administrators, and the professors of the ancient universities. Its acquisition and possession was therefore a 'badge of their own rank as effectively as any coat of arms' Honey (1989: 48) states. Reflecting the geographical location of the court, what became Standard English had a regional base – the South of England, in particular London and the Home Counties. Beyond the court and the literati, ordinary people continued with their local ways of speaking. By the eighteenth century these provincial accents were deemed unacceptable in genteel society and stigmatised. By contrast, speaking RP became a marker of and entry ticket to 'polite society': 'A gentleman was known as much by his correct pronunciation as by his wealth or breeding. English became a tool for snobs, and a useful ally for hierarchs' says Bragg (2003: 234). Upper-class parents from around the UK began to send their offspring to private schools to have their regional accents 'corrected', and RP became standardised across the British ruling classes. Into the twentieth century, it remained the speech of Britain's key institutions, such as the BBC. It was the speech of those 'who needed to command but rarely to mix' Morrish (1999: 20) suggests.

The expansion of higher education in the nineteenth century helped diffuse Standard English. As a result it became the 'educated accent'. Into the mid-twentieth century universities acted as its guardian. Standard English was offered in state schools to pupils from a range of social backgrounds, delivered by an army of university-educated teachers. Some of these teachers imposed that English on their pupils, as one of Eustace's (2012) hospitality workers explained – and hated – when she reflected on how her school teachers tried to force her to drop her working-class Glaswegian accent which was deemed 'bad English' and in need of correction.

From the 1980s, however, it became 'virtually taboo' to talk about talk and heretical to suggest that schools should teach their pupils to talk any other way than they did, claims Honey (1989: 11). The alleged rise of meritocracy and death of class in Britain were said to be making accents irrelevant, he states. Regional accents started to be more acceptable and promoted. The BBC switched to favour 'modified' RP for formal, state announcements and allow regional accents for everyday programming. RP was consigned to museums – literally, recorded as part of the National Sound Archive in the UK (Morrish, 1999). Indeed attitudes have changed since Eustace's worker was at school. Some Scottish accents are now ranked second to RP in terms of positive perceptions in public polling (*Daily Record*, 2008).

Of course, despite the frequent pronouncements of its death, class is still very much alive in Britain (Crompton, 2010) and its markers continue to hierarchialise. What George Bernard Shaw stated in the preface to his satirical play *Pygmalion* – that 'It is impossible for an Englishman to open his mouth without making another Englishman hate and despise him' (2010: 3) – is as true today as it was then. It was British sociologist A.H. Halsey who remarked that there is a snobbery 'that brands the tongue of every British child' (quoted in Honey, 1989: 1). In this respect, speech is the most obvious indicator of social class according to Fox: 'Your accent and terminology reveal the class that you are born into and raised in … And whatever you do accomplish, your position on the class scale will always be identifiable by your speech, unless you painstakingly train yourself to use the pronunciation and vocabulary of a different class' (2004: 82). Bourdieuian without Bourdieu, Maconie (2009: 127) notes that speech contains 'linguistic mantraps and trapdoors'. He provides the example of British upper-middle class family names that are pronounced very differently from how their spelling would suggest: 'All those Featherstonehaughs ([pronounced] Fanshaws) … and Cholmondleys (Chumleys) are really there to act as a kind of password into rarefied social strata. If you know the pronunciation, you're in'.

It was the Norman invasion of 1066 that shaped the linguistic landscape of Britain. With the invasion two languages collided and two linguistic codes created that distinguished its users into socially superior and subordinate. Norman French was established as the 'polite language' of the ruling class. Those speaking French 'felt distinctly superior to … follow-islanders, the Celts' (Gillingham, 2009: 75). The twelfth-century English historian William of Malmesbury cheered this development as socially ameliorating, a civilising force because the French had 'polished manners' (quoted in Gillingham, 2009: 73). This power-loaded linguistic distinction remains. Some of the words used in UK English today appear interchangeable but have subtle social differences which can be traced back to this Francofication. A meeting can 'start' (old English) or 'commence' (French), with the latter carrying 'a touch more cultural clout' according to Bragg. As a consequence, Bragg points out, class has become 'buried in language' (2003: 59).

Individuals thus have different 'linguistic capital' in which some is more desirable than others. A hierarchy of accents provokes attitudes and ascribed personality traits. People who continue to speak the less acute, 'clipped' form of RP for example, are regarded as intelligent, ambitious, self-confident and wealthy. They are also perceived physically to be good-looking, tall and clean. Other accents are often perceived to be more friendly, generous and honest. According to a poll conducted by the Aziz Corporation, business people from the Home Counties in England (the home of Standard English) are rated in polls as sounding most successful (*Metro*, 2002). Other accents in the UK all fare less well but not equally so. Educated Scottish, Welsh and Irish English are well received. Middling are a 'cluster' of northern English accents, of which Yorkshire is the higher rated. The accents consistently less well received are London Cockney, Liverpool Scouse and the Brummie of the West Midlands, all of which are reported by Honey (1989) to be deemed unpleasant and ugly.

SPEECH AND SYMBOLIC VIOLENCE IN EMPLOYABILITY

Social perceptions created through speech matter, Honey (1989) notes, because they affect individuals' employability. What we say and how we say it make us more or less marketable according to one consultant in a report by the then Institute of Personnel and Development (IPD) (cited in Younge, 1997: 5).[1] Providing social information, speech sends out signals to employers and is an important part of first impressions in interviews. Job interviewers are often as interested in how applicants talk as much as in what they say. Communicating with confidence and enthusiasm is key to success in employment interviewing according to career development consultant and psychologist Rob Yeung (Yeung, 2014). Job advertisements regularly refer to wanting applicants who are 'well spoken' (cf. Honey, 1989; Jackson et al., 2002). High-end financial services providers such as Glasgow-based Morgan Stanley Dean Witter, for example, evaluate job applicants' voices, with company notes to assessors providing guidelines on applicants' vocal volume (quiet to loud), pitch (low to high), pace (slow to fast), and articulation (clipped to rounded).

Workers with strong regional accents can still experience employment discrimination, having difficulty obtaining, maintaining and progressing in jobs.[2] For example Stacy Holloway lost her job as a medical secretary because her employer believed that her accent was 'common' (Novaresse, 1997). 'Let's face it', said the previously mentioned consultant from the IPD report, 'people with a Scouse accent ... sound whiny and people with Brummie accents ... sound stupid' (cited in Younge, 1997: 5). Apparently having a Glaswegian accent is a barrier to career advancement, while a Cambridgeshire one boosts a career (*Daily Record*, 2011). As the consultant said in the IPD report, to get ahead a job applicant has to have the right accent, preferably RP, which despite the 'democratisation' of accents in the mass media, continues to be perceived well.

Individuals with less or without the desired linguistic capital have to choose between adapting to what is required or suffering symbolic violence through social marginalisation and condemnation. Symbolic violence is exacted by dominant classes upon superordinated classes. The violence is not physical but symbolic in that it involves the denial and denigration of the legitimacy of the habitus of subordinates by superordinates (Bourdieu, 1991a). Opting to do what is required to gain social legitimacy rather than suffer this violence, some people modify their accents. Even in the 1980s when Clive Myrie joined the BBC as a news reporter, he felt that he had to change his accent to fit in. Born in Lancashire in northern England, 'I was surrounded by people from the home counties' he said, 'so my flat vowels got elongated because it felt as if that was what I needed to do' (quoted in O'Kelly, 2017: 4). Although the clipped form of RP can today sound comical, the benefits of Standard English possession are not lost on the aspirant provincial middle and working classes, who often pay to learn it through elocution lessons with voice coaches for themselves and their children.

This verbal impression management is not new. In Shaw's *Pygmalion* (written in 1912), professional phoneticist Professor Henry Higgins brags to bystanders that he can identify any accent. One of the bystanders asks Higgins if a living can be made from phonetics. 'Oh yes, quite a fat one' Higgins replies, 'This is an age of upstarts. Men begin in Kentish Town with £80 a year, and end in Park Lane with a hundred thousand. They want to drop Kentish Town: but they can give themselves away every time they open their mouths. No I can tame them' he states (Shaw, 2010 [1916]: 17). The meaning is clear: Higgins earns a nice living by helping social aspirants switch codes linguistically. At the end of this conversation Higgins has made a bet with the other man, Colonel Pickering, that with training, he can take a poor girl selling flowers in the street and transform her: 'You see this creature with her kerbstone English: the English that will keep her in the gutter to the end of her days ... in three months I could pass that girl off as a duchess at an ambassador's party' (p. 19). Hearing this brag, the flower girl, Eliza Doolittle, declares that she wants to be transformed. She wants to be off the streets but knows what is hindering her: 'I want to be a lady in a flower shop stead of sellin' at the corner of Tottenham Court Road. But they won't take me unless I can speak more genteel', she explains. The bet is accepted. Higgins' task is to make Eliza speak differently, changing not just how she speaks but also what she says: 'not only how a girl pronounces, but what she pronounces' (p. 56).

Whilst Shaw's play is fictional, in the real world speech modification is a tactic often used by politicians. The voice, according to Karpf (2011: 33), is a 'vital political instrument', helping politicians sell themselves to the public. And so politicians' speech, not just their looks, comes under media scrutiny. It was widely reported in the UK press that George Osborne, the then Conservative Party Shadow Chancellor and 'toff' educated at an expensive private school, received voice-coaching lessons in an attempt to lower his vocal tone and sound 'less posh' to make him more relatable to the electorate (Walters, 2008). Of course Osborne was only following another successful Conservative politician, Margaret Thatcher, in trying to modify his voice to better appeal to the electorate. Thatcher, who had elocution lessons to soften her 'shrill' voice when she became leader of the Conservative Party in the 1970s, was said thereafter to have a strident voice, a sexy voice and a persuasive voice depending upon her audience and intent (Watts, 2000).

Thatcher and Osborne are not alone in wanting to change how they are perceived by changing their speech; it seems that many of us worry about how we are perceived aurally by others. Number three in the Top 10 academic bestselling books in Blackwell's London store at the time of Osborne's voice-coaching was *Get Rid of Your Accent* by Linda James and Olga Smith (*THE*, 2008). In the BBC TV series *Who Would Hire You?*, which we discussed in the previous chapter, participants went through a mock recruitment process to improve their employment chances by offering advice on their dress sense and body language, but also speech.

Attempts to transmute speech are an attempt by workers to sell themselves to employers in order to boost their employment prospects. It is an intervention by workers for their personal benefit, as Eliza Doolittle and Michelle Dockery (see Box 6.2) personify. In the same way that in Chapter 2 we noted that some workers can enhance their aesthetic appeal as a way of getting in and getting on in their working lives, some workers transmute their speech to do likewise, to get in and get on at work.

Box 6.2   From downstairs to upstairs

Michelle Dockery is an actress, famously featuring in the internationally successful period costume drama *Downton Abbey* TV series. Early in her career though she recognised that her accent was holding her back, and struggling to find work realised that it had to change if she was to have a career in acting. At an audition for *The Sound of Music*, the other youngsters 'were all annunciating perfectly' she says, 'And when I was then asked what experience I had, I replied, "Well I've done lots of shows around Essex but I ain't done nuffink up the West End." I instantly suspected that I'd blown it. And I had'. Today, with an elocution make-over, her accent is now more upstairs than downstairs. She is a new Eliza and likewise doing very well in her career.

(*Source*: *OK! Magazine*, 2011)

This linguistic code switching suggests that social hierarchy is, as Hanks (2005: 75) states, 'transposed into stylistic hierarchy', the basis of which are 'different verbal styles'. This hierarchy does not just reflect positional differences but also creates legitimacy and authority. Different styles are recognised and accorded status by the producers and receivers: 'Through speaking a language one is embedded in a universe of categorization, selective distinctions and evaluations' (2005: 77). Through repetitive practice, most obviously in the context of familial socialisation – or as a feature of elocution lessons – knowing what to say and how to say it acquires 'symbolic capital' and having 'proper' speech. Not doing so can perpetuate social subordination, and incur symbolic violence and social stigma.

MIND YOUR LANGUAGE

It is not just individual workers who know that speech matters, affecting the perceptions of employers; employers too are aware that the spoken word can affect customer and client perceptions. Language is used extensively to market companies and their products, and persuade customers to buy and buy again (Sedivy and Carlson, 2011). This language is not just that used in marketing materials but also that uttered by employees. Speech is the 'verbal presentation' of the organisation explains employer Paul Kerr, and 'can be pivotal to business success' (quoted in Ward, 2000: 6). Along with dress and body language, employee speech projects an organisation's image. As the previously mentioned IPD consultant commented: 'people in front-of-house positions, from telephonists to account managers are therefore expected to speak, as well as dress, in a particular way' (Younge, 1997: 5). Consequently, organisations want employees with speech that appeals positively to customers and clients (Schneider and Bowen, 1995). What employees say and how they say it to customers and clients therefore matters. As one of our retail focus group participants stated, 'If their voice is right, they can sell the product, that's what the company is looking for'. In our employer surveys there was a clear demand for employees with the right voice and/or accent. In the survey of fashion retailers in Manchester, over 27 per cent of employers cited voice and accent as very important or essential in work that involves interacting with customers. In the Glasgow survey of retailers, hotels, restaurants, bars and cafés, 44 per cent of employer stated that employee voice and/or accent were important features of company image and business success. When employers seek to mobilise and manipulate workers' speech for organisational benefit, it folds into aesthetic labour.

Employers thus attempt to hire employees with the 'right' speech. In call centres, employees are invisible to customers so their voice-to-voice interaction becomes salient. For call centre jobs in Glasgow, the first stage of the recruitment process typically involves a telephone interview with the employer in which the 'The smile that's so important in any sales operation has to be translated into a voice that sounds like someone who could be your friend' (Johnstone, 1997: 13). Similarly at Hotel Elba, job applicants who telephoned the company were asked a number of questions about themselves; it was the usual casual questions about what they were doing at the moment, what work experience they had, etc. It was, Moira the human resources manager said, 'a general chat'. Again however it wasn't just what the callers said but how they said it that mattered. The company were looking for the aural smile: 'Just from the voice', she continued, 'you can quite often tell on a phone call if they've got enthusiasm. You can pick that up right away'.

Some of the older participants in our banking focus group noted the change from what might be termed 'old bank' to 'new bank'. In old bank job applicant selection focused on qualifications, usually basic school-level qualifications, and most applicants were in their mid-teens. Applicants good at maths and English were preferred. In new bank the emphasis was on applicants' 'people skills', particularly communication skills. Banking is now about selling not telling they said: 'They've become very focused on making sure they've got the right sales people on the front row. Folk who can't communicate are in the back', said Angus, a thirty 30-something bank clerk. The banks no longer hire school-leavers but prefer graduates with interactive service experience, e.g. those who have worked in hotels as receptionists during their study. The interview process helps filter out the undesired and filter in the preferred accents and voices. As one of our focus group bank workers noted, 'by interviewing you they already know what you sound like'. How this filtering process is executed was explained by a worker at another bank: 'The phone bank actually call you at home as part of the interview process. Off the cuff, they tell you it will be today; they don't tell you when it will be. It's so that when you pick up the phone you give your normal answering 'phone voice'. Hotel Elba used the same tactic. It would telephone job applicants ostensibly to check their interview availability. In reality the call served as a screening device, enabling the company to assess how the applicants spoke: 'they had to have the correct tone and a nice voice' human resources manager Moira said. In practice, needing to have a nice voice also served to screen out callers from the lower social classes: 'We didn't want someone who spoke in a guttural manner' Moira explained.

Hotel Elba and the banks are succeeding in their recruitment strategies. Other employers however have more difficulty. A manager of a small restaurant chain in Glasgow, TNT, had advertised a number of job vacancies. Despite a good number of applicants the manager decided not to make any appointments, claiming that local workers had 'poor language skills' with the 'Glasgow dialect' particularly problematic. The manager recognised that, as a small firm, it did not have the resources of a larger company to provide training for these applicants, and instead had to hire not develop staff with the right speech 'skills'. In our survey of fashion retail in Manchester, almost 9 per cent of employers reported that it was very difficult or impossible to recruit employees with the right voice or accent.

TRAIN TO GAIN

Whilst some employees already have the right speech, others need to acquire it. Even those employers who can hire workers with the right speech still provide speech training. In new bank, new recruits watch videos about how to answer the telephone said one of the focus group participants: 'Irrespective of what type of day you're having, you've got to [smiles] and say "Yes, can I help you?"'. In training its call centre agents to build rapport with customers, Glasgow-based Response Handling Limited instructs these agents that they need to sound confident on the telephone, that having the right attitude is manifest through having the right vocal tone on the telephone with customers. Another call centre, this time that of an auto insurer, instructs its employees to be 'upbeat' when talking to customers and close the call 'with feeling', and it formally assesses employees' tone of voice. 'It's a performance', our focus group participants explained; customers need to 'hear the smile in your voice'. Employers thus evoke what Eustace (2012, after Cameron, 1995) refers to as 'verbal hygiene practices', seeking 'organizational control of linguistic practices' to modify or transform workers' voices to better appeal to customers (2012: 334). This point is illustrated in Bain's (2001) study of US call centres in Alabama (see Box 6.3).

Box 6.3   Sweet honed Alabama

The number of call centres and call centre workers throughout the world has grown dramatically in the past few decades. In the quest for cheaper labour, to take advantage of relocation grants, subsidies and tax breaks, and sometimes to avoid trade unions, many banking, insurance and telecommunications, utilities and travel companies have shifted their operations out of the US and Europe. English-speaking workforces are particularly sought after, hence the move to 'off-shore' operations from the UK to countries such as India. However some companies remain in their home countries and others return. In the US companies serving the national markets prefer to locate in states where the workforces are perceived 'not to have an accent'. To create jobs, Birmingham in Alabama was keen to attract call centres. Training was provided 'cost-free' to employers and focused not only on basic work discipline – punctuality and attendance, etc. – but also 'non-accent training'. This speech training was seen as particularly important because the local Alabama accent is perceived elsewhere in the US as 'dumb' and workers needed to tone down their local accent.

(*Source*: Bain, 2001)

As the Hotel Elba example highlights, it is not just telebanking and call centre workers with only voice-to-voice customer interaction who have their speech transmuted by employers; workers with face-to-face interaction also have their speech shaped, using 'kind of script things' according to our focus group participants. In this way, organisations don't just shape how workers speak but also what they say. Scripts outline the questions and responses to be executed by employees and thus guide the length and tone of the interaction. Such scripts were also expected by management to ensure the delivery of the desired type of service, and to be a way for companies to differentiate themselves in competitive markets. Leviathan, a designer retailer, had just changed its required telephone technique, Jacinta said: 'We were training on it the other day. It used to be just "Leviathan, hello" but now they've introduced "Good morning, Leviathan Glasgow, Jacinta speaking, how can I help you?" They want the personalised service'. Across Glasgow retail and hospitality, employers prescribed what was said and how it was said by employees with customers. One focus group participant working for a well-known American clothes retailer described a training video which aimed to create an 'I can' culture amongst frontline staff: 'We've got this thing now, it's like the training is "I can", you're never to say "Oh, I don't know." It's always "I can get that for you," "I can help you in the fitting room" … there was a video for like an hour on this'. The use of particular words is meant to appeal to customers' aural senses and helps portray the company in a particular way. Employers have prescriptions and seek to ensure that those prescriptions are followed. 'You get waitresses', one of the hospitality focus group participants explained, 'that instead of saying "potatoes" they'll say "tatties"'. In this case the worker's slang was not acceptable. 'It's the way you speak that's most important' said one of the retail focus group participants; 'It's all part of the sale' her colleague continued.

In some cases, employers simply want to ensure that employees are comprehendible to customers. Our Glasgow retail and hospitality focus group respondents told us that it was important for staff to be able to communicate properly with customers. Some requirements were basic, e.g. not being 'rough' or using slang with customers. However a tension can arise for employers in wanting employees to be comprehendible and appearing 'natural'. In one of our Glasgow focus groups, a telebanking worker explained that 'Regional accents are hard to deal with. I'm not saying anything out of turn but I find the Welsh extremely difficult [laughs], I find it really difficult. I have on two occasions gone [mouths "What are they saying?"] to my boss'. Conversely, another banking clerk noted how much customers liked the Glasgow accent: 'If you are speaking to someone down south [England], they say "Oh, that's a lovely accent." They always comment, it's the first thing they say to you, "Oh I love 'phoning Glasgow; it's a lovely accent"'. However another worker from the same bank qualified this claim. He noted that their bank did not want any Glasgow accent but one that was comprehendible to customers from outside the city: 'They are absolutely adamant that the people they have got answering the phone do not talk a hundred miles an hour, have quite a clear accent'.

To be understood by the tourists that the rebranded city wants to see flock to Glasgow to eat, drink and shop, retail and hospitality workers need to speak Standard English and not just Glaswegian to local customers. However for working-class Glaswegians, Standard English connotes distance and formality. To appear friendly and informal would mean speaking Glaswegian Scots.[3] Some employers proscribe Scots and prescribe Standard English. Some employees understand this managerial stipulation and actively engage its need, others do so reluctantly, others try to resist, as Box 6.4 illustrates.

Box 6.4   Diya ken?

Archie is a subscriber: 'If I am speaking to someone in the company I adopt a more English style to the way I speak ... I haven't got an English accent but can make myself sound English'.

Betty acquiesces: 'If ye've got visitors here you wouldnae say "Aye right well whit are ye wantin'?" then you'd say "Can I help you, what would you like?" cause yer telt to say that'.

Margaret resists: 'A couldnae chynge for the wye they were daen it: "Good afternoon sir, what would you like sir, would you like this sir?" ... it's as phoney as hell, it's no me'.

(*Source*: Eustace, 2012: 337, 338, 341)

BRANDING THE TONGUES OF EMPLOYEES

The linguistic demands made upon these workers in terms of how and what they speak are based on a hierarchy and a belief that some ways of speaking are better than others. In the same way that Halsey (quoted in Honey, 1989) noted that speech brands the tongue of every child into both acceptable speech and speech associated with different social classes, employee speech also helps brand organisations in the profit and not-for-profit sectors. The prescribed speech is believed by employers to be more appropriate to good customer service generally, and can also help define and promote a particular type of service by organisations.

Some employers are explicit in wanting to manipulate customers' aural senses through employee speech. At Telebank, a UK-based banking call centre, the work requires a mixture of technical abilities – abilities that can be low level, e.g. keyboard skills – and social competencies. The latter are difficult to pin down Callaghan and Thompson (2002) admit, but essentially boil down to personality traits such as enthusiasm and communication skills. These skills centre on verbal tone, pitch and fluency, and are manifest in employees being enthusiastic and energetic on the phone with customers. This emphasis is important because it is through voice-to-voice interaction that Telebank differentiates itself from its competitors. As one of the bank's mangers explained:

> Their guys know all about banking products, my guys know all about banking products. Their guys will have to know about systems, my guys will have to know about systems. That's all roughly the same. The differentiator is how they communicate with the customer. It is the overriding skill that they've got to have. (cited in Callaghan and Thompson, 2002: 241)

Audibly maintaining enthusiasm and energy on the phone with customers is thus paramount. The bank wants employees who 'consciously use their voice as a tool to shape and control conversational mood' (p. 242). To this end, the company assesses employee oral performance and how it is likely to be aurally perceived by customers: 'looking for sentence shape, are they melodic, are they using good pitch, or are they monotonous, have they got the one tone they always speak at' another manager said (p. 241–2). What the company does not want is 'energy drop' in the service interaction: 'Energy drop is where you've got someone who's started a sentence, sounded quite bright, and then it drops off' the same manager explained (p. 242).

As Pettinger (2004, 2005) has noted with corporate clothing, the aestheticisation of workers' speech also differs depending upon the organisation's market segment. Our Glasgow retail and hospitality focus group respondents were required to differentiate between types of customers and speak differently to those various types. As part of their training, managers asked new hires how they would approach customers depending on those customers' age: 'We always like to know how they would assess the customer before they get down to selling', said Eleanor, a bar/café manager. 'If it's younger people that come in, they're less formal … it's "Hi how you doing? What can I get you guys?" If it's older ladies it's different, it's "Good morning" or "Good afternoon"'.

Once again product market distinctions were evident amongst employers, with upmarket and mid-market ones having different linguistic codes and so different speech demands. As a male hotel worker explained in one of our focus groups, 'if you work with the general public, at an ordinary level, three stars, then your accent is not too important. But when it gets to five stars and you're working in posh places, you should be able to pronounce things clearly and properly'. Another, this time female, hotel worker in the same group agreed: 'It's about recruiting the right staff for the market', and going on she explained, 'I think that [hotels] try and recruit people that are ultimately going to fulfill their guests' expectations. At different places people are looking for a different thing'. Working in an upmarket designer fashion retailer selling to affluent customers, one worker described how there was a list of proscribed and prescribed words when talking to customers and describing outfits: 'You weren't allowed to say "nice" or "lovely". You had to say that's "exquisite", that's "glamorous", that looks such and such'; 'You have to say "fabric" and not "material" and it's "luxurious"', said her colleague; the first then explaining 'There's a type of customer who would really like that language'. This links back to Bragg's (2003: 59) point that some words have 'a touch more cultural clout', denoting and enforcing hierarchy, prescribing words such as 'exquisite' rather than the more prosaic 'lovely' reflects the class buried in language: 'exquisite' has Latin (Norman) origins and 'lovely' is Old English (Celtic), and so denotes upper/middle and working class respectively.

Adherence to the script in this upmarket fashion retailer was strict, with management monitoring and correcting workers. Scripts also existed in mid-market fashion retail stores but adherence could be less strict:

At [mid-market company] for example, I would just go up and say 'Do you need a hand with sizes?' or something, but in [upmarket company] I wasn't allowed just to go up and say 'Can I help you at all?' ... You had to strike up a conversation. You were actually a sales person but you had to go up there ... to say things like 'It's a nice day outside', just to start a conversation with a complete stranger.

Interestingly, these retail workers noted how the use and efficacy of scripts varied by worker; some made the script seem natural, others stilted: 'When you're give a script some people can say it and it will come out completely unnatural and you can tell they've been told. Whereas some people can make it sound as if it's not a script' said one of the retail focus groups participants.

For customers, an employee going through an obviously scripted interaction can depersonalise the interaction. The customer knows that he or she is receiving standardised service from which the employee is not supposed to deviate. Having to wait whilst the employee goes through the script can also slow the interaction. Even the managers amongst our focus groups bemoaned the imposition of scripts amongst workers answering company telephones, even in retail: 'It used to be when you answered the phone it was "Hello, [company name]." Now you've got to say "Hello or Good morning, [company name]" and then which department you are and your name, and it's ten minutes before you get to the customer', explained one.

Nevertheless employers do not just monitor employees' verbal interactions with customers, they will also sanction employees who cannot or will not adhere to the speech demands of what to say and how to say it. For example, we were told the story in our focus group of banking workers of a bank teller facing managerial sanctions due to perceptions of poor performance, not just because of the way that she looked because also because of the way that she spoke: 'I mean she was brilliant [at bank telling] but because of the way that she looked and the way that she spoke he [the manager] took an instant disliking to her'. Another bank worker explained how 'customers expected the girls to speak to them in a certain way'. 'In all of the jobs I've had', a female hospitality worker explained in a focus group, 'accent has been important. When I was working at Café Chat one girl got laid off because they thought she spoke common'. How workers speak can be 'under the microscope' of employers explained another worker.

A CHANGE OF HABIT

The invoking of verbal hygiene practices is most acute in offshored call centre operations. Globalisation is having a major impact on services. Some services are spatially bound, for example the provision of hotel rooms: a tourist visiting Glasgow cannot stay in a hotel in Mumbai. However, as with manufacturing, some routinised services can be spatially relocated. Call centres are one such industry. Enabled by ICT, call centre operations can be offshored from the advanced to the developing economies. Relocation usually occurs to save costs, which in the case of India, a popular offshore destination for UK and US call centres, means cheaper labour and infrastructure costs. The additional twist compared to manufacturing is that it is not just the source of production which is changed through spatial relocation but also the nature of production. Voice-to-voice interaction occurs between customer and employees often without the two sharing the same mother tongue.

As a consequence, in US and UK operations offshored to India, agents are required to limit their Indian mother tongue influence (MTI) and modify or switch their accents to have either non-identifiable, non-country specific neutral accents or the accent of the customer. Employers argue that this requirement protects the workers from customer prejudices (Taylor and Bain, 2005). However, there are other reasons for this 'vocal aesthetic demand' according to Nath (2011: 717; see also Ramjattan, 2019). First, workers must be aurally comprehendible to those customers. Second, adopting the speech of customers generates empathy between workers and customers. Third, it masks the location of the workers and so deflects potentially uncomfortable questions from customers about the geographical location of workers.

The prescribing of speech in this way requires a habitus of employees that is not their own and has to be acquired, most obviously through training. Anil is an illustrative example, a composite of the 50 call centre agents in outsourced US call centres in India studied by Poster (2007) (see Box 6.5).

Box 6.5   Anil goes American

Anil has a job that involves posing as an American. For eight hours a day, he talks, thinks, and positions his body as an American while he is on the phone with US customers. His supervisor tells him he must also do so during his breaks and when talking to his own colleagues. At home, he has become unaccustomed to hearing Hindi from his parents and siblings, and has asked them to speak English. Acting American has four components in Anil's job. One is the 'voice and accent'. He has learned American diction, voice modulation, rhythm (including number of beats per second), and grammar training. He knows Americans speak much slower than Indians, and emphasise their 'r's. Facial expressions are part of this posing. Even though the customers cannot actually see him, Anil's shopfloor manager paces up and down the aisles shouting 'smile and dial!' Second, Anil needs an 'alias' to announce his American identity to the customers. The US client gave him the name 'Arnold.' He must use this name with his own colleagues, and speak to them in English. Third, he practises American conversational skills. Anil is expected to use small talk to suggest indirectly that he is in the US. He has learned the local lingo, and knows that Americans shop at Walgreens, eat at McDonalds, and drive Ford Fiestas ... In order to get a sense of how to put the whole package of American-ness together, he has been watching

(Continued)

Friends and *Baywatch* in his training sessions. Finally, Anil has practised a script, to be used for the looming question from customers: 'Where are you calling from?'. From experience, he knows he will be asked this question many times during his shift. He has been given a carefully prepared set of responses by his supervisor.

(*Source*: Poster, 2007: 272)

Technical training in these companies' operations' 'hard skills' is short, lasting only a week or two. However 'soft skills' training lasts up to three months and teaches employees about American voice and accent as well as geography, business and culture: 'You have to sound similar to them [the customer]' one call centre worker explained in Poster (2007: 286). Employees are encouraged to speak English not just in the interactions with customers but with colleagues at work and even when out with work, in the home and amongst friends. Employees are even encouraged to adopt American names to help develop work personas. Likewise in Nath's (2011) study, workers were provided up to one month's speech training to learn how to speak like Americans or Britons. 'The words are "box, "fox",' said one female worker. 'The trainer says "You should say 'bAx'. The training tells you to roll your "Rs" and drop your jaw. Training was real hard. Every single word you are so conscious'.

Even so, workers complained that the training was insufficient. They had to respond to customers in different countries, for example the US and UK, and deal with the multitude of accents within both of those countries. As one male worker explained:

You will go *mad* with this accent training thing. There are 50 states in the US, with different accents and different dialects. Some [customers] speak slow and some speak fast. You've got to keep changing your accent *and* your speed, tone and all. I change depending on their address that pops up on the screen, if they talk fast, you should, if they talk slow *you* should. (Nath, 2011: 716; emphasis in the original)

Knowing the need to have a neutral accent or talk the American or British way to work in call centres, some workers paid for their own pre-hire training:

I actually took voice and accent training before joining. Some people told me that I have a lot of MTI. I used to feel very upset and wanted to change it. At my first interview I got through but in the final round they told me I had a communications problem. I even started crying ... I was rejected for voice and accent. ... I took then one more month of training and in the third interview I got through. (Female worker, Nath, 2011: 720–21)

Employers were thus hiring workers with some identifiable capacity to talk the required way, but as is often the case with aesthetic labour this capacity was then augmented by employer-led training – and with good reason; some customers would try to identify call centre workers' 'real' accents. In such cases prolonged or tricky verbal exchanges followed between customer and worker, disrupting the service encounter and lengthening call handling times: 'You speak in the [altered accent]', explained one worker, 'but you can lose a word or two and they [the customer] say "Where are you?"' (Nath, 2011: 715).

Work was therefore complex. Workers were required to quickly read different customers' accents and mirror those accents through voice alteration. Performance had to be convincing. Management monitored workers and provided feedback on workers' accents. Pay was linked to performance, which caused anxiety amongst the call centre workers. One worker reported being 'on edge' during calls. Workers worried about their being able to shift to the required accent and convincingly perform that accent in order not to disrupt call-time targets: 'Your customer service percentage AHT (average handling time) – everything will be affected by the way your accent is' said a female worker (p. 715). As a consequence, these call centre agents could suffer psychologically and financially if they lacked the 'adequate aesthetic skills' (p. 722) Nath states.

This psychological distress, however, was not confined to performance anxiety. Some workers disliked the need to adopt foreign accents. They felt that it involved having to dissociate themselves from their own country. In aestheticising their labour through management-enforced speech alteration, they felt that they were being made to be ashamed of their nationality. To echo Bragg's (2003) point, they were being made to feel that how they spoke had a 'stigma' that they had to hide. The work is thus physically and psychologically tough, Nath states, because workers have to deny their own and have to fake another identity at work. Poster goes further on this point. She says that Anil represents a new trend in interactive service work that she calls 'national identity management' (2007: 273) by companies. She claims that the imposition of another identity on Indian employees by requiring them to change their speech results in those employees losing control over their sense of local identity, and can result in some cases in multiple personality disorder: 'I am two individuals – "Jeff" at work, and "Gaurav" in my social life' said one call centre employee. Poster believes that this 'psychic split' (p. 295) can serve as a coping mechanism to help employees distance themselves from their required artificial persona. In the case of Gaurav, customers could be abusive to Jeff whilst his 'real' self was shielded from this abuse: 'They are not abusing me, they are only talking to Jeff', he said.

It is clear from Poster's study, however, that employee responses to this verbal hygiene practice are mixed: some assimilate, others accommodate it, some acquiesce to it, and others resist it. Just over 10 per cent of respondents happily assimilate, believing that the requirement to sound American makes good business sense and can help them in their personal development, i.e. it enables them to have a relatively good job and later perhaps enter the US to study. The bulk of respondents, just over 40 per cent, accommodate this demand, disagreeing with it in principle but complying for more or less the same pragmatic reasons as the assimilators. Another group, just over 30 per cent, object, not wanting to be perceived as American, but then some do and some don't act upon this objection. A final small group, just over 10 per cent, actively resist, refusing to adopt American speech and identity. Ultimately, whilst some employees dislike this demand being placed upon them, many are aware of how their interests are aligned with those of their employer and managers in that demand. By deceiving their customers, economic development is furthered in India by inward investment and the creation of jobs. And it should be noted that many of these jobs, whilst lower paid than similar jobs in the US or UK, are better paid relative to other jobs in India and so are regarded there as good jobs – jobs for the new Indian middle class.

CONCLUSION

This chapter has sought to redress the relative lack of attention given to speech within research on aesthetic labour. As we have highlighted, speech per se has not been neglected as the focus of study. Bourdieu and others have long since pointed out that speech is a social construct that socially defines, differentiates and discriminates. It also helps or hinders employability. Having the right speech boosts employees' social and economic opportunities. Having the right speech helps them into employment and can be part of their work once employed.

In their pursuit of organisational competitiveness and profitability, private sector employers in interactive services are currently recognising the importance of positively affecting the aural senses of customers and seeking to shape employee speech, proscribing and prescribing what is said and how it is said. Having employees with the 'right' speech helps create a particular image for organisations or at least provides them with differentiation in competitive markets.

As the weight of research on the labour process indicates, such interventions are most salient in voice-to-voice service interactions in call centres. However our research reveals that it also exists in face-to-face service encounters such as those in retail and hospitality. Employers attempt to hire employees with the right speech, provide speech training, and then monitor employee verbal interactions with customers and clients: ultimately, they will sanction employees who cannot or will not conform. Workers lacking the required speech become the victims of symbolic violence – either denied access to jobs or required to undergo training and the imposition of verbal hygiene practices. This violence is not physical but one that seeks to subordinate or alter workers' identities as employers impose other, more organisationally beneficial ones. In this respect, the globalisation of call centres means that some workers are required to jettison their native identity, manifest to customers through speech, and attain a new identity through the adoption of another linguistic code. Some workers will accept, others will detest this imposition.

This identity management broadens the scope of what employers seek to control in the services labour process through the aural service encounter. It is not just speech per se; employers are messing with employee identity. Through speech, employers want their employees to adopt the linguistic code of another social class or fake being another nationality. With national identity management in offshored call centre operations, Poster (2007) rightly believes that race, and not just gender, now needs to be factored into the analysis. We believe that with spatially fixed face-to-face services such as retail and hospitality it also requires that class be brought back into the analysis, a point that we pick up in Chapter 7. Yet in asserting that this induced linguistic code switching creates an interaction based on deception, Poster is missing the point. This deception is not an unfortunate outcome but intended by management. Through the imposition of verbal hygiene practices, employers want to deceive the senses of the customer, and manipulate customer and client perceptions of the employee and henc, the organisation. The condemnation of employer attempts to mobilise and manipulate workers' speech is a point to which we return in the concluding chapter.

NOTES

1. The forerunner of the CIPD – the Chartered Institute of Personnel and Development, and the professional body in the UK for human resource professionals.
2. This is not just a UK phenomenon as a recent experimental study in the US found. The study by Timming (2017b) used the aural dimensions of aesthetic labour to highlight how job applicants speaking Chinese-, Mexican- and Indian-accented English were much more likely to face discrimination in seeking a customer-facing role compared to native candidates speaking American English. Interestingly, at the top of the hierarchy was the British-accented English accent.
3. Lowland Scots or Lallans, with the Lowlands being the broad geographic area in which Glasgow is located, is often mistaken for badly spoken English, even by many of its speakers. In fact, it is categorised as a 'traditional language' by the Scottish Government, was established in Scotland by the Middle Ages, and is sometimes regarded as a distinct Germanic language.

7

BEAUTY AND THE BEAST

This chapter examines what we think of as the 'dark side' of aesthetic labour, namely the extent to which, in some organisational contexts, it legitimises and normalises the overt sexualisation and discrimination of workers based on their appearance. The chapter begins by considering the sexualisation of (usually) female employees before moving on to engage with broader debates about appearance discrimination against those considered unattractive or what is usually described as 'lookism'.[1] The chapter initially considers the sexualisation of service workers through aesthetic labour. We place this discussion within a broader context in recognising debates about sexualisation in contemporary society, in particular drawing on the work of Hakim (2010, 2011) and Walter (2010). Having recognised this broader debate, we then go on to examine sexualisation and labour drawing on earlier work in which we considered how organisations sanction, subscribe to or strategically use employee sexuality (Warhurst and Nickson, 2009). We also begin to introduce key elements from debates about lookism, including the notion of 'the essence of the business' and 'bona fide occupational qualification' (BFOQ). Specifically, we consider debates about the extent to which organisations can legitimately claim that sexualising employees is in the business interest and thus a BFOQ. We conclude this section of the chapter by recognising arguments on how this process of sexualisation still remains highly gendered, with much greater impact on female employees.

The chapter then moves on to consider the issue of lookism as another dark side of aesthetic labour. In assessing lookism we consider arguments which have been made for and against hiring people based on looks, before moving on to consider attempts to legally address this issue in different countries. Importantly, whilst we recognise that a number of elements that we have highlighted with our research on aesthetic labour are equally seen in discussions of lookism, we further argue for the importance of class – something rarely, if ever, considered in the lookism literature, which has largely focused on the legal aspects of appearance discrimination.

SEXUALISATION IN SOCIETY

There is an increasing belief that, in the words of Walter (2010: 10), contemporary society is now characterised by a 'new hypersexual culture', which 'redefines female success through a narrow framework of sexual allure'. Whilst Walter is deeply critical of the highly sexualized culture being created, others such as Hakim (2010: 499) eulogise the 'sexualized culture of affluent market societies', entreating women (and to a much lesser extent men) to use what she calls their 'erotic capital'. Hakim suggests erotic capital is multifaceted with six elements (or seven if fertility is included), these being beauty, sexual attractiveness, social skills, liveliness, social presentation, and sexuality itself. She further argues that erotic capital exists alongside economic, cultural and social capital, and is seen as an asset in 'mating and marriage markets' (2010: 499) but also more broadly in the media, politics, advertising, sports, the arts, everyday interactions, and labour markets. Consequently, whilst both of these writers agree that there is increasing sexualisation of women, they disagree significantly on what it means for women, generally or specifically, within a workplace environment.

In considering the workplace aspects of hyper sexualisation Walter focuses upon two broad areas: first, the depressing reality of working in a sexualised role, such as a 'glamour model', pole and/or lap dancer and prostitute; and second, inequality in areas such as leadership and management roles, pay and reward, and attitudes towards work–life balance, and in particular responsibility for raising children. Underlying this discussion is her recognition of how stereotypical attitudes about women's role in society and within workplaces often lead to negative outcomes. Additionally, she highlights how judgements about women are measured not by their abilities but by their sexualised appearance. In a similar vein, Hakim also recognises how opportunities in the labour market may be linked to appearance. She explicitly states how 'erotic capital can be crucially important in certain occupations and industries, becoming part of work roles' (2010: 509). Such work roles encompass industries, which we have discussed at some length in this book, such as hospitality, as well as what are coyly called 'entertainment industries' (p. 509), such as women working as strippers, burlesque artists, erotic dancers, lap dancers, call girls, and nightclub hostesses. Other occupations where Hakim suggests that erotic capital is considered important for both men and women mirror a number of the occupations that we highlighted in Chapter 3, including actors, singers, models, and TV presenters. Finally, Hakim also notes the discussion around the beauty premium for good-looking people and the plainness penalty for those deemed to lack aesthetic capital, issues we highlighted in Chapter 2. Unlike Walter though who decries the focus on appearance in a hyper-sexualised culture, Hakim believes that erotic capital has the potential to give women an advantage, such that 'in the labour market, erotic capital can be more important than economic or social capital' (2010: 512), especially in the leisure and entertainment industries.

SEXUALISATION IN INTERACTIVE SERVICE WORK

It is within this context of an increasingly sexualised culture that we consider the process of sexualisation in interactive service work. In an earlier work (Warhurst and Nickson, 2009) we outlined three forms of sexualised work in interactive service work: that which is *sanctioned by management*; that which is *subscribed to by management* (and both employee-driven); and that which is a *management strategy* (and organisationally driven). As we discussed in Chapter 3 our definition of aesthetic labour talked of the embodied capacities and attributes possessed by workers at the point of entry into employment, which are then mobilised, developed and commodified by employers through processes of recruitment, selection, training and monitoring, to transform them into 'competencies' or 'skills' which are then aesthetically geared towards producing a 'style' of service encounter. McDowell (2009) recognises how customer expectations of the service encounter and its attendant 'good service' will impact on who is likely to be deemed appropriate by the organisation to offer such service. As McDowell further notes this appropriateness will often be raced, classed and gendered (see also Macdonald and Merrill, 2009; McDowell et al., 2007). For Belisle (2006) this process has consequences for what interactive service employers are seeking in their employees. In particular Belisle suggests that, 'whiteness, heterosexual attractiveness, and acceptance of class subordination ... remains central to service work' (2006: 143). This process of 'typing' service jobs can then take many forms, as we have highlighted throughout the book, though it is argued that women are much more likely to find themselves sexualised in the service encounter (see for example Adkins, 1995; Hall, 1993; McDowell et al., 2007; McGinley, 2007a, 2007b).

Although the primary focus of this section of the chapter is on those organisational contexts which seek to overtly and strategically sexualise their employees, it is important to note that sexualisation of young women, in particular, is commonplace even in ostensibly non-sexualised environments. Adkins (1995), Erickson (2004) and Hall (1993), for example, have recognised the manner in which hospitality organisations in particular tacitly encourage sexuality as part of the performative aspects of their frontline employees. We had many similar examples of this tacit sexualisation in our research. In answer to the question of what 'tasty' meant in their recruitment advert described in the opening chapter of the book, Moira, the human resources manager of the Elba Hotel, acknowledged that in reality 'I would say in [the owner's language] that would be quite sexy'. In a similar vein, Emma, a focus group participant who worked in a Glasgow city centre style bar, recognised that 'I think if you go for a bar job and there's a pretty girl sitting next to a not so pretty girl and they've both got the same experience or whatever, the pretty girl will get it every time'. Eleanor, another manager of a city centre style bar and restaurant, noted that employing good-looking staff was integral to allow for flirting with customers: 'It's a kind of incentive for staff ... if they're going to flirt with customers they'll make more money out of them tips wise'. She went on to acknowledge that this approach was often used as a deliberate managerial ploy: 'What we tend to do is if you get a group of guys in we send the girls over to serve them, and if you've got group of girls in it's the young guys that'll go over and serve them'. Clearly, then, lots of hospitality organisations recognise the commercial benefit of mobilising and developing employee sexuality, although ultimately these organisations are reluctant to do so in ways that might suggest a deliberate corporate strategy. Consequently, there is a need to consider organisational contexts where the use of employee sexuality is the required look, integral to the employment relationship, and so creates a style of service that is deliberately and strategically sexualised through the employees' aesthetic labouring.

In this section of the chapter, therefore, we examine what we have described as organisationally driven sexualisation (Warhurst and Nickson, 2009), focusing on three contexts – Hooters, working as a cocktail server in a casino, and A&F – in which the organisations seek to overtly and strategically sexualise their employees. In the words of Gumin (2012: 1770), such organisations are characterised as 'plus sex' businesses which 'primarily sell food, clothing or services, but use the image of the "sexy" employee to distinguish themselves'.

Hooters

Hooters are perhaps the best-known example of an organisation seeking to overtly sexualise their employees. Indeed, they are often held up as the exemplar organisation for what Moffitt and Szymanski (2011) describe as a 'sexually objectifying environment' or more straightforwardly 'breastaurants' (Avery, 2016) or 'sextaurants' (Gumin, 2012).[2] Hooters are characterised by Bruton (2015: 622) as 'part restaurant and part venue for sexual titillation'. Key to this process of sexual titillation is the employment of young, attractive, slim and sexy women or the so-called 'Hooters girls', who – in the words of the company's website – portray the 'pretty face' and 'sex appeal' that are key elements of their brand. Once employed, 'Hooters girls' are dressed in sexually provocative clothing which seeks to draw attention to the physical or sexual attributes of women's bodies and encourages the 'male gaze' (Moffitt and Szymanski, 2011). There is much debate about the place of Hooters and other restaurants of that ilk in the American business landscape. On the one hand Hooters has now been 'mainstreamed', including being featured as a successful business in *Fortune* for example. Indeed, according to the company's website they now have over 400 restaurants in 29 countries. Similarly, Avery (2016) notes that the 'breastaurant' sector is the fastest growing sector of the casual dining industry in the US. On the other hand, others such as Rhode (2010: 108) are highly critical of the company:

> Customers of a 'family restaurant' who want what a Hooters' spokeswoman described as a 'little good clean wholesome female sexuality' are no more worthy of deference than the Southern whites in the 1960s who didn't want to buy from blacks, or the male airline passengers in the 1970s who liked stewardesses in hot pants.

This latter point is one that is discussed later in the chapter, as the manner in which American airline companies moved away from overtly sexualising their employees was, in part, driven by decisions taken in the courts. In that sense, Hooters has famously survived a legal challenge by the US Equal Employment Opportunity Commission (EEOC) on the basis that the company brand is 'female sex appeal' and so all waitresses must fit that aesthetic (Avery, 2016). As Corbett (2011: 646) notes, the case brought by the EEOC never went to trial, although the company had staked out a legal argument that 'being female was a BFOQ for being a Hooters girl'. Corbett further recognises how the EEOC seemingly had the better of the legal argument based on precedent, but Hooters mounted an aggressive public relations campaign, which made the EEOC's position look 'foolish' (2011: 646). Consequently the company reached a settlement with the EEOC which permitted them to continue their recruitment practice of hiring Hooters girls.

A further issue which is highlighted by Avery (2016) is the question of whether waitresses in Hooters, and other such 'breastaurants', are subordinated or empowered by their work (see also Newton-Francis and Young, 2015; Rasmusson, 2011). For example, some women commodified in this way may see it as a 'good job' (McGinley, 2007a) and in Loe's thinly disguised (1996) ethnographic study of 'Bazooms' it is noted that over 800 women applied for the 60 jobs available. On the other hand, Avery questions whether the investment in (to use Hakim's term) erotic capital made by 'breastaurant servers' is worth it financially in terms of enhanced tips, given the extent of sexual harassment experienced in these jobs (and see Box 7.1).

Box 7.1   Working in a sexually objectifying environment (SOE)

Research undertaken by Szymanski and colleagues found that one of the main reasons for women working in an SOE, such as Hooters, was financial; the financial reward from tipping was suggested as being much greater than for non-appearance-focused restaurants. However, women working in an SOE feel a good deal of ambivalence towards their working environment, which expects them to flirt, feign sexual availability, and generally flatter male customers. Consequently the women accepted that they would be subject to the male gaze as they are constantly on display. A number though also reported more extreme forms of sexual objectification, which saw instances of sexual harassment, such as being grabbed, having pictures taken of sexual body parts, and having lewd comments directed to them. Participants in the research spoke about feeling 'uncomfortable' in the presence of what were often seen as 'creepy' customers. Negative emotions from these experiences included feelings of disgust, anger, degradation, sadness, and anxiety. Coping strategies used by the women working in such environments included minimising sexual objectification by joking and laughing off the attention of men or seeking to ignore uncomfortable comments. Clearly this relatively passive response is one that is bounded by the organisational context, which limits the potential to more actively respond, such as asking the customer to stop. Waitresses also attempted to establish clear boundaries, e.g. by highlighting their non-single status, as well as cognitively and emotionally separating themselves from their work and non-work personas. Whilst much of the above discussion highlights the negative aspects from working in such an environment, the research did also find that women saw some perceived benefits as well, with participants in the research reporting increased self-esteem from the compliments and expressions of approval that they often got from customers. Overall, however, the work by Szymanski and colleagues concluded that sexualised working conditions were associated with less job satisfaction and negative psychological and vocational health outcomes for waitresses working in such an environment.

(*Sources*: Moffitt and Szymanski, 2011; Szymanski and Feltman, 2015)

Whilst Hooters, and other such 'breastaurants', are the most emblematic organisations in terms of their attempts to overtly utilise the sex appeal of their waitresses, other examples do exist. One such organisational context is working in a casino.

Working in a casino

The work by McGinley (2006, 2007a, 2007b) and Frey (2015) highlights the manner in which a number of casinos seek to sexualise the role of cocktail waitress, and to a lesser extent of blackjack dealers, by creating a hypersexualised environment. What is interesting about this work is the manner in which it considers the gendered nature of such sexualisation and the different experiences of men and women in such an environment, a point to which we return below. The process of sexualisation for women is explicit in both the process of recruitment and, once employed, in appearance standards and dress codes. As McGinley (2007a: 262) notes, 'casinos openly and self-consciously sell sexual appeal by limiting cocktail serving jobs to women dressed in alluring outfits', hiring women who are 'young, shapely, smiling, and thin' (2007a: 259). Frey (2015: 96, 97) similarly describes the recruitment process in Borgata, a 'trendy, stylish, and ultra-modern casino, catering to a hip crowd' and oozing 'sexiness'. The cocktail waitresses, or in company parlance 'Borgata Babes', were expected to be 'part fashion model, part beverage server' (2015: 97). Once employed the 'babes' were expected to wear tight-fitting, sexy costumes consisting of skirts and bustier tops designed by a well-known American fashion designer and high heels. Additionally, cocktail waitresses were also expected to maintain an 'hourglass' figure. The interesting element of Frey's work is that it is reported in the context of 22 female servers suing the company for amongst other things creating appearance standards that made them look like prostitutes and also creating a 'sexually humiliating and objectifying atmosphere based on sex stereotypes' (2015: 99). The company defence was premised on the notion that their appearance, grooming and clothing requirements were not uncommon in the casino workplace, and that employees were aware of such standards when they signed their contracts. Ultimately the court found in favour of the company, supporting the casino's view that the cocktail servers had to remain within a certain weight requirement, as part of maintaining the desired 'sexy' image sought by the casino, and that the company's appearance policy did not subject women to an 'atmosphere of sexual objectification' (p. 103).

What is interesting in the work of McGinley and Frey is the description of how the women's experiences differed from those of men working in this environment. Whilst cocktail servers were exclusively women, men would work as cocktail hosts. In such a role men would be expected to maintain a 'well-defined, healthy appearance' (Frey, 2015: 97) and had to conform to a much more conservative dress code of trousers, a t-shirt, and black shoes. Clearly there are very different expectations in terms of how women and men are aestheticised in the casino, and as Frey notes 'a fitted bustier and tight skirt as compared to black slacks and a t-shirt do not a unisex, gender neutral uniform make' (p. 111).

McGinley (2007a) similarly considers the very gendered notions of sexualisation and how these tend to be primarily focused on women rather than men. In recognising this point she advocates that casinos should be given two choices. The first would be to de-sexualise the job of cocktail server and look to recruit both men and women to the role. The second choice would see the casinos keeping the sexual component of the job, but both men and women would be hired for the job and once employed would be expected to dress in equally sexy outfits (and see Box 7.2).

Box 7.2   Tallywackers: the male version of Hooters

Tallywackers was a short-lived restaurant in Dallas and was characterised as both a gay bar and 'Hooters for women'. Opened in 2015, the 'chestaurant' was meant to be the first of a planned chain. The all-male waiters were 'chiselled' and scantily clad in skimpy outfits consisting of red tank tops and boxer briefs. Waiters were expected to straddle the line between being a 'sexy waiter' and 'male stripper', though some customers were asked to leave for groping waiters. Prior to getting the job, as part of the recruitment process all prospective employees were made to parade around the restaurant in the outfit worn by waiters. The 24 waiters who were initially employed by the owner of the restaurant were whittled down from a pool of more than 120 applicants. As the owner, Rodney Duke, noted, 'We want to hire a wide variety of men. Everyone has a different type. The younger ones, the older ones, the muscular ones, the not-so-muscular ones. We want to have eye candy for everyone'. At the time of the opening an industry analyst opined that 'Men are far more likely to visit a restaurant that has attractive, scantily clad women than women are to visit a restaurant that has attractive, scantily clad men', perhaps highlighting the likely challenges facing the restaurant. The restaurant closed abruptly in 2016, though there have been suggestions that the owner intends to resurrect the concept in the future.

(*Sources*: Gubbins, 2016; Holley, 2015; Nieuwesteeg, 2015; Quilantan, 2015; and see www.dailymail. co.uk/video/news/video-1188670/Restaurant-Tallywackers-male-version-Hooters.html)

The sexualisation of both women and men can be seen in the final organisational example of A&F.

A&F

Walters (2016: 1) notes how the company 'embeds its brand of sexuality onto its workforce' through its 'looks policy'. The policy aims to ensure that employees embody the desired brand image, which is unashamedly about the creation of a look which is representative of a 'youthful All-American lifestyle' (Mohamedbhai, 2013, cited in Nickson and Baum, 2017: 547). What is interesting is the manner in which the company, much as with the other examples discussed above, has, until very recently, been unapologetic about this image. In a newspaper profile the company's then CEO, Michael Jefferies, emphasised that the brand image was about 'youth and sex, creating an idealized image of clean-cut, frat-boy hunks, and a conventional, cheerleader-type look for girls' (Saner, 2012). The consequences of such a look are nicely captured in the description by Walters (2016: 2) of the manner in which A&F 'often greets its shoppers with a massive poster depicting a young white-looking guy with his mouth slightly agape. He poses shirtless with his upper groin area visible above the A&F jeans waistband' – so in effect a picture of a half-naked man. As a further variant of this point, Williams and Connell (2010: 357) describe the interior of an A&F store in which 'a well-toned and muscular young worker stands shirtless next to a huge poster that could be a photograph of his chest'. Walters (2016) notes how these 'shirtless greeting' employees are selected by store managers to act as models. The same author also highlights how A&F design and staff the store in such a way that male customers are served by female customers and vice versa, and consequently 'this gendered and sexualized positioning indicates that A&F purposefully assigns workers to interact with customers under pretences that customers regularly interpret as sexually inviting' (p. 3). As with our earlier discussion above of working in a sexualised environment, the vast majority of A&F employees interviewed by Walters did not welcome the sexual attention, and a number of them, particularly female employees, found this process of sexualisation discomforting.

THE VEXED ISSUE OF CUSTOMER HARASSMENT: WHEN THE 'LOOK' LEADS TO INAPPROPRIATE BEHAVIOUR

There are concerns, as highlighted in the discussion above, about the extent to which employers profit from giving customers opportunities to discriminate against or sexually harass service workers. As we noted in the discussion of Hooters and casinos there are certain organisational contexts where appearance and conduct are regulated by management to present female employees as attractive and sexually available, creating the conditions for sexually harassing behaviour. It is not just in these overtly and strategically sexualised environments where such harassment occurs though, with sexual harassment being a pervasive problem in interactive service work generally (Waudby and Poulston, 2017; Yagil, 2008). For example, a survey by the trade union Unite of employees working in the UK hospitality sector found that 89 per cent of the participants had experienced one or more incidents of sexual harassment in their working life, with the most likely source of this harassment being customers (Topping, 2018). Similar research in the US showed that 58 per cent of hotel workers and 77 per cent of casino workers surveyed have been sexually harassed by a customer (UNITE HERE Local 1, 2016).

Clearly customer-perpetrated harassment is widespread in hospitality, often taking the form of sexual harassment of young workers (TUC, 2018). Despite the pervasiveness of this sexual harassment, and the damaging consequences for employees, the philosophy of the contemporary service economy, within which 'the customer is always right', constructs the superiority of customers over employees (Madera et al., 2018). The implication of this customer sovereignty is that they can misbehave through sexually harassing behaviour, with employees being expected to engage with it, tolerate it (Coffey et al., 2018) or, even more ominously, accept it as part of the job (Good and Cooper, 2016; Huebner, 2008). Such a situation is often exacerbated by feelings of helplessness on the part of employees due to the lack of obvious means of redress, with young workers in particular feeling powerless (Waudby and Poulston, 2017). For example, in 2013 the UK government repealed legislation that had been introduced in the Equality Act 2010 which sought to protect employees against third-party harassment such as from customers. The provisions had given a legal remedy if the employer knew that a third party had harassed an employee on at least two other occasions and had failed to take reasonably practicable steps to prevent it. Justification for the repeal was based on the fact that the provisions had been little used since their introduction and a recognition that employers have little or no control over the actions of a third party. Concerns have been expressed that the repeal of the legislation will mean employees will have little protection from their employer when facing harassment from customers (TUC, 2018). In a similar vein, even with the existence of third-party harassment protection in Australia there has been no reported cases of employees seeking redress (Good and Cooper, 2016). Good and Cooper's study of frontline male and female workers in retail and hospitality found to a large extent the power of customers in service transactions would act as a constraint to complain formally. Instead, employees were more likely to take informal action, sometimes involving them attempting to directly, either by themselves or with colleagues, stop customer sexual harassment (see also Coffey et al., 2018). Given the situation described above, Wang (2016) argues, in a legal sense, for a more explicit recognition of employer responsibility for customer harassment, as currently employees face significant challenges in holding an employer accountable for creating an environment that potentially encourages customers to sexually harass employees. Indeed, at the time of writing there is currently discussion in the UK of the need for a new law to make employers responsible for protecting their staff from sexual harassment at work. It is suggested such a new law would have the effect of shifting the burden of dealing with sexual harassment from individual employees to employers (Labour Research Department, 2019; and see Box 7.3).

Box 7.3 'Men only' – the scandal of the Presidents Club Dinner

In 2018, the *Financial Times* carried a story from an undercover reporter about the experience of 130 hostesses who had been employed to work at an event hosted by the Presidents Club charity. The dinner at the Dorchester Hotel was men only and attended by 360 leading figures from British business, politics, finance and entertainment. Hostesses, who were employed by an agency, Arista, were expected to be 'tall, thin and pretty' and instructed to wear skimpy black outfits (which were purchased by the charity) with matching underwear and 'sexy' black high heels. The women had to sign a five-page non-disclosure agreement, with no opportunity to read it or to take a copy with them. Prior to the dinner starting a team of hair and make-up artists prepared the women for the evening. The women were also given wine to drink prior to the dinner starting. During the course of the dinner there was widespread sexual harassment, with hostesses reporting being groped, subject to lewd comments and repeated requests to join diners in their bedrooms, despite a full-page warning in the accompanying brochure for the dinner that no staff should be sexually harassed. Arista also had what was described as an 'enforcement team', i.e. suited men and women whose job was to tour the ballroom to ensure that less active hostesses interacted with the dinner guests. Following a huge public outcry the dinner, which has been held annually since 1985, will no longer take place, and the Presidents Club charity was forced to close. A subsequent report from the Charity Commission noted the treatment of the female staff 'fell short of what would be expected in the 21st century', noting as well that the dress code was not 'acceptable in a charitable environment'. As the Chief Executive of the Charity Commission noted, 'raising funds for charity does not absolve trustees of their legal duties or moral responsibilities'. As a final postscript to the story, the agency which supplied the hostesses subsequently signed an agreement with the Equality and Human Rights Commission (EHRC) promising never to expose their staff to such 'deplorable' conditions again.

(*Sources*: Davies and Weaver, 2018; Marriage, 2018; Neate, 2018; Rudgard, 2018)

Certain organisations, then, clearly attempt to overtly and strategically sexualise their employees. As we also noted this process is usually directed at women. In this context, the examples described above highlight questions with regard to notions of the essence of business and BFOQ. In two of the examples, Hooters and casinos, employers have survived legal challenges to their sexualising of female employees. This situation seems strange given the precedent set by a famous case in the early 1980s, *Wilson v. Southwest Airlines Company* (1981). Cavico et al. (2013: 96) note the importance of this case as a 'leading BFOQ sex appearance case'. The same authors also recognise how the company sought to develop a 'love' marketing campaign – 'spreading love all over Texas'. In support of such a campaign it sought to hire exclusively attractive female flight attendants and ticket agents and dress them in sexy hot pants and 'go-go boots' to appeal to male business fliers. When the company was taken to court by a male plaintiff for refusing to hire men for flight attendant and ticket agent roles, it offered a BFOQ defence on the basis that hiring attractive women was necessary for the continued financial success of the airline. However the courts rejected the company's position, stressing that the primary goal of the company was to carry passengers and not to promote female sexuality as a means to titillate and entice male customers (Gumin, 2012). In essence the court rejected the notion that the airline could hire women due to their sex appeal. Within this context the manner in which organisations such as Hooters and the casinos are able to maintain an overtly sexualised approach in their recruitment of female employees, in particular, seems puzzling.

Despite some employers arguing for the fundamental necessity of sexualised attractiveness it seems extremely questionable the extent to which this goes to the very essence of their business. It could reasonably be argued that in working at Hooters and in a casino the primary job of the waitresses is to serve food or drink, not display their sexuality. Similarly in retail, sexual attractiveness is not a necessary quality for an employee to greet and assist customers, work a cash register or fold clothing. As Frey (2015: 112, emphasis in original) argues, 'sexy dress and appearance codes should be a BFOQ *only* for jobs where "female sexuality [is] reasonably necessary to perform the dominant purpose of the job which is forthrightly to titillate and entice male customers"', i.e. where sex or sex appeal is the primary commodity being sold (see also Gumin, 2012; McGinley, 2006, 2007a, 2007b). Mears and Connell (2016) neatly capture this distinction in their description of 'display work'. Thus, whilst recognising that the aesthetic labouring of hospitality and retail workers involves some display, it is not the reason for the job existing. This situation can be compared to certain jobs (a number of which we have discussed earlier in the book), such as modelling or sexual entertainment, where physical appearance is the service provided by display workers. Indeed, in their conceptualisation of 'display work' Mears and Connell use three exemplifying occupations – fashion modelling, porn acting and stripping – and consequently they note that 'display work is often sexualized work; in fact, some display workers are explicitly engaged in sex work' (2016: 336). Thus, it is only in these occupations that are explicitly engaged in display work where there would be an argument in support of such overt sexualisation in support of the essence of the business, and therefore a genuine BFOQ. In the other organisational contexts, such as Hooters, in which we described these practices, many would argue that this is just an extreme form of the everyday appearance discrimination or 'lookism' which pervades many organisational contexts, and especially those involving customer interaction. Hence the chapter now turns to consider the issue of lookism and attempts at legal remedies for appearance discrimination.

LOOKISM AND LEGAL INTERVENTION

All employers discriminate between applicants for a job. The issue though with such discrimination is the criteria through which decisions are made. Some discriminators are deemed legitimate – the use of qualifications for example or work experience. Some discriminators were once deemed legitimate but are now proscribed, a worker's race or sex for example. The list of protected characteristics has grown recently across the advanced economies to include, for example, age, disability, religion, and sexual orientation. However some discriminators remain a grey area; looks is one such grey area. Lookism is defined by Ayto (1999: 485) as 'prejudice or discrimination on the grounds of appearance (i.e., uglies are done down and beautiful people get all the breaks)'. The term is an Americanism first used in print by the *Washington Post* in the late 1970s (Tietje and Cresap, 2005). Tietje and Cresap observe that 'In our society aesthetic capital, like other kinds of capital, is unequally distributed' (p. 32). As a result of this unequal distribution of aesthetic capital, lookism, or what Bruton (2015) describes as looks-based hiring (LBH), has increasingly entered the lexicon of disadvantage and discrimination, and has a particular resonance with regard to securing employment, particularly in customer-facing roles.

When lookism becomes discriminatory or exclusionary in an employment context some would suggest that this can be considered abnormal, pernicious and unfair. Bruton (2015), for example, notes how critics of lookism would contend that it compounds social disadvantage for the unattractive, places less emphasis on substantive accomplishments, reduces workforce efficiency as employers disregard 'actual qualifications', undermines people's self-esteem and job aspirations, perpetuates false stereotypes, and is stigmatising. Throughout our research we had innumerable instances of how people who were perceived as unattractive would face discrimination. A typical example came from Catherine, a focus group participant, who was working in a stylish city centre restaurant in Glasgow. She relayed a story of a potential employee coming into the restaurant and being immediately judged on how they looked:

> A girl came in for an application form and he [the restaurant manager] said 'Sorry, we don't have anything'. Later I said 'Yes we do', and he said 'She's too ugly to work here'. I said 'You can't say something like that, that's terrible', and he goes 'Yeah, I can, this is the industry, that girl can't work here'. I was shocked.

However, dismay at such overt discrimination is by no means a universal view and Corbett (2011: 630) recognises that appearance discrimination is something that society is 'morally ambivalent' towards. Others, then, would contend that employees should be able to use their physical capital (or in Hakim's case their erotic capital) in the same manner as other skills and attributes. Barro (2003: 7), for example, suggests that 'a worker's physical appearance – to the extent that this characteristic is valued by customer and co-workers – is as legitimate a job qualification as intelligence, dexterity, job experience, personality and so on'. This school of thought can be summed up in Pagliarini's (2014: 280) observation that 'aesthetics should be considered a legitimate hiring criterion for all types of job positions, not just because that historically "looks sell"'.

Indeed, moving beyond moral or economic arguments about lookism in terms of legal views on LBH, Cavico et al. (2013: 102) note that 'in the vast majority of jurisdictions, appearance discrimination, particularly in the form of attractiveness, is not a protected characteristic ... and thus as a general rule, it is legal to discriminate based on appearance'. Although there is limited legal protection with regard to physical appearance that is not to say it is not subject to much debate. There are debates between those who favour such legislation and those who are against. Moreover, even for those advocating for legal intervention there are arguments as to how it should be best framed. In essence, for those who argue for legislative intervention to address the issue of lookism such arguments take one of three positions:

- Reinterpret existing legal frameworks which cover equality to include appearance as an additional protected characteristic.
- Develop national-level discrimination laws, which explicitly address appearance discrimination.
- Develop state or local discrimination laws, which explicitly address appearance discrimination.

This section of the chapter considers three jurisdictions where prohibitions against appearance discrimination have been introduced: France, the US and Australia. France is one of the few countries to have developed legislation at the national level (Huggins, 2015). The legislation to prohibit discrimination based on physical appearance was introduced in France in 2001 and sought to address what the then Minister for Employment and Solidarity described, using similar terminology to Bourdieu, as the unacceptable violence of such discrimination (Viprey, 2002). The 'expansive' law covers all forms of physical appearance including mutable aspects such as piercings, tattoos, clothes and hair, and immutable aspects such as facial traits, weight and height (Huggins, 2015). Any finding of appearance discrimination carries both civil and criminal liability and covers organisations and individuals, such as CEOs, who could potentially be imprisoned for up to three years in prison (Barth and Wagner, 2017). At the time of its introduction a primary driver for the legislation was debates in the US about the extent to which US airlines discriminated on the basis of appearance, particularly in terms of having weight requirements according to Huggins. As a final point it should be recognised that appearance can be a recruitment criterion if there is a clear business purpose, such as playing a Disney character or modelling (Barth and Wagner, 2017).

Beyond the national level legislation enacted in France, in the US and Australia there are a small number of jurisdictions at state and city level which have introduced legislation. In the US Michigan included height and weight as a prohibited form of discrimination in 1977 (Cavico et al., 2013). In a similar vein San Francisco added a prohibition against height and weight discrimination to its human rights law in 2000. Rhode (2010) suggests that one of the most well-known prohibitions on appearance-related bias is a 1992 ordinance in Santa Cruz, California. Initially the proposed ordinance banned discrimination based on height, weight *and* appearance. After much protest and negative publicity, the Santa Cruz City Council replaced 'appearance' with 'physical characteristics', which are defined as a 'bodily condition or bodily characteristic of any person which is from birth, accident, disease, or from any natural physical development, or any event outside the control of that person including physical mannerisms' (cited in Adamitis, 2000: 210). It should also be noted that the Santa Cruz ordinance allows employers to discriminate on the basis of voluntary aspects of appearance. Recognition of this point highlights again the importance of mutable and immutable characteristics. Consequently, voluntary mutable aspects of appearance, such as tattoos and piercings, wearing make-up and having an unconventional hairstyle, can clearly impact on employment chances – a point we highlighted in Chapter 4. This sense of employer latitude, even within the context of prohibition of appearance discrimination, is also seen in the legislation in Washington DC. Cavico et al. (2013: 100) suggest that Washington DC's anti-discrimination laws 'are considered some of the broadest in the nation preventing employers from discriminating based on "looks" and actually identifying "personal appearance" as a protected class'. However, as Gumin (2012: 1780) recognises, 'the drafters saw fit to include an additional defence for businesses specific to appearance discrimination. Employers may assert that their act of discrimination is part of a "prescribed standard" with a "reasonable business purpose"'.

The Australian state of Victoria has also developed legislation to prohibit appearance discrimination. Under the Victorian *Equal Opportunity Act 1995* it is unlawful to treat someone unfairly or discriminate against them because of their physical appearance. The Act specifically refers to discrimination on the basis of physical features, and seeks to prevent employers from treating people less favourably because of these characteristics. It defines physical features as a person's height, weight, size and shape and bodily characteristics such as scars, skin conditions and birthmarks. Again, though, it should be acknowledged that, as with other statutes described above, there is still scope for employer discretion on appearance when aligned to the purpose of the business (Waring, 2011).

Though the national and local statutes described above seem to have the potential to address concerns about appearance discrimination, in a strict legal sense their impact has been very limited. In France there has been a handful of complaints and convictions, despite surveys showing that anything between 20–30 per cent of employees believe they have been discriminated against based on their appearance (Barth and Wagner, 2017; Huggings, 2015). In the US context Rhode (2010) notes that there has been little or no take-up of the legislation, with only a small number of complaints about appearance discrimination in the workplace. For example, she notes that there had not been a single complaint in Santa Cruz. As she further recognises a positive interpretation of the lack of take-up in the legislation would suggest 'in some jurisdictions, the same tolerant attitudes that led to passage of the laws may help account for their circumscribed role; employers may be less likely to discriminate or articulate their biases openly' (2010: 139). Furthermore, it is argued that the existence of the legislation may also discourage discriminatory behaviour on the part of employers. Indeed, within the context of France it is suggested that the legislation has served to raise a broader awareness of discrimination based on appearance. According to Huggins (2015: 940–41) the legislation has shone a spotlight 'on the ways in which weight, and looks more generally, should not be a determinant factor in employment decisions', creating a social shift in perceptions about appearance discrimination (and see also Barth and Waring, 2017, for a discussion of the development of an awareness-raising video and training materials for managers in a French company, which seeks to change mindsets to ensure that they look beyond appearance and concentrate instead on a person's skills).

However, less positively, Rhode (2010) and Waring (2011) highlight concerns about the framing of legal prohibitions, the potential embarrassment complainants may experience in bringing these cases forward, the evidentiary burden of proving appearance discrimination, the willingness of courts to accept employer prescriptions on appearance as a necessary business purpose, and lastly the limited remedies for victims of such discrimination.

Many of these issues are highlighted in the work that we undertook with our Australian colleagues on the legislation introduced in Victoria.

In conjunction with the Victoria Equal Opportunity and Human Rights Commission (VEOHRC) we examined enquiries received by the Commission about 'physical features'. In the period 1995–2005 there was a total 1,876 enquiries, which represented around 1.5 per cent of the total enquiries submitted to the VEOHRC. From these enquiries 800 complaints were subsequently made, of which the majority, 639, were in the area of employment, with a significant number of complaints, 435, coming from women and 204 from men. Of the 639 cases detailed analysis was undertaken on 106 individual cases from 2000–2005. In the 106 cases reviewed it was possible in 89 cases to reveal the sex of the claimant, with 62 per cent of complainants being women. What is noteworthy, however, is that the proportion of male complainants rose over the period. Although a number of cases were in service industries such as retail and hospitality, surprisingly the highest number of complaints were in the manufacturing industry. Interestingly, when broken down by sex there were more cases of men complaining about physical features in manufacturing, whilst in hospitality and retail the vast majority of cases were brought by women.

Our research of the Victorian data shows that the majority of claims are made by women in interactive services, broadly classified, though there are also claims by men in service work – and perhaps more surprisingly, there are a number of cases of men, and to a lesser extent women, submitting complaints in industries such as manufacturing and transport and storage. Overall, though, the number of complaints remain relatively small and it is unclear how many complainants were ultimately successful in proving discrimination based on physical features as the VEOHRC data did not report final outcomes.

In sum, an employer can, as a general rule, discriminate based on appearance in the form of judgements of attractiveness. However, employers still need to ensure that an appearance standard is not connected to a protected characteristic which could trigger a discrimination lawsuit. Consequently, due to the lack of direct legislation to prohibit appearance discrimination plaintiffs must prove that the discrimination is based on other protected characteristics such as sex, race, religion, age or disability, as Box 7.4 highlights.

Box 7.4   When a looks policy becomes discriminatory: the case of Abercrombie and Fitch

A&F has regularly found itself in court with their looks policy being challenged as discriminatory with regard to protected characteristics such as race, disability and religion. Most famously in 2004 the company agreed a $50 million settlement with a number of plaintiffs from minority ethnic groupings, including African Americans, Latinos and Asian Americans. The plaintiffs had either failed to get jobs or were excluded from salesfloor positions as their natural physical features did not fit the company's conception of 'natural classic American style', which was characterised as being pretty, and crucially, white. In the UK an employee with a prosthetic arm won damages for unlawful harassment after she was been forced to work in the stockroom because she did not fit the company's strict policy on appearance. More recently, the US Supreme Court ruled that the company had violated the civil rights of a young Muslim woman who was not hired due to wearing a head scarf.

(*Sources*: Corbett, 2007; Saner, 2012; Talbot, 2015)

Having considered some of the debates highlighted in the lookism literature the next section of the chapter goes on to consider one aspect of an individual that is often overlooked in these debates, that of social class. In particular, it highlights how being from the 'wrong' social class can act as an exclusionary mechanism in at least some parts of the aesthetic economy.

CLASS IN FRONTLINE SERVICE WORK

As we have noted in our earlier chapters many of the particular 'skills' in personal presentation, self-confidence, grooming, deportment and accent that service sector employers are seeking are liable to be linked to the parental social class of the job applicants. As such the style labour market in particular tends to draw on young workers from the middle class (e.g. Boyle and De Keere, 2019; Gatta, 2011; Williams and Connell, 2010), which to a large extent accounts for the attractiveness to employers of students. By virtue of their cultural capital, these workers are perceived to be more appealing to consumers. For example, as we found in Hotel Elba a typical customer-facing worker was in his or her twenties, a graduate and well-travelled. The company deliberately placed job advertisements in the *Sunday Times* rather than the local evening newspaper in order to recruit the sons and daughters of the middle class. Aesthetic labour, especially within the style labour market, thus tends to be sourced from the middle rather than working class, reflecting what we already noted as Hochschild's (1983) outgoing middle-class sociability. Thus, as product and producer are conflated in interactive services, so the social background of employees becomes an issue and also important in creating employability and the capacity to do work so that having or contriving to have 'middle-classness' becomes key in both getting and doing these jobs and clearly has implications for others in the labour market (Warhurst et al., 2017; see also Bolton et al., 2019).

Indeed, in an earlier work we have considered the extent to which the growing reliance on 'middle classness' creates a new 'labour aristocracy' (Warhurst and Nickson, 2007b) of employees working in high-end service settings. For example, writing in a UK context Crang and Martin (1991: 106) note that for such jobs in Cambridge:

> ... the cultural and social background of employees is used by employers as a criterion of selection and discrimination: as one manager of a fashion retail store said to us, the residential origin of his employees is an important consideration: none came from the large council estates in ... as they were not the 'right kind of people' he was looking for. They lacked the 'cultural capital' ... to display and sell the middle class clothes in the store.

As an interesting spin on the point above about only recruiting from certain residential areas Eleanor, a manager with extensive experience in a number of style-driven restaurants and bars in Glasgow, acknowledged that in overtly stylish places sorting for jobs via CVs would often be done on the basis of applicants' addresses: 'It's unfortunate what goes on … they look at addresses, they have no idea of how they speak or what they look like, but they look at the address and if it's not the right address they don't want them'.

Work by Gatta (2011) and Williams and Connell (2010) in the US highlights the manner in which high-end retailers seek to employ middle-class, often student, workers. For example, Williams and Connell argue that employers in high-end retail recruit class-privileged workers, noting how these workers are typically 'middle class, conventionally gendered, and typically white' (2010: 350; and see Box 7.5).

Box 7.5 When the look is white and middle class

Historically debates about intersectionality have tended to focus only on race and sex in attempts to explain labour market 'sorting' and discrimination. Class was omitted. Research in the US, though, has identified a high degree of segregation and the creation of occupational niches in hospitality and retail organisations based on class, race and ethnicity. These niches favour white employees for frontline positions, with unskilled Latino immigrants and darker-skinned Black women much more likely to be marginalised and facing discrimination. A study of the clothing retail industry characterised this process as reflecting 'tri-racial aesthetic labour', a three-tiered hierarchy which saw managers favouring white beauty standards and white employees, with lighter-skinned and racially ambiguous-looking Asian, Black, Hispanic and multiracial employees being employed as a means to diversify brand representations. Darker-skinned Black women were much more likely to face discrimination. The same study also found that the vast majority of employees were likely to be middle class by dint of their currently undertaking a four-year college degree. Similarly a study of two restaurants in Los Angeles found the majority of servers were young, white or mixed white and well educated, usually denoting having a degree. A very small number of frontline staff were African Americans or Latino immigrants. The study did highlight, though, that second generation Latino immigrants, who were often bilingual English-Spanish, had greater opportunities to progress compared to more recent immigrants benefitting from what is characterised as their 'in-betweeness' in a workplace divided between class-privileged white workers and unskilled immigrants.

(*Sources:* Crenshaw, 1989; Walters, 2018; Wilson, 2016, 2018a, 2018b)

Gatta recognises how, whilst a student, she was recruited to work as a 'Besty's Girl' in the eponymous dress boutique as she 'fitted' with the company image being a young white middle-class girl who was friendly, energetic, and would look good in the clothes sold in the shop. This recruitment process is characterised as employers often making instantaneous 'blink' decisions based on their first impressions of prospective workers

As Gatta notes, 'in many ways the blink moment can indeed be code for race and class bias' (p. 62). At the point of recruitment there was no attempt to discern whether workers had any product knowledge. Only later would employees receive training in the high-end products that they were selling. Williams and Connell (2010) also acknowledge this informality in the recruitment process, noting the manner in which the high-end retail outlets they studied 'matched' employees with the brand image. In creating this match they show how stores used several strategies, including hiring customers directly off the shop floor. As a variant on the idea of employers matching with employees, many of our focus group participants talked about how they would often first shop or eat in a retail or hospitality outlet prior to going in and asking about potential vacancies to, in the words of one focus group participant, 'get to know the type of place, the type of clientele they have, and whether I would want to work there'.

As Williams and Connell further acknowledge 'only stores that sell merchandise considered refined, stylish and upscale – in a word, only stores that are "cool" – can rely on a steady stream of middle class worker-consumers willing to take their low-quality jobs' (p. 354). Employees consent to their aestheticisation and commodification because they identify with the brand as consumers, to the exclusion of their interests as workers (see also Besen-Cassino, 2016). These worker-consumers, who are often students, are thus prepared to accept low-wage jobs and objectively poor job quality, suggest Williams and Connell, because they gain access to product discounts and do not need the income to support themselves (cf. Cutcher and Achtel, 2017; Johnston et al., 2019; Misra and Walters, 2016).

In a different retail context, that of the bookshop, Wright (2005) suggests that those working in the UK book trade see themselves very differently from, and superior to, other retail workers. Drawing on interviews with 30 managers and workers (including 15 shop-floor workers) in three high street bookchain retailers, Wright suggests that the bookshop industry and the appreciation of books and reading, which were deemed essential to getting a job in the bookshop, are 'ascribed a certain value that places the trade in general in a hierarchal position over other trades and in particular in hierarchal positions over other workers' (p. 311). Thus, even while bookshop workers, as with other retail workers, are low paid they see themselves as distinct as a result of the product they are selling and their personal attributes and characteristics. For example, with regard to the product 'the workers and managers in this study were keen to emphasise an almost evangelical aspect to the role of the bookshop workers, based in part on the belief in the inherent value of books and reading' (Wright, 2005: 303). Consequently, as he further argues, 'the bookshop is allowed to stand for a type of retail that obfuscates processes of commodity exchange and emphasises more apparently noble ideas' (2005: 304). In terms of personal attributes and characteristics, 27 of Wright's interviewees were graduates and they invested in their work a high degree of appreciation of the cultural goods being sold, and which was dependent on the persona of a well-read, cultivated self, built on appropriate cultural capital and 'middle classness'.

This sense of workers having appropriate cultural capital is also apparent in Johnston and Sandberg's (2008) ethnographic account of 'cosmetics girls' working at an 'exclusive' department store. The predominately female employees were recruited not only because of their physical attractiveness, but also on the basis of their understandings of class and taste as Bourdieu (1984) would recognise and appreciate. In this way employees were expected to embody the organisational aesthetic and in doing so also 'embody a certain style, taste and class as representatives of the organization and the brand/s it sells' (Johnstone and Sandberg, 2008: 398). As Johnston and Sandberg note, this means that the employees deemed most suitable for employment in this store were middle-class women as opposed to the 'higher classes' or working-class women. These middle-class women would thus have the 'right' appearance, be confident in interacting with often high-class customers, and when needed would have the ability to defer to such customers. Importantly, and as with the work discussed above of Gatta, Williams and Connell and Wright, many of the women employed in the store were also consumers of the store, and thus understood what it stood for in terms of the required style as well as reinforcing the notion of a worker-consumer.

Within this context of middle-class students increasingly colonising entry-level jobs in industries such as hospitality and retail (see for example Barron, 2007; Curtis and Lucas, 2001; Martin and McCabe, 2007), it is worth considering the particular case of young working-class men because it is often suggested that their inability to secure and maintain service sector employment will often be related to their inappropriate embodiment. McDowell (2009) suggests that for young working-class men, whose fathers usually worked in manufacturing, their labour market opportunities will often be restricted to jobs in industries such as hospitality and retail. However, such working-class men will often find that employers in these industries find these 'stroppy, macho, often awkward young men' (p. 194) are less appealing than young women from the same class, working mothers, migrant workers and increasingly, as we have noted above, middle-class students of both genders. Thus, 'fit and healthy young [working class] men may now be counted among the culturally oppressed, as their embodiment, their looks, their stance, their embodied hexis, seem threatening to potential employers and customers' (p. 194). In addition to the views of employers there is also the view of these potential employees towards service work, and research has suggested that working-class men, and particularly older working-class men, are usually antipathetic towards interactive service work, expressing concerns about job quality and the cultural acceptability of working in what are often perceived as women's jobs (Lindsay and McQuaid, 2004; Nixon, 2009).

That said, it should be recognised that McDowell (2009: 196) also notes that some working-class men were prepared to 'knuckle down and produce the sort of deferential performance and servile docility essential to holding on to their jobs'. McDowell also states that often the young men she interviewed would highlight the 'masculine' elements to their job, citing the example of how young men working in a sports shop would see themselves as giving advice to sportsmen rather than necessarily enacting feminised and servile service. Roberts (2011, 2013) reports research on young men aged 18–24 who were not students and who were working in retail. Of the 24 young men interviewed by Roberts, three-quarters were described as coming from working-class backgrounds. The research found the idea of interactive service work was not necessarily anathema to these young men, with a number noting how they enjoyed the customer service aspects of their jobs, particularly the full-time workers he studied. Rather like McDowell, Roberts also found evidence of these young men recasting their jobs in a masculine manner, e.g. emphasising the technical or product knowledge they had, and especially when they had the opportunity to use their knowledge and expertise in assisting customers. Other mechanisms were also highlighted by Roberts to make sense of this type of work, and he cites one interviewee who noted that:

> People might be like 'I swear they're gay because they work in a shoe shop or a fashion shop'. And it's not the case. We just like fashion. There's a great advantage as well ... like really attractive women come in every day and you get to serve them, so that's a bonus. (Roberts, 2013: 677)

It is clear then that some working-class young men can make sense of their jobs in interactive service roles. If there is an acceptance that there is the potential for young working-class men to access these type of jobs then it would seem important that they are fully aware of what is needed to access them. This point would seem to highlight how class disadvantage can potentially be overcome by potential employees recognising how they need to offer appropriate emotional and aesthetic labour. In that vein the research that we conducted with the Wise Group, discussed earlier in the book, to train the long-term unemployed in appropriate emotional and aesthetic labour skills for working in industries such as hospitality and retail, offers insight as to how their employment might be achieved through a tailored training programme (see also van den Berg and Arts, 2019, for a discussion of how in the Netherlands an awareness of personal aesthetics is integral to working with the unemployed to ensure they are 'presentable' and in 'ready-for-work-mode' when they are seeking employment). Overall, such research shows how current use of aesthetic labour by employers is infused by social class, and which works to the benefit and detriment of different classes.

CONCLUSION

This chapter considered what we characterise as the 'dark side' of aesthetic labour. In particular it highlighted how, in certain organisational contexts, there are attempts to overtly sexualise employees as a deliberate corporate strategy through aesthetic labour.

Within the chapter three organisational exemplars were considered: Hooters, working in casinos and A&F. The chapter recognised that, at best, there is a degree of ambivalence from employees who work in such environments, with many expressing concerns at the sexual harassment they routinely experience from customers. There is an important issue that arises with this discussion in terms of the extent to which the overt sexualisation of (usually female) employees can be justified both as a BFOQ and as a necessary business requirement. As the chapter highlighted, the manner in which Hooters and a number of casinos have survived legal challenges to their appearance standards and dress standards seems perverse, given the earlier decisions in cases brought against the airline industry that rejected the promotion of female sexuality as a key ingredient to business success This discrepancy is not to suggest that there are no occupations for which appearance might be a genuine BFQQ. Here reference to Mears and Connell's (2016) notion of 'display work' is helpful in highlighting that there may be 'genuine' looks-based businesses or occupations, such as acting in pornography and stripping, where sexualised work moves explicitly into sex work.

Arguably the issue of overt sexualisation of employees is the most extreme manifestation of the broader debate around the manner in which in many employers are prepared to overtly discriminate on the basis of physical appearance and attractiveness. As we have noted in previous chapters, aesthetic labour is premised on the notion of employers employing people as they have the right look, whether that look be 'sexy', 'attractive', 'neat and tidy' and so on. Many remain uncomfortable, though, at such practices as underlined by our recognition of debates within the now voluminous literature on lookism. In considering the literature on lookism we acknowledged the increasingly polarised debates between those who are supportive of LBH and those who are against the idea of recruiting an employee primarily based on their appearance. In recognising the views of the latter group the chapter also considered debates around the desirability and feasibility of legislative intervention to make appearance discrimination illegal. Having considered the (lack of) legal impact of the legislative interventions in France, the US and Australia, it is unsurprising to see authors such as Corbett (2011) asserting that, despite discrimination based on physical appearance being one of the most widely practised forms of discrimination, it is unlikely that it will ever be covered by discrimination law in any meaningful way. Instead, employees are more likely to seek recourse through the law courts and employment tribunal systems through linking appearance discrimination to other protected characteristics such as sex, race and disability. However, as we discuss in the concluding chapter the experiences in France since the introduction of legislation may point the way in terms of opening up debates about appearance discrimination by creating a social shift in perceptions from introducing legislation as a means to change attitudes.

The final part of the chapter examined the manner in which discriminatory and exclusionary practices may also extend beyond obvious corporeal aspects to also include social class. Here the lookism literature is largely silent and it is only in the more sociologically oriented accounts of aesthetic labour from ourselves and others that class in explicitly recognised. Discussion of social class highlights how aesthetic labour, and particularly in the style labour market, is often equated with middle classness. This situation poses potential challenges for those from working-class backgrounds in seeking to compete against, for example, students for frontline service work. In particular, we would suggest that these challenges are especially acute for young working-class men whose embodied hexis may be seen as inappropriate to potential employers.

In sum, whilst in Chapter 2 we recognised how the aesthetic economy is ostensibly premised upon choice within which both employers and employees want the freedom to establish aesthetic identities, what much of our discussion in Chapters 3–6 and this chapter shows clearly is that in a clash of aesthetics when the aesthetic of the employee is mismatched with that of the employer there is likely to be only one winner. Employees' right to freedom of expression, through appearance by dress for example, must be subordinated and even surrendered to that of their employers who can use these employees to create the desired organisational identity – even if such an identity is a reflection of the 'dark side' of aesthetic labour.

NOTES

1. It is interesting to note that the lookism literature largely emanates from the US and follows a socio-legal tradition. It is equally noteworthy that this literature has expanded significantly in recent years. For useful overviews see Bruton (2015), Corbett (2011) and Pagliarini (2014).
2. Other 'Breastraunt' chains include Twin Peaks, Spice Rack and Tilted Kilt (Avery, 2016).

8
THE FUTURE OF AESTHETIC LABOUR

This book has demonstrated the importance, extent and consequences of aesthetic labour. We have shown how it is manifest in the workplace as an employer strategy, whilst also contextualising it within wider social and economic trends. This final chapter provides an overview of the origins, operation and outcomes of aesthetic labour. It charts our initial research in Glasgow focused on frontline workers in the retail and hospitality industries and then moves across the range of different occupations and industries and sectors in which other research has revealed aesthetic labour. The chapter also outlines workers' individual and collective responses to aesthetic labour, and our initial surprise at the lack of resistance to it and trying to make sense of the absence of evidence for resistance. Given that lack of resistance, and even the challenge to it, we end by asking whether, despite its dark side, we all need to embrace aesthetic labour or challenge its underlying premise.

THE ORIGINS, OPERATION AND OUTCOMES OF AESTHETIC LABOUR

Our research interest in aesthetic labour started in Preston but was developed in Glasgow as the city sought to reinvent itself as services driven and became the focal city for much of our empirical research. Although still offering itself as a retail and hospitality destination hub, some of the shine has faded from Glasgow's style mile. The city, after successfully repositioning itself for the putative post-industrial era, was hit by the Global Economic Crisis from which it, Scotland and the UK as a whole have still to recover over a decade later. Consequently there is empty retail space along the 'Golden Z' that loosely comprises the city's three-street style mile. Nevertheless, new retail and hospitality outlets have also opened, including an impressive restoration of Miss Cranston's original tearoom, accompanied by the obligatory new retail experience next door. Moreover, with economic restructuring in the advanced and increasingly developed economies, services now dominate other major cities beyond Glasgow. Some of these other cities now have their own versions of the 'style mile'. In the US, for example, cities such as Chicago have sought to reinvent themselves – in Chicago's case offering a 'Magnificent Mile' that claims to be a global shopping destination. What we found in Glasgow therefore has far wider resonance.

As employers have become more adept at managing the service interaction, so aesthetic labour has become more prominent. It existed in the past as Miss Cranston's tearoom in Glasgow illustrates. However, whilst past research noted the importance of looks in interactive service work, the importance of those looks was never fully explored, as Mills (1951) and Hochschild (1983) most obviously exemplify. However, if marginalised in research, it was becoming more important to employers and it is now, we have demonstrated, a key requisite of many workers in interactive services. As we saw though in Chapter 3, it is not just in interactive services where the look of employees matters; the concept of aesthetic labour is now applied widely to a range of workers in different occupations, industries and sectors – from airline cabin crew to actors, from traffic wardens to TV presenters across the private and public sectors. Even female academics are now exhorted to have makeovers in order to boost their organisational visibility and career prospects (Inge, 2018). If the data from the Skills and Employment Survey are right, in the UK at least, around 52 per cent or 16.3 million jobs require the deployment of aesthetic labour, whether to look good or sound right (Felstead et al., 2007). As the expanding research based developed by us and then others shows, this represents a clear strategy on the part of many employers. It has gone from the margins – the style labour market – to the mainstream of services and beyond. Indeed, according to van den Berg and Arts (2019: 310), aesthetic labour is now ubiquitous – an 'integral part of labour'.

Although we are cautious about the grander claims of a transformational aesthetic economy based on a new 'expressive age' or 'age of look and feel' (see, respectively, Böhme, 2003; Postrel, 2004), we do recognise that what happens in workplaces can both drive and reflect wider socio-economic developments. In this respect, the increased salience of aesthetic labour is part of the increased aestheticisation of everyday life. This aestheticisation is not just evident in the aesthetics of organisations such as style bars, restaurants and cafés, and boutique hotels, it also permeates the sense of self for many people and helps them create and maintain their employability, as we explained in Chapter 2. Workers are exhorted to dress for success and enhance their impression management with employers and colleagues (Wellington and Bryson, 2001). What is notable about this 'aesthetics in organisations' is that it is driven by individuals (supported by a warehouse of guides and self-help manuals) for those individuals' benefit, i.e. it helps them sell themselves to get into work and get on in work. Those benefits are tangible. A raft of data highlights a beauty premium, with workers who are perceived to be better looking earning more and having better careers (Hammermesh, 2011; Sierminska, 2015). Conversely, a penalty exists for those not deemed to be attractive (Rhode, 2010). Body work has followed by which these individuals undergo the nips and tucks of what is now called aesthetic surgery supported, if not encouraged, by the beauty industry and its expanding workforce (Jones, 2010; Westwood, 2004). Whilst most emphasis on this personal aestheticisation still centres on women, men too are now being encouraged to follow suit as the beauty industry seeks to expand its market base.

No doubt there is a link between this personal aestheticisation and the demands of employers. Certainly, as Mills (1951) noted, employers are very happy to draw on the aesthetic capital of individual workers, such as 'The Charmer', in order to boost sales. However, as we explained in Chapter 3 it is when employers seek to capture and commodify worker corporality that a step change occurs and a strategy based on aesthetic labour is pursued. This strategy centres on affecting a particular style of service based on that corporality that appeals to the senses of customers and clients. In the process, it becomes driven by employers for their organisations' benefit and individual workers' aesthetic capital becomes transmuted into aesthetic labour. It is a strategy intended to exploit the habitus of workers in order to generate (exchange) value for employers. For workers it becomes a feature of their employment relationship and manifest in their recruitment, selection and training for the job, and continues in the job through its monitoring, management and reward.

Different styles of service require different aesthetics. As a shorthand, workers need to look good and sound right for the style of service being offered by the organisation. This shorthand of looks and sound is useful but reflects the emphasis placed on the visual and aural senses, at least in Western culture (Fine, 2009; Gurney and Hines, 1999). These senses align with the key operationalisation of aesthetic labour in workplaces: the clothing or workwear of employees, and their body language or comportment, appeal to the visual senses, as well as speech – what is said and how it appeals to the aural senses. In this book we have sought to explain how and why each is operationalised in organisations as a feature of aesthetic labour.

In Chapter 4 we outlined the role of workwear. This workwear comprises organisational uniforms, appearance standards and dress codes. It can improve employee identification with the organisation and so positively impact employee performance to the benefit of employers (Nath et al., 2016; Nelson and Bowen, 2000). Just as importantly from the employers' perspective, all are intended to communicate the organisation brand or identity (Byrne, 2018; Rafaeli, 1993). This workwear can involve off-the-shelf or bespoke clothing depending upon the market segment or sector of the organisation (Pettinger, 2004, 2005)

For example, the Glasgow boutique hotel, Hotel Elba, had the latter, with its 'little Chinese tunic' designer-styled uniforms. As such, this workwear is prescribed by employers. Our Glasgow employer survey revealed that 90 per cent of retail and hospitality organisations had defined appearance standards. Employers also proscribe particular appearance, banning tattoos and certain types of jewellery for example.

Such managerial prescriptions and proscriptions of workwear seem to be mostly accepted by employees. Most workers either seemed to like what they we being asked to wear – as we reported, one of our airline cabin crew trainees said 'you feel good about yourself' – or accepted the business case and the role of workwear in projecting the organisation's brand or identity. Even so, management still monitored workwear and how it was being worn, through 'grooming checks' for example, as several of our focus group participants explained. This monitoring was backed up by disciplinary action for transgressions. Sanctions included the withholding of tips from employees and employees being sent home. It is noteworthy that despite claims that the enforcement of uniforms, appearance standards and dress codes might violate human rights, employers do have the legal right to impose them (Middlemiss, 2018).

There is now a huge volume of self-help literature on body language and how individuals can use it for personal benefit. The non-verbal communication of employees' body language can also be used for organisational benefit. It can convey emotional messages (Fast, 1971) to customers and clients that can both positively and negatively affect the service offering, giving out the right or wrong 'vibes', commented one of our retail managers in Chapter 5. The management of employee body language, employers believed, helps make the sale or at least improve customer or client perceptions of the service offered by organisations.

These emotional messages through body language, and in particular the smile, are the most obvious link between aesthetic labour and emotional labour (see Hochschild, 1983). As a trainer we reported in Chapter 5 explained about airline cabin crew selection, 'You can be as bright as a button [but] if you walk into that room and don't smile, it's over'. This type of body language requirements held for other interactive service work training. For example, in Hotel Elba eye contact with customers was emphasised. In this regard, employers again prescribed and proscribed forms of body language: if making and maintaining eye contact was prescribed, crossed arms was proscribed, both in training and in work. Again, it was also monitored by managers, and even recorded.

As verbal impression management, what employees say and how they say it, also matters to employers, as we explored in Chapter 6. We showed that the management of speech can work to individuals' advantage, most obviously helping them obtain employment. To this end, there is a long history of individuals having explicit and implicit elocution lessons in schools in the UK to transform their speech. The chapter then shifted the emphasis onto employers, and how they also realise that speech can be a verbal representation of their organisation (see Ward, 2000), affecting customers' and clients' perception of that organisation. To maximise the organisational benefit from speech, these employers seek to control and, when necessary, change the speech of their employees to better appeal to the senses of those customers and clients.

Hotel Elba is an exemplar of this employer emphasis and intervention: 'We didn't want someone who spoke in a guttural manner' the human resources manager explained to us, and the hotel actively filtered out job applicants if they didn't speak nicely and exude enthusiasm through their voice. Its importance to employers was underlined by their reported recruitment difficulties based on what they perceived as the unattractiveness of the Glasgow accent – at least the working class Glaswegian accent. Employers both provided training in speech to new employees and prescribed the speech of existing employees, using scripts to shape what was said and providing guidance on the 'correct' tone to influence how it was said. As with workwear and body language, management would monitor and enforce these prescriptions. One of our focus group participants even claimed that one of her colleagues was dismissed from the café that they worked in because of the way she spoke, being 'too common'.

What is striking in each case – workwear, body language and speech – is how employers have sought to capture and commodify what already exists, and was already being managed by individual workers for their personal benefit. To echo Hochschild (1983) in her observation about emotion management, recognising the organisational benefits, employers now manage the aesthetics of their employees and organise it more efficiently and have pushed it further. However, stringent employer demands sometimes induced what might be termed 'performance anxiety' in some workers, which, despite the general acceptance of it by many of our research participants, highlights the potential dark side of aesthetic labour.

We focused on two particular aspects of this dark side in Chapter 7: how aesthetic labour can exacerbate the sexualisation of employees; and give rise to employment discrimination based on worker looks. With regard to the first, critics and advocates both agree that the sexualisation of life and work is now more pervasive in the advanced economies. Claims that the interaction between employees, particularly female employees, and customers or clients in service work can be sexualised are not new (e.g. Adkins, 1995; McGinley, 2007a, 2007b). However, with aesthetic labour we argue that this sexualisation becomes an overt and deliberate organisational strategy driven by management, most obviously in organisations such as Hooters. Nevertheless, the legitimacy of this sexualisation as a bona fide occupational qualification in most service occupations is questionable. Certainly, whilst male workers at companies such as fashion retailer A&F are also now being sexualised, it is female workers who are most likely to be sexually objectified as a feature of their work. As such, this outcome of aesthetic labour would seem to run counter to equal opportunities as well as leading to sexual harassment (Rhode, 2010). Relatedly, we would argue that it is also regressive. It is noteworthy that the promotion for Hakim's (2011) book on erotic capital featured images of women from the 1950s. As we highlighted in Chapters 3 and 4, the 2019 dress code of Norwegian Air stipulates the wearing of high heels and appropriate make-up and jewellery for its female cabin crew. Unsurprisingly, it was criticised in Norway for being retrograde: 'While the rest of society has moved on, Norwegian is stuck in the Mad Men universe of the 1950s and 60s,' said Ingrid Hodnebo, a women's spokesperson for Norway's Socialist Left Party; and 'Uniform requirements are one thing' echoed Anette Trettebergstuen of the country's Labour Party, 'but to impose heels and make-up is going too far. The year 1950 rang and it wants its rule book back'.

This lack of equal opportunities is a theme that runs through criticism of 'lookism'. Some forms of discrimination are considered legitimate in employment decisions. Worker aesthetics, some argue, are as legitimate a selection criterion for a job as worker intelligence (e.g. Pagliarini, 2014). Most countries would seem to agree with this position. There are very few jurisdictions that outlaw discrimination on the basis of appearance. However, in one that does – the State of Victoria in Australia – our research showed an increasing number of complaints about lookism. Most, but not all, of these complaints arise within the service industries but interestingly there has been a rise in complaints by men, though women still make most complaints. Our research in Glasgow also suggests that class is a key feature of this type of discrimination, for example refusing to consider applicants whose CV suggested that they came from the 'wrong' part of the city. It is middle-class habitus that is deemed more attractive by employers. The consequence is that workers with a working-class background are deemed less employable, even for ostensibly working-class jobs. In the absence of anti-lookism legislation, other protected characteristics, such as sex, race and disability, are typically used to prosecute cases of alleged appearance discrimination by employers. Because class is not a protected characteristic, we believe the working class remain vulnerable in labour markets in which aesthetic labour is a feature.

Clearly, then, aesthetic labour is prevalent in economies dominated by services and its operation and outcomes matter for workers and employers and society more widely. It is not surprising therefore that there are a number of responses to it.

LOVE IT OR LOATH IT: RESPONSES TO AESTHETIC LABOUR

At the outset of our exploratory research on aesthetic labour we knew that we had identified an employer strategy around the recruitment and use of workers based on their corporality. However, we were open minded about what we might discover about that strategy. Nonetheless, steeped in labour process theory, aware of the contested nature of the employment relationship, and also aware, through the theory of practice, of the manner in which the body is regarded as a form of physical capital, which often results in symbolic violence, we anticipated finding evidence of two issues at least. The first was an employer reticence to acknowledge that they were recruiting on the basis of worker appearance, partly because it represents the explicit appropriation of workers' bodies and not just their hearts and minds (cf. Hochschild, 1983; Thompson and Warhurst, 1998), and partly because of its discriminatory intent. Despite finding the advert in the *Lancashire Evening Post* that sparked our initial interest in this area, we still felt that most employers might be reluctant to openly admit that their recruitment and selection of employees could be driven by looks rather than experience or qualifications. The second issue that we expected to find was a degree of employee resistance or at least resentment to aesthetic labour, and their employers' and managers' attempt to control the way that they look and sound through dress, body language and speech once employed. On both counts we were wrong.

From the outset, employers and managers were open to us about their use of aesthetic labour. They were candid about how they sought to ensure an appropriate fit between their organisation's brand or identity and the employees' who best represented it, and their belief that such a strategy appeals to customers and clients. Employers and managers were unfazed when we asked questions about it through surveys, interviews or focus groups. As Moira, the human resource manager from the Elba Hotel explained in Chapter 1, the owner was explicit in wanting 'pretty attractive looking people' and advertising this desire in recruitment material. Her task was to deliver those attractive people. However, employee responses were more mixed and the varieties of response have been borne out as the scale of research on aesthetic labour has expanded. From this research, we would suggest that employees can approve, accommodate or resist attempts by employers to manage and transmute how they are visually and aurally presented in the workplace, as we now discuss below.

Individual employee responses in the workplace

As we have noted throughout this book, employees are clearly expected to subordinate or alter their corporality in response to employer-imposed, organisationally beneficial requirements as to how they look, dress, stand and speak. Employees without the required aesthetic capacities and attributes can be regarded, at best, as lacking the right skills and at worst, become the victims of symbolic violence (Bourdieu, 1991) – either denied access to jobs or having to deny their own identity and style for those of the organisation. Despite the potential for symbolic violence and the sense of invasiveness that the imposition of standards of appearance may create – and mirroring the description of the view of the call centre employees studied by Poster (2007) in Chapter 6 – we found that most of the employees in our research accepted aesthetic labour, either approving or accommodating employer use of it.

As we noted in Chapter 3, aesthetic labour is a twist on the 'person-organisation fit' approach to human resources (Kristof, 1996). We would suggest that in large part, and especially in what we identified as the style labour market, there is often employee self-selection, i.e. workers choosing to work in an organisation for which they may already have an existing affinity, often as consumers. This self-selection then facilitates the person-organisation fit. Where employees approve of aesthetic labour by embracing the organisational ideal, they would often talk in positive terms about working for a particular brand. Indeed self-selection can, at least initially, be because employees not only understand the brand but also positively wish to associate with it. This position was particularly evident in the style labour market (Williams and Connell, 2010). In their research of fashion retail, Cutcher and Achtel (2017) usefully highlight how, when first recruited, all of their respondents were positive about the brand for which they worked and its aesthetic labour requirements. Over time, however, some of these employees developed a deeper attachment to the brand, 'engendering feelings of love, pride and playfulness' (2017: 686). In this respect, these employees willingly approve organisationally prescribed aesthetic demands and accept those demands.

Of course, as we have demonstrated, the nature of the person-organisation fit can differ significantly and be shaped by factors such as the type of industry (e.g. retail or acting), sub-sectors within the industry (e.g. electrical retailer vs fashion retailer), the product market (e.g. high end or low end) and departmental differences (e.g. back-of-house jobs or frontline jobs). Consequently, employer aesthetic demands will vary from requiring employees to be simply neat and tidy to exuding sex appeal. Any particular organisationally prescribed look will often encompasses a variety of elements, such as being female, young and sexually attractive or older, male and so looking like an experienced tradesperson, and we would suggest that potential employees will often be aware of those differences and will seek to work in an environment in which they are most likely to fit the look.

Other employees simply accommodate to the employer aesthetic demands, even when they may find them a heavy burden (see for example, Tsaur and Tang, 2013).[1] As we discussed in some detail in Chapters 4 and 7, within a legal framework that heavily supports the managerial prerogative around creating the desired organisational brand or identity, it seems an element of pragmatism emerges on the part of employees. They will be aware that in applying for a job there may be certain appearance or speech requirements and accept these requirements as simply a part of that job. Many responses from our research participants were along the lines of 'it's perfectly acceptable for organisations to manage your appearance because it's important to their businesses'. This point was underlined by one employee who regarded her company's 'uniform police' as a 'good thing'. In this respect, they too accept aesthetic labour but do so because they believe it makes good business sense and if they want the job they need to conform to its requirements.

Employees in our research largely accepted prescriptions on their appearance, and we found few or only minor examples of overt employee resistance or resentment, one example being the female employee in Chapter 4 who explained that in Hotel Elba some workers tried to customise their uniforms in the non-prescribed ways and which invoked the disapproval of management. With a strong managerial prerogative that allows employers to develop appearance standards that are in the business's interests – and the attendant employment contracts that enable employers to have the right to direct, monitor, evaluate and even discipline employees who do not fit the required look – the lack of resistance we found in our research is, in retrospect, not surprising. The story that we relayed in Chapter 7 of Catherine finding the overt discrimination against a person considered 'ugly' as being 'terrible' was very much an isolated expression of concern amongst the employees to whom we talked.

It is noteworthy, though, that over time, some respondents in Cutcher and Achtel's (2017) research also changed their attitude to aesthetic labour from enthusiastically embracing it to being more ambivalent and simply accommodating it, with some eventually feeling disaffection. Equally noteworthy, however, is that their research does not detail any active acts of resistance. We think that the issue of resistance to aesthetic labour requires further research. It might be that there are two counter prevailing processes that explain the lack of empirical evidence: first, that it is counter-productive for the employee or, second, that instead of resisting employees simply exit. With regard to the first possibility, as we noted in Chapter 4, when there were examples of employees not complying with organisational expectations then employers would respond with a variety of often punitive actions, such as sending employees home from a shift or withholding tips. Over and above these examples, it was clear that if a person did not consistently conform to the aesthetic expectations of the organisations, ultimately they would either be managed out of the organisation or would choose to leave voluntarily. This second possibility – voluntary exit – is one that is not just noted but championed by Postrel (2004). She recognises that in the context of the aesthetic economy and heightened emphasis on aesthetics not every employee will accept managerial aesthetic prescriptions, and that some workers' identity or at least sense of self can clash with those prescriptions. In these cases, employees not willing to match their aesthetic identities with that of their employer are free to go elsewhere for employment. Thus, from Postrel's perspective, employees do not resist – instead they exit, voting with their feet.

Collective responses beyond the workplace

Beyond individual employee responses, there are collective possibilities for addressing how companies choose to use aesthetic labour. Prominent amongst these possibilities are customers, trade unions and civil society organisations, and regulation through state-enacted legislation.

In considering how customers may influence the choices made by organisations' use of aesthetic labour, as we noted in Chapter 3, there is now an increasing amount of research evidence (e.g. Quach et al., 2017; Tsaur et al., 2015) that the appearance of employees can have a positive effect on customers – especially if those employees are deemed attractive. Consequently, as we found in our research, an argument proffered by employers and managers is that they are simply responding to customer preferences for aesthetically pleasing employees.

However, we also noted in Chapter 3 that organisations in different product market segments can have different aesthetics and so require particular looks from their employ-ees. Consequently, some organisations may find that some markets are more receptive to certain types of aesthetic labour than others. One recent, and startling example is A&F. The company were long-time eulogists of aesthetic labour, with an explicit looks policy. However, the company announced in 2015 that it intended to abandon this pol-icy. The shift was driven by changes at the top of the organisation and the departure of Michael Jefferies as CEO. As we noted in Chapter 7, Jefferies unapologetically talked of the brand being about youth and sex, staffed by pretty women and handsome men. When he stepped down in 2014 it was decided that the policy would go with him (Kasperkevie, 2015). A letter sent to regional and district managers noted the shift in company policy to recruiting frontline staff on their ability to offer excellent customer service and not solely on their looks. As the letter noted, 'we will not tolerate discrimination based on body type or physical attractiveness and will not tolerate discrimination in hiring based on any category protected under the law' (Jung, 2015). Additional changes were a new, looser dress code allowing employees greater individual choice, and a change to the name of sales staff from 'model' to 'brand representative' as a means to more fully align with their new approach on customer service and not employee looks (Zeitlin, 2015). Although there may be a view that this decision reflects a sudden recognition of the ethical consid-erations of their previous hiring policy and/or as a result of the company's many run-ins with the law, which we highlighted in Chapter 7, in reality the reason is likely to lie much more pragmatically around bottom-line considerations. For example, a number of commentators pointed to the major fall in sales as the biggest reason, in part due to the 'exclusionary' marketing approach adopted by the company underpinned by its focus on employing young, attractive workers, and the company's refusal to create large-size clothes and to stock pants over a size 10 (Berfield and Rupp, 2015; Moore, 2014). It remains to be seen if public pronouncements on the policy shift translate into changes in practice in the company's approach to recruitment and selection.

Although given greater impetus by the #MeToo movement in recent years, concerns around the potentially damaging consequences of the sexualised form of aesthetic labour have, as we noted above, existed for many years. Consequently, the idea that a 'sexy' look is essential to some jobs in hospitality and retail organisations has been vigorously challenged in some countries. Hooters, for example, opened its first restaurant in the UK in 1996 with the intent of having a further 36 restaurants by 2012 (Rowe, 2013). Although a small number of additional Hooters did open in the UK they were met with significant protests from a range of campaigners and shut soon after opening having attracted insufficient numbers of customers (BBC, 2012). Other planned restaurants were not opened in part due to opposition from campaigners. However, this recognition of the lack of success of Hooters in the UK has to be seen in the context of Avery's (2016) recognition, which we noted in Chapter 7, that the 'Breasturant' sector is the fastest growing sector of the US casual dining industry. Indeed, whilst some national markets may not be receptive to Hooters, others seemingly are, with reports suggesting a significant expansion of the company in South East Asia for example (Whitehead, 2016).

It is important to note here that these two companies might be considered as being emblematic, even extreme, examples of aesthetic labour. Consequently, A&F changing strategy and jettisoning its looks policy and Hooters finding limited success in the UK would suggest that consumers could have some influence on the use of aesthetic labour, at least indirectly. The danger, though, is to believe that the market alone will decide the fate of aesthetic labour. In reality, these examples appear to be isolated and our recognition of the rise of the aesthetic economy and the growth of the beauty industry and aesthetic surgery suggests that an obsession with appearance is not going away any time soon. Similarly, in an organisational setting for every story about the likes of Virgin Airlines now not requiring cabin crew to wear make-up there are many other stories of airlines seeking to employ young, slim, pretty women, who are expected to wear high heels and make-up as we noted in Chapters 3 and 4. Indeed, the weight of evidence from our research and that of other researchers globally suggests that employers will continue to use aesthetic labour to ensure that their employees embody the organisational brand or identity in response to what they think appeals to customers and clients.

If the market will not intervene because consumers are largely indifferent towards or indeed supportive of aesthetic labour then other potential sources of intervention, such as trade unions, become more salient. With aesthetic labour, organisations are clearly seeking to shape the employment relationship, which opens up a possible negotiating and bargaining role for trade unions. As we noted in Chapter 1, the employer right to direct, monitor evaluate and even discipline employees within the workplace can be mediated sometimes by trade unions (Kaufman, 2004). In reality, however, low union density in some key industries that might be obvious sites for union action is a challenge. In the UK trade union density is less than five per cent in hospitality and just over ten per cent in retail (DBEIS, 2019). It is less than five per cent in both industries in the US (Bureau of Labor Statistics, 2019). The likelihood of formal, direct trade union intervention in this area is therefore very unlikely. Instead, trade unions are more likely to indirectly influence this issue, especially in terms of sexual harassment. As we noted in Chapter 7 the requirement to sustain a particular look will often mean that some employers either tacitly or in some instances explicitly seek to sexualise their female workers, in particular, as part of an organisational strategy. This practice is especially true for hospitality employers, though as we noted, it can also apply to certain retail environments. Not surprisingly, as we noted in Chapter 7, workers in the hospitality and retail industries are most likely to experience sexual harassment by customers. Trade unions in both the UK and US have had some success in raising awareness of the issue of customer harassment, leading to organisations seeking to make workplaces safer (e.g. see TUC, 2018; UNITE HERE Local 1, 2016). In this regard, trade unions and other campaigning organisations are shining a much needed light on the unacceptable sexual harassment from customers faced by service workers.

These attempts to hold employers to greater account have been given more impetus recently by the #MeToo movement. For example, as we noted in Chapter 7, the outcry from many organisations and individuals that followed the scandal of the President's Club Dinner led to the dinner being scrapped and the disbanding of the President's Club charity. Furthermore, in the UK the umbrella organisations for trade unions and employers, the Trade Union Congress (TUC) and Confederation of British Industry (CBI) respectively plus the Equality and Human Rights Commission (EHRC) and Fawcett Society[2] have all supported the re-introduction of legislation to protect employees against third-party harassment such as that from customers (Fawcett Society, 2018). Overall, however, the ability of trade unions to directly intervene and mediate organisations' use of aesthetic labour appears to be minimal.

The final area to consider is that of state-enacted legislation. As we discussed in Chapter 7, the vast majority of jurisdictions do not seek to intervene on the question of whether it is lawful to employ workers on the basis of their appearance. In the small number of jurisdictions that have developed prohibitions against appearance discrimination in employment, the impact in a strict legal sense has been very limited in terms of the number of cases brought to court and the number of successful claimants. Instead, employees are more likely to win an appearance discrimination case if it can be tied to a protected characteristic, such as age, race or disability. For example, the Australian airline Virgin Blue lost a claim centred on employee looks but which was filed under age discrimination (Ainsworth and Cutcher, 2008). That said, we did acknowledge the potential for specific legislation on appearance discrimination to potentially change the attitudes of employers' and society more generally towards appearance-based discrimination. In France, for example, it is argued that the introduction of legislation has created a social shift in perceptions about appearance discrimination (Huggins, 2015). As Barth and Wagner (2017: 146) recognise, whilst an obsession with attractiveness and the importance of appearance is unlikely to disappear, opening up debate at societal and workplace levels has the potential to 'change mind-sets far more than prescriptions and injunctions', citing their own research on appearance-related prejudices in French workplaces. This point about whether legislation has changed social and workplace attitudes is also one worthy of further research, we suggest, and may be more fruitful an avenue than research trying to identify workers who have not been hired because of their looks. The latter avenue is particularly difficult, in part because workers are rarely told by prospective employers that the reason they are not being hired is because of their appearance. In part, it is because we suspect that it can be uncomfortable for workers who do know to come forward to relate their experience and make complaints to organisations with statutory responsibility for monitoring and enforcing equal opportunities (Warhurst et al., 2020).

In the context of a society that appears obsessed with physical appearance and attractiveness (Corbett, 2011), the mainstreaming of aesthetic labour as an organisational strategy in interactive services is difficult to challenge, and even mediate. Moreover, without this challenge and given the wider socio-economic influences on the workplace, aesthetic labour will likely continue as an organisational strategy for the foreseeable future.

LEARN TO LOVE THE BOMB OR EXPLODE THE CODE?

In making this point that aesthetic labour will continue as an employer strategy, we want to avoid making grand claims about aesthetic labour as the future of (service) work. Analyses of the development of advanced economies are littered with grand claims for epochal shifts in the nature of work and employment that have failed to materialise – though they boosted the careers of the academics making them. We are more cautious. Employers continually need to reinvent the labour process in order to create competitive advantage, and where the private sector goes the not-for-profit sector often follows. In the early twentieth century employers appropriated worker knowledge through scientific management. From mid-century they then appropriated worker feelings through emotional labour. Over the turn of the twenty-first century it is now worker corporality that is being appropriated with aesthetic labour. Employers' use of this corporality to gain competitive advantage or simply to project a desirable organisational brand or identity is, we repeat, not new but it has become more important in services and more prevalent as it has been diffused from the margins of the style-driven and 'exotic' services to the mainstream services of the high street. Its longevity will depend on how long it provides that advantage. As it further diffuses across services, that advantage will diminish comparatively. However, we suggest that it will likely continue in some form. Whilst new strategies emerge, the old ones never quite disappear. We doubt that anyone would seriously argue that versions of scientific management and emotional labour have been totally jettisoned by employers. Likewise, going forward, it is likely that in turn aesthetic labour will be displaced by a new strategy though will remain one of a range of options for employers and managers to produce a style of service encounter between workers and customers or clients.

In analysing this use of aesthetic labour, we have focused on the recruitment, selection, training, monitoring and management of employees. Although it is a key feature of the employment relationship, we have left open to further empirical examination the rewards for these employees. The UK 2006 UK Skills Survey found no statistically significant pay premium gained by employees who state that they are required to look good or sound right as part of their jobs (Felstead et al., 2007). However, other studies have noted both a pay premium and pay penalty for those deemed to be attractive and unattractive respectively in their jobs, and which is more salient in services (e.g. Hamermesh, 2011). Indeed, in certain occupations, such as working as a sales assistant or waiter/waitress, the payoff to appearance is high, according to Sierminska (2015). In our research we found that employees in the style labour market did receive enhanced remuneration but not necessarily centred on pay. Rather they gained other non-financial benefits such as discounted or even free clothing and grooming. In part, it was the existence of these benefits that triggered our redevelopment of the concept of a labour aristocracy for the twenty-first century (Warhurst and Nickson, 2007b). At the boutique Hotel Elba, Moira, the human resources manager, explained that new female and male staff were given free haircuts and makeovers. Thereafter, discounts were then available to these staff at that particular hairdressing salon. In addition, staff were given vouchers for a shoe store, with any prescribed purchased shoes expected to be able to be worn both in and outwith work. Other researchers have also noted these non-financial benefits, including access to prestigious events for employees in this style labour market (e.g. Cutcher and Achtel, 2017; Walls, 2007). That said, the allure of these benefits can soon wear thin, as the perceived glamour of working in the style labour market rubs up against the mundanity, graft and low wages of much of the work for which these workers are employed (Misra and Walters, 2016; Williams and Connell, 2010). However, further research is needed into this issue, both in terms of the scope of the total remuneration packages of employees and its impact upon those employees in terms of recruitment and retention. This research would benefit from being mixed method and encompassing both employers and employees, we suggest, and able to then capture the what as well as the how and why of the relationship between aesthetic labour and remuneration. Such research might also benefit from being internationally comparative. With aesthetic labour now identified in a range of advanced economies, many of which have differing employment regimes (Gallie, 2007), the influence of contextual national employment policies, institutional arrangements, including skill formation systems, and the power of organised labour for example, might help further develop a better understanding of the operation and outcomes of aesthetic labour within organisations.

Likewise we acknowledge that further conceptual development would be useful. First, some researchers have made suggestions for *deepening the understanding of aesthetic labour*. Despite aesthetic labour potentially appealing to customers' and clients' five senses, we have focused on just two of those senses – the visual and aural – in our examination of the workwear, body language and speech of employees. In Chapter 3 we did note the small body of evidence that suggests the other senses may also have a role in aestheticising organisations' physical environment as well as employees. We therefore accept Karlsson's (2012) suggestion that aesthetic labour research should move beyond the scope of 'looking and/or sounding the part' to explore the operation and outcomes of the other senses. Would it not be possible, he asks, to add new words to the vocabulary of aesthetic labour such as 'smelling nice, tasting delicious, having a gentle touch?' (p. 61). He notes research by Stephen and Zweigenhaft (2001) that revealed that waitresses who touch customers receive more tips than those who do not. Interesting research is now also emerging by Leanne Cutcher and her colleagues on older workers and aesthetic labour (e.g. Ainsworth and Cutcher, 2008; see also Nickson and Baum, 2017). We are supportive of this focus and with regard to Karlsson's list, we would hope that the analytical scope of future research also extends to include a more overt focus on race, disability and the sexualisation of employees in service organisations that are intended for homosexual consumers for example. It would be useful, in this respect, if future research on aesthetic labour drew on the concept of intersectionality, which, after its narrow beginnings, now includes race, sex and class (Kerner 2012).

Second, some researchers have looked to *embed existing understanding of aesthetic labour in broader conceptualisations* of service work. Given the point that we raised in Chapter 3 about their complementarity – emotional labour focused on the commodification of employee feelings and aesthetic labour focused on the commodification of employee corporality appearance within services – it is not surprising that some researchers have attempted to better enjoin them. The obvious example is Bryman's (2004) concept of Disneyisation. Bryman argues that Disneyisation is the process by which the principles of Disney theme parks are coming to dominate the rest of the world and is 'a homogenising trend that creates a standard world … diffusing through the economy, culture and society' (p. vii). One if its key dimensions is 'performative labour' or the tendency for interactive service work to be viewed as 'akin to a theatrical performance' (p. 103) that helps companie differentiate themselves in crowded markets and provides 'a template' (p. 12) for the service sector. Significantly, it is both aesthetic labour and emotional labour that are the 'primary forms' of work as a performance, 'suggesting that the two may often go hand in hand ... important weapons in the battle for differentiation' (pp. 123, 127). Understanding how aesthetic labour potentially works with or as part of other managerial strategies requires further research therefore, we suggest.

Third, there is what might be thought of as *conceptual spin-offs from aesthetic labour*. Prominent in this regard is the concept of 'athletic labour' developed by Huzell and Larsson (2012), who participated in our international project to develop comparative understanding of employer aesthetic demands. Analysing aesthetic labour in Sweden, they note that Swedish employers use the aesthetics of employees not only to sell goods and services but also as a marker of employee health at the point of recruitment. Understanding this health helps employers to better forecast their likely sick pay outlay and reduce employee costs – which is an issue in Sweden. Whilst this athletic labour is reported by employers to be less prevalent than aesthetic labour per se in Sweden (29 per cent vs 59 per cent), it opens up the possibility of developing further conceptual innovation. In particular it suggests a new layer of theorisation based on the drivers of employers' use of employee corporality, in this case adding the making of cost savings to what we have argued is the producing of a style of service (see Karlsson, 2012).

This engagement with aesthetic labour as a concept is welcome. However, we believe that there needs to be a clear distinction between embracing the concept and embracing the practice. As we noted in Chapter 7, there is a debate about whether employers' use of aesthetic labour is pernicious and unfair or that reference to workers' aesthetics is legitimate both as a hiring criterion for employment and as a feature of their work. Our research to date suggests that customers and clients and many employees accept aesthetic labour. However, we have concerns about the dark side of aesthetic labour and how it exacerbates the sexualisation of women and, increasingly, men, and how it creates a new form of employment discrimination that also excludes many of the workers already most vulnerable in the labour market.

We have advocated an engagement with aesthetic labour, at least for the unemployed. In our earlier discussed work with the Glasgow-based Wise Group that helps the long-term unemployed get back into work in Scotland, we did so mindful that, at that time, 20,000 workers were unemployed in Glasgow but there existed 5,500 unfilled jobs. The vast majority of these jobs were in the retail and hospitality industries and just a mile away from the working-class district in which the Wise Group was based. Driven by a belief in equity and pragmatism, we supported the development of a new training programme for these unemployed workers based on our research. We wanted to see the long-term unemployed equipped with aesthetic skills. They were trained in how to dress for work, answer the telephone and engage customers. We wanted them to understand that employees could affect the appropriate bodily dispositions by adopting an approach in which workers recognise that they can and should don masks for tasks or simply sur-face act (Nickson et al., 2003), what Moss and Tilly (2001) call 'code switching'. Feedback indicated that the trainees valued the course. However, our colleague Anne-Marie Cullen was unable to track the progress of these trainees as the programme was axed following a tabloid newspaper's 'exposé' that public funds were being spent on training Glaswegians who, as we noted in Chapter 1, were 'too grubby to get a job'. The hypocrisy of the *Sun* newspaper condemning the training of working-class Glaswegians for having makeovers to improve their employability whilst supporting middle-class politicians who have had makeovers to improve their electability could not have been more stark. It is a social injustice that compounds social inequality, an example of the symbolic violence experi-enced by these already vulnerable workers.

More recent research by van den Berg and Arts (2019) on aesthetic labour training for the unemployed, which we noted earlier in the book, suggests that this symbolic violence cuts deeper. Drawing on their research of Dutch municipal welfare and employ-ment services, van den Berg and Arts argue that aesthetic labour has become of 'pivotal' (p. 298) importance in navigating precarious labour markets. It is both a practice and a pedagogy, they point out: a set of practices that the unemployed must do to obtain jobs and a set of instructions to become trained in those practices. The practices signal that the unemployed are work-ready; the pedagogy the technique through which the unemployed become work-ready. In this respect, such training is again positioned as a pragmatic response to the demands of the labour market as it provided unemployed clients with labour market adaptability. In making the distinction between practice and pedagogy, van den Berg and Arts also make the point that aesthetic labour is a 'disciplin-ing and civilising offensive' (p. 310) that is different from previous employer strategies: it does not just manifest in practices – wearing certain clothes, speaking in particular ways – it is also a technique and benchmark for self-development that requires workers to calibrate the work-self. Without this calibration, the unemployed are denied access to basic citizenship rights such as the right to work. As such, van den Berg and Arts argue that aesthetic labour is now 'constitutive of social inequalities' (2019: 310) and that these inequalities will only increase if the aestheticisation of workers continues.

Thus, code switching might not be sufficient. Whilst morally we might suggest that appearance-based discrimination, particularly in respect of immutable physical features, is wrong and should be proscribed, preferably through law, some seemingly mutable fea-tures of appearance can also be difficult to overcome. As one of us has noted elsewhere with other colleagues, in the same ways that middle classness is embodied, so is poverty. This poverty leaves physical scars – poor teeth and skin for example. Such features are dif-ficult to 'mask'. While aesthetic skills training can help blunt the blink moment and help enhance some job opportunities, it will neither eliminate the potential biases in the blink moment nor alter the way that the labour market works (Warhurst et al., 2017).

It might be time to explode the code. This alternative to code switching means, in the case of aesthetic labour, pressing employers and society generally to accept diversity and be open to a range of idioms of service interaction (Moss and Tilly, 2001). We would support Barth and Wagner's (2017) point about the importance of opening up debate in workplaces and society about the aestheticisation of individuals and business models premised on aesthetic labour. Importantly, this debate was opened up due to the introduction of legislation in France that outlaws appearance discrimination. We think such legislation has the potential to send an important signal to employers, employees and trade unions about what is acceptable management practice.

Exploding the code would help address social inequality and social injustice in the labour market and within workplaces but might also serve a wider purpose. The UK's All Party Parliamentary Committee on Body Image (APPG on Body Image, 2012) noted that research shows growing dissatisfaction with body image and the rise in cosmetic surgery. The report also showed that developing and maintaining the ideal body is regarded as more important than maintaining good health. Indeed, the quest for the ideal body is associated with eating disorders, and dissatisfaction with body image can damage individuals' mental health and well-being. By way of remedy the Group recommended the promoting of a positive body image, particularly for children and young people. More recently, the UK's Children's Society (2018) reported that children's everyday experience was now littered with comments and jokes about people's looks, bodies and sexuality. It also noted the widening gap recently between girls' and boys' levels of happiness with their appearance. Calling for change, it urged a rethink of the school curriculum to promote well-being. Relatedly, studies show that brains are plastic and can change with experience during life but also that some changes can be ingrained very early in life, amplified by parental decisions, and have a lasting effect on individuals including incidences of depression and anxiety (see Critchlow, 2019). The science then affirms that nature and nurture have an effect. The last influence has led some to argue for parenting classes on childrearing. A series of recent UK Governments have provided or been encouraged to provide early years inventions through these parenting classes (e.g. Curtis, 2008; Richardson, 2011) and with a particular emphasis on the development of children's 'soft skills' of which aesthetic skills are part.

Such solutions push responsibility for dealing with the increasing aestheticisation of work and life onto individuals or parents and schools rather than challenge the legitimacy of employer and societal demands (see Warhurst et al., 2017). As with cosmetic surgery, these solutions represent remedial intervention, shoring up with socialisation and skills training the perceived aesthetic capital deficits of individuals to support their employability. The real issue is whether having to adopt middle-classness or overt sexuality in the workplace is really desirable and should be challenged. We think it should. In this respect, what is needed is systemic change. An example of the need for this wider change is presented below in Box 8.1.

Box 8.1   Discrimination, not a lack of training, is the problem

Karen Daly-Gherabi, the managing director of the consultancy hired by more than 25 UK universities to provide female academics with makeover advice, justifies advice this by reference to externalities – stereotyping and the need to conform to it. 'The programme is not designed to challenge society', she said, 'but to prepare women to better deal with the obstacles faced' (quoted in Inge, 2018: 9). The quality of these academics' work accounts for only 10 per cent of their chances of being promoted the company's workbook states, 30 per cent depends upon their image. Do not challenge the situation is the message, buy into it, or more specifically, buy a designer handbag, new clothes and restyle your hair. This approach to career management concerned one academic so much that she dropped out of one of the consultancy's courses, pointing out that it 'positioned women as the problem' (2018: 9) rather than problematising the stereotyping and discrimination that underpinned the course's need.

Recognition of this failure to identify the real source of the problem is needed and appears to be happening, at least on the streets of Glasgow. In the mid-2010s, two decades after our initial interest in aesthetic labour, a small poster appeared on the lampposts of Glasgow's streets (see Figure 8.1). In its own small way, it signalled a pushback against the aestheticisation of the economy and society not just in Glasgow but elsewhere. It challenged the view that workers must conform to the demands of employers and socio-economic mores and laid the blame for any feelings of inadequacy that individuals might have about their appearance squarely at the feet of society. It is society that is at fault, not individuals, it says

Figure 8.1   Pushback against aestheticisation

We noted earlier in the book how aesthetic labour needs to be seen in the context of a more general aestheticisation of the economy and society. Changing the economy and society is no easy task. However, we believe that it is time to question the outcomes of business models premised on aesthetic labour and, more widely, the aestheticising of individuals in society. Naming the problem and its source is an important first step.

NOTES

1. The research by Tsaur and Tang highlighted the burdens of aesthetic labour in airlines and hotels in Taiwan. These burdens included organisational aesthetic requirements and training, such as clothing and appearance standards, deportment requirements and the burden of aesthetic training; customer service pressures, such as customer criticisms of their appearance and having to match customers' service image requirements; and burdens in time off work, such as investing personal time to maintain an appropriate aesthetic.
2. The Fawcett Society is a UK charity that campaigns for gender equality and women's rights at work, at home, and in public life.

APPENDIX: BRIEF DETAILS OF THE RESEARCH PROJECTS

Aesthetic labour was an original area of enquiry. The primary research reported in this book was undertaken by us sometimes with colleagues from what both Korczynski (2002) and Karlsson (2012) have called the 'Strathclyde group' – and occasionally with colleagues in other universities and countries. It consisted variously of both quantitative and qualitative research, with surveys, focus groups, interviews and document analysis, as the outlines of the different research projects below show.

In 1997, a small-scale exploratory research pilot project funded by Glasgow University was initiated with the aim of discerning the nature of aesthetic labour. This pilot was quickly followed by a series of focus groups and a small number of interviews over 1997–98 funded jointly by Glasgow and Strathclyde Universities. Initially four focus groups were conducted, with each focus group containing between three to seven participants. In total, across the focus groups there were 21 participants (14 female and seven male). Participants ranged in age from 20–50. The focus group participants were recruited through responses to an advertisement in a widely read local Glasgow daily newspaper, the *Evening Times*. The advertisement sought individuals from the service sector who were involved in face-to-face or voice-to-voice interaction with customers. Within an overarching focus on aesthetic labour an interview guide was developed to assess recruitment and selection, training, working and management practices, and the service encounter. Individuals with similar work experiences were grouped together, resulting in a banking and customer service group, a retail group, a café/bar group, and a group of managers from a range of companies across the service sector. Subsequently one further focus group was undertaken, which brought back together six selected participants (five female and one male) from the four initial groups. This additional focus group was conducted to allow for further clarification and triangulation of some key issues that arose in the initial four focus groups. The focus group data were complemented by a small number of semi-structured interviews with managers in a range of hospitality and retail organisations. These interviews generally lasted 90 minutes. All interviews were audio recorded and subsequently transcribed verbatim. In addition, as part of our pilot research a review was conducted of job advertisements in several Glasgow newspapers in order to ascertain the selection requirements being signalled by companies to prospective applicants.

The significant publicity from the first research project led to unsolicited material being sent to us by workers in Glasgow's service industries. It also led to interest in our work from the Wise Group, an intermediate labour market organisation headquartered in Glasgow. This organisation works to help the long-term unemployed back into work in Scotland. Initially we worked with the organisation to develop a two-week pilot training course on self-presentation skills for the unemployed, drawing on our work on aesthetic labour. Following this initial collaboration with the Wise Group we moved towards a more formal collaboration with an Economic and Social Research Council (ESRC) PhD studentship. This studentship was awarded to Anne Marie Cullen. The studentship developed an examination of employer skill demands and training provision for unemployed people interested in interactive service work, with the intention of helping the unemployed back into work by targeting job opportunities in the hospitality and retail industries. The research took a multi-stakeholder perspective with data collected from employers, training providers and unemployed job seekers undertaking training. For the employers 12 managers were interviewed from a range of hospitality and retail organisations. Additionally, interviews were conducted with key informants from Glasgow City Centre Partnership and the Glasgow Employers Coalition. Interviews were also conducted with 14 representatives from a range of training providers, which, similar to the Wise Group, worked with the unemployed to help them into or back into work. Lastly, the perceptions of unemployed job seekers towards interactive service work were explored. Participants were recruited from existing trainees enrolled in a variety of courses at the Wise Group, with 31 participants in total. Participants were equally split between men (n=16) and women (n=15) and ranged in age from 18–48 (and see Cullen, 2008, 2011, for a fuller discussion of the research).

Whilst these projects allowed us to initially identify and start to develop some of the theoretical and potential policy implications emerging from the concept of aesthetic labour, we felt that we needed to extend our analysis by further assessing the empirical extent of aesthetic labour with larger-scale survey data. Two surveys followed that were jointly funded by the then Scottish Executive (now Scottish Government) and the UK's ESRC research centre for Skills, Knowledge and Organisational Performance (SKOPE) at the Universities of Oxford and Warwick. One was an employer survey, the other an employee survey of the Glasgow retail and hospitality industries.

The employer survey consisted of a core series of questions for all of the organisations and then some tailored specific questions for hotels, bars/restaurants and retail outlets. Examining current and future supply and demand, the focus of the questionnaires was on recruitment, selection, training and management practices, including elements such as the importance of appearance to businesses, appearance standards and dress codes. For the employers' survey, 1,023 questionnaires were distributed to hotels, restaurants/bars/cafés and retail outlets in Glasgow, encompassing all the different types of product market orientations from high-end fashion retailers through to supermarkets, for example. After distributing the questionnaires it became apparent that certain businesses were part of a group where the recruitment and selection of staff tended to be conducted by a central office, therefore reducing the number of possible responses. Additionally, 29 questionnaires were returned due to the property no longer existing or the questionnaire was returned uncompleted. As a result, the total number of reachable responses was reduced to approximately 950, which generated 147 returned responses – a response rate of 16 per cent. In their overview of response rates to surveys in business and management research, Mellahi and Harris (2016) suggest that there is no absolutely agreed 'gold standard' for an acceptable response rate and response rates should not be considered in isolation in judging the validity and quality of a study. Nevertheless we would acknowledge that this was a low response rate and not within the 35–50 per cent guideline suggested by Mellahi and Harris as being a good indicator of an appropriate response rate in business and management research. Indeed, to ensure a better response rate to our later survey of fashion retailers in Manchester described below we adopted a number of the suggestions highlighted by Mellahi and Harris for improving response rates.

Covering similar issues as the employer survey, for the employee survey 324 questionnaires were distributed to students who worked in the Glasgow retail and hospitality industries. Recognising prior research that highlighted that the vast majority of students who worked did so in the retail and hospitality industries (e.g. Barron, 2007; Curtis and Lucas, 2001; Lucas, 1997; Martin and McCabe, 2007), it was felt that this was an appropriate population to access. From the 324 questionnaires, 207 completed questionnaires were returned, a response rate of 64 per cent. Additionally, in order to further explore the issues identified in the questionnaire in more detail, qualitative data were also generated from five focus groups, involving 22 undergraduate students (eight male, 14 female), who were working or had recently worked in the retail or hospitality industries. All focus groups were audio recorded and subsequently transcribed verbatim.

As noted in Chapter 1 we were also approached to conduct research with a Glasgow-based further education college that was running a self-presentation course for tourism students that drew on our research. The course focused mainly on providing training for aspiring airline flight attendants. Data were generated through both quantitative and qualitative methods. A questionnaire (n=27 students, 20 female, seven male) explored students' expectations and experiences of the course, and in particular their awareness of the aesthetic requirements of airlines. Additionally two focus groups explored these issues in more depth with students (n=14, 12 female, two male). Further data were generated through semi-structured interviews with the course leader and the two course tutors responsible for delivery of the course, both of whom had previously worked as cabin crew. Although delivered by the college, the course was devised and assessed by a private company, anonymised here as AirTrain. Consequently, interviews were conducted with the owners of AirTrain, who had also previously worked in the airline industry as a senior flight attendant and a managing director. This material was complemented with covert participant observation undertaken by Johanna Macquarie (neé Commander) in another private training provider, FlightTrain. This participation involved attending a two-day course delivered by FlightTrain which aimed to prepare course participants for the recruitment and selection process of airline companies in the industry. A training diary was kept by Johanna which logged details and comments from the 11 other participants (eight female, three male) and the course leader. Course content ranged from the writing of application forms through to sessions on what to wear to and how to act when attending the interview. The aim of the course was to teach participants to 'think, act and look like cabin crew', which differentiated it from the other course in that less attention was given to teaching some of the 'harder' tasks performed by cabin crew in favour of enabling a greater focus on the softer skills.

As we further developed our work on aesthetic labour we started to engage with debates about lookism and became aware, through the socio-legal literature on lookism, of attempts in a small number of jurisdictions to legislate against appearance discrimination. With funding from Sydney University and working with colleagues from that university, Richard Hall and Diane van den Broek, we were given an opportunity to assess the impact of attempts to legislate against appearance discrimination in one jurisdiction that had introduced such legislation, the state of Victoria in Australia. Under the Victorian Equal Opportunity Act (1995) it is unlawful to treat someone unfairly or discriminate against them because of their physical features, which are defined as height, weight, size or other bodily characteristics including attributes such as hair length or colour. These physical features can include primary, immutable attributes inherent to the person's 'natural appearance', as well as secondary or mutable. At the time we conducted the research there had been no assessment of the operation or impact of the physical features provision. We were granted access to the archive of the first ten years of the law. Consequently we assessed all cases brought to the Commission from 1995 to 2005, and those enquiries and complaints that included a claim of 'physical features' discrimination were identified. Overall, there were 1,876 enquiries and 800 subsequent complaints related to physical features. Of that number, 639 were complaints in the area of employment.

In addition, contextual data were gathered through two interviews with Victorian Equal Opportunity and Human Rights Commission (VEOHRC) case managers. The research team was granted access to the VEOHRC archives in Victoria and necessarily worked on-site in the VEOHRC offices examining the individual case files, which pertained to employment, with the data covering all industries and occupations. Ultimately, detailed analysis was only possible for cases occurring after 1998–99, as due to their obligations under the Public Records Act 1973 (Vic) the VEOHRC destroys case files after seven years. Analysis of the data focused on a number of issues:

- The number of employee physical features cases (enquiries and complaints) each year filed under the Equal Opportunity Act 1995.
- The percentage of these cases in relation to the total number of employment cases received by the VEOHRC.
- The percentage of employment-related cases in relation to the total number of cases received by the VEOHRC in relation to other services covered by the Act.
- Identification of the industries and occupations from which the employment-related cases arose.
- The disaggregation of complaints by sex for industries and occupations.

As well as our survey described above in Glasgow with a range of hospitality and retail outlets, we wanted to conduct a more in-depth survey of a particular niche in interactive service and chose to focus on a segment of the retail industry that had been identified as often having heightened aesthetic requirements, i.e. that of clothing, footwear and leather goods retailers (see for example Pettinger, 2004, 2005). With funding from the Nuffield Foundation and support from the then sector skills council for retail, Skillsmart, this survey was undertaken in the Greater Manchester area as part of a broader comparative project with teams from Australia and Sweden. The survey was administered to a sample of 500 clothing, footwear and leather goods retailers in Manchester. From the sample of 500 fashion retailers a final response rate of 35 per cent (n=173) was achieved, which as discussed above was in line with what Mellahi and Harris (2016) suggest is an appropriate response rate for business and management surveys. The questionnaire included sections on recruitment and selection, the importance of appearance, dress codes and appearance standards, skills demand and whether skills shortages in potential recruits, or skills gaps in the current workforce existed. Similar surveys were administered in Stockholm by the Swedish team of Patrick Larsson and Henrietta Huzell, and in Sydney by the Australian team of Richard Hall and Diane van de Broek. Each country team had its own funding source.

Further details of these research projects and full findings can be found in, respectively, Warhurst et al. (2000), Nickson et al. (2001), Nickson et al. (2003), Nickson et al. (2005) Warhurst and Nickson (2007a), Warhurst et al. (2012) and Nickson et al. (2012).

BIBLIOGRAPHY

Adamitis, E. (2000) 'Appearance matters: a proposal to prohibit appearance discrimination in employment', *Washington Law Review*, 75(1): 195–223.

Adkins, L. (1995) *Gendered Work*. Buckingham: Open University Press.

Ainsworth, S. and Cutcher, L. (2008) 'Staging value and older women workers: when "something more" is too much', *International Journal of Work Organization and Emotion*, 2(4): 344–57.

Allen, V. (2010) 'Opening day queue at shop that's only for the beautiful', *Daily Record*, 27 March, p. 39.

All Party Parliamentary Committee on Body Image (APPG on Body Image) (2012) *Reflections on Body Image*. London: APPG on Body Image/YMCA.

American Society of Plastic Surgeons (2018) *Plastic Surgery Statistics Report 2017*. Available at: www.plasticsurgery.org/documents/News/Statistics/2017/plastic-surgery-statistics-full-report-2017.pdf (accessed 10 February 2020).

Anderson, T., Grunert, C., Katz, A. and Lovascio, S. (2010) 'Aesthetic capital: a research review on beauty perks and penalties', *Sociology Compass*, 4(8): 564–75.

Anýžová, P. and Matějů, P. (2018) 'Beauty still matters: the role of attractiveness in labour market outcomes', *International Sociology*, 33(3): 269–91.

Arkin, A. (1995) 'Tailoring clothes to suit the image', *People Management*, 24 August, pp. 18–23.

Armstrong, S. (2008) 'Now male autocuties are coming under fire', *Guardian*, 17 September, p. 3.

Avery, D. (2016) 'The female breast as brand: the aesthetic labour of breasturant servers', in M. Crain, W. Poster and M. Cherry (eds), *Invisible Labor: Hidden Work in the Contemporary World*. Oakland: University of California Press, pp. 171–92.

Ayto, J. (1999) *20th Century Words: The Story of the New Words in English Over the Last Hundred Years*. Oxford: Oxford University Press.

Bain, P. (2001) 'Some sectoral and locational factors in the development of call centres in the USA and the Netherlands', Occasional Paper 11. Glasgow: Department of Human Resource Management, University of Strathclyde.

Baker, P. (2018) *Obesity Statistics*. London: House of Commons Library.

Baldamus, W. (1961) *Efficiency and Effort: An Analysis of Industrial Administration*. London: Tavistock.

Barber, K. (2016) '"Men wanted": heterosexual aesthetic labour in the masculinization of the hair salon', *Gender and Society*, 30(4): 618–42.

Barro, R. (2003) 'The economics of beauty', *Across the Board*, 40(3): 7–8.

Barron, P. (2007) 'Hospitality and tourism students' part-time employment: patterns, benefits and recognition', *Journal of Hospitality, Leisure, Sport and Tourism Education*, 6(2): 40–54.

Barry, K. (2007) *Femininity in Flight: A History of Flight Attendants*. Durham: Duke University Press.

Barth, I. and Wagner, A.L. (2017) 'Physical appearance as invisible discrimination', in J-F. Chanlat and M. Özbligin (eds), *International Perspectives on Equality, Diversity and Inclusion* (vol. 4). Bingley: Emerald, pp. 127–49.

Barton, L. (2001) 'Dressing down Friday', *Guardian*, Office Hours section, 5 March, p. 6.

Bauman, Z. (1998) *Work, Consumerism and the New Poor*. Buckingham: Open University Press.

Baxter, C. (2005) *The Glasgow Visitor Guide*. Glasgow: Colin Baxter Photography Limited.

BBC (2003) 'Fitness firm targets "larger employees"'. Available at: http://news.bbc.co.uk/1/hi/uk/3023525.stm (accessed 1 March 2020).

BBC (2006) 'China seeks good-looking sailors'. Available at: http://news.bbc.co.uk/1/hi/world/asia-pacific/4762803.stm (accessed 10 February 2020).

BBC (2007) 'Men "face pressure to look good"'. Available at: http://news.bbc.co.uk/1/hi/health/6900650.stm (accessed 10 February 2020).

BBC (2010) 'UBS dress code scrutinises staff underwear'. Available at: www.bbc.co.uk/news/business-12023033 (accessed 10 February 2020).

BBC (2011a) 'UBS to revise 44-page dress code'. Available at: www.bbc.co.uk/news/business-12207296 (accessed 10 February 2020).

BBC (2011b) 'Free parenting class trial to run in England'. Available at: www.bbc.co.uk/news/education-15312216 (accessed 10 February 2020).

BBC (2012) 'Bristol Hooters restaurant closes'. Available at: www.bbc.co.uk/news/uk-england-bristol-16932892 (accessed 10 February 2020).

BBC (2017) 'Russia's Aeroflot airline accused of "sex discrimination"'. Available at: www.bbc.co.uk/news/world-europe-39653381 (accessed 10 February 2020).

BBC (2019) 'Men warned about Botox and cosmetic surgery risks'. Available at: www.bbc.co.uk/news/newsbeat-48015133 (accessed 10 February 2020).

Beale, C. (2004) 'Beale on … HSBC'. Available at: www.campaignlive.co.uk/news/206330 (accessed 20 February 2020).

Belisle, D. (2006) 'A labour force for the consumer century: commodification in Canada's largest department stores, 1890 to 1940', *Labour/Le Travail*, 58: 107–44.

Bell, D. (1973) *The Coming of the Post-Industrial Society: A Venture in Social Forecasting*. New York: Basic Books.

Bennett, O. (1998) 'Down with design', *Independent on Sunday*, 15 November, p. 2.

Benson, S. (1983) '"The clerking sisterhood": rationalization and the work culture of saleswomen in American department stores 1890–1960', in J. Green (ed.), *Workers Struggle Past and Present: A 'Radical' American Reader*. Philadelphia: Temple University Press, pp. 101–16.

Bentley, T. (1995) 'Uniformity versus diversity', *People Management*, 24 August, p. 20.

Berfield, S. and Rupp, L. (2015) 'The aging of Abercrombie & Fitch'. Available at: www.bloomberg.com/news/features/2015-01-22/the-aging-of-abercrombie-fitch-i58ltcqx (accessed 7 April 2020).

Bernstein, B. (2003) *Class, Codes and Control*. London: Routledge.

Besen-Cassino, Y. (2016) *Consuming Work: Youth Labour in America*. Philadelphia: Temple University Press.

Bixler, S. and Nix-Rice, N. (1997) *The New Professional Image*. Avon: Adams Media Corporation.

Black, P. (2004) *The Beauty Industry: Gender, Culture and Pleasure*. London: Routledge.

Blackman, L. (2008) *The Body*. Oxford: Berg.

Böhme, G. (2003) 'Contribution to the critique of the aesthetic economy', *Thesis Eleven*, 73(1): 71–82.

Böhme, G. (2010) 'On beauty', *Nordic Journal of Aesthetics*, 21(39): 22–33.

Bolton, S. (2004) *Emotion Management in the Workplace*. London: Palgrave.

Bolton, S. (2010) 'Old ambiguities and new developments: exploring the emotional labour process', in P. Thompson and C. Smith (eds), *Working Life*. London: Palgrave, pp. 205–24.

Bolton, S. and Boyd, C. (2003) 'Trolley dolly or skilled emotion manager? Moving on from Hochschild's Managed Heart', *Work, Employment and Society*, 17(2): 289–308.

Bolton, S.C., Laaser, K., McGuire, D. and Duncan, A. (2019) 'A neglected pool of labour? Frontline service work and hotel recruitment in Glasgow', *European Management Review*, 16(3): 567–78.

Bonnaccio, S., O'Reilly, J., O'Sullivan, S. and Chocchio, F. (2016) 'Nonverbal behavior and communication in the workplace: a review and an agenda for research', *Journal of Management*, 42(5): 1044–74.

Borland, J. and Leigh, A. (2014) 'Unpacking the beauty premium: what channels does it operate through and has it changed over time?', *Economic Record*, 90(288): 17–32.

Bourdieu, P. (1974) 'The school as a conservative force', in J. Eggleton (ed.), *Contemporary Research in the Sociology of Education*. London: Methuen, pp. 32–46.

Bourdieu, P. (1984) *Distinction: A Social Critique of the Judgement of Taste*. London: Routledge.

Bourdieu, P. (1990) *The Logic of Practice*. Cambridge: Polity Press.

Bourdieu, P. (1991a) *Language and Symbolic Power*. Cambridge: Polity Press.

Bourdieu, P. (1991b) 'Price formation and the anticipation of profits', in J.B. Thompson (ed.), *Language and Symbolic Power*. Cambridge: Polity Press, pp. 66–102.

Bourdieu, P. (1992) *Outline of a Theory of Practice*. Cambridge: Cambridge University Press.

Bourdieu, P. (1998) *Practical Reason: On the Theory of Action*. Stanford: Stanford University Press.

Bourdieu, P. (2004) *Distinction*. London: Routledge.

Boyle, B. and De Keere, K. (2019) 'Aesthetic labour, class and taste: mobility aspirations of middle class women working in luxury retail', *The Sociological Review*, 67(3): 706–22.

Bragg, M. (2003) *The Adventure of English*. London: Sceptre.

Braiden, G. (2007) 'Bid to get A-list status for "first style bar"', *The Herald*, 1 March, p. 11.

Branigan, T. (2010) 'Only the pretty need apply', *Guardian Weekly*, 12 November, p. 44.

Braverman, H. (1974) *Labour and Monopoly Capital*. New York: Monthly Review Press.

Breward, C. (2011) 'Aestheticism in the marketplace: fashion, lifestyle and popular taste', in S. Calloway and L. Federle Orr (eds), *The Cult of Beauty*. London: V&A Publishing, pp. 192–204.

British Association of Aesthetic Plastic Surgeons (2018) 'Cosmetic surgery stats: dad bods and filter jobs'. Available at: https://baaps.org.uk/about/news/1535/cosmetic_surgery_stats_dad_bods_and_filter_jobs) (accessed 12 February 2020).

Brody, D. (1960) *Steelworkers in America*. New York: Harper & Row.

Brown, S. (2017) 'PhD Barbie get a makeover! Aesthetic labour in academia', in A. Elias, R. Gill and C. Scharff (eds), *Aesthetic Labour: Rethinking Beauty Politics in Neoliberalism*, London: Palgrave Macmillan, pp. 149–63.

Bruce-Gardyne, T. (2005) 'Glasgow' in *The Glasgow Visitor Guide*. Grantown-on-Spey: Colin Baxter.

Bruton, S. (2015) 'Looks-based hiring and wrongful discrimination', *Business and Society Review*, 120(4): 607–35.

Brydges, T. and Sjöhom, J. (2019) 'Becoming a personal style blogger: changing configurations and spatialities of aesthetic labour in the fashion industry', *International Journal of Cultural Studies*, 22(1): 119–39.

Bryman, A. (2004) *The Disneyization of Society*. London: Sage.

Bureau of Labor Statistics (2019) *Union Members 2018*. Available at: www.bls.gov/news.release/pdf/union2.pdf (accessed 13 February 2020).

Bunt, K., McAndrew, F. and Kuechel, A. (2005) *Jobcentre Plus Employer (Market View) Survey 2004*. Norwich: Her Majesty's Stationery Office.

Burkeman, O. (2000) 'Hey, good looking …', *Guardian*, 16 June, pp. 6–7.

Butler, C. and Harris, J. (2015) 'Pills, ills and the ugly face of aesthetic labour: "They should have discriminated against me"', *Work, Employment and Society*, 29(3): 508–16.

Butler, S. (2014) 'Primark pays $10m more to Rana Plaza victims', *Guardian*, 17 March, p. 17

Byrne, S. (2018) *Dress and Appearance Survey 2018*, XpertHR. Available at: www.xperthr.co.uk/survey-analysis/dress-and-appearance-survey-2018/163588/ (accessed 11 February 2020).

Callaghan, G. and Thompson, P. (2002) '"We recruit attitude": the selection and shaping of routine call centre labour', *Journal of Management Studies*, 39(2): 232–54.

Calloway, S. (2011) 'The search for a new beauty', in S. Calloway and L. Federle Orr (eds), *The Cult of Beauty*. London: V&A Publishing, pp. 10–22.

Calloway, S. and Federle Orr, L. (eds) (2011) *The Cult of Beauty*. London: V&A Publishing.

Calnan, M. (2016) 'Discrimination pay-out for waitress told to be "easy on the eye"', *People Management Online*, 4 July.

Cameron, D. (1995) *Verbal Hygiene (The Politics of Language)*. London: Routledge.

Carlisle, S. and Hanlon, P. (2011) 'Wellbeing, consumer culture and the "new poor"', Oxfam Discussion Paper. Available at: www.gci.org.uk/Documents/dp-whose-economy-papers-complete-series-010911-en.pdf (accessed 12 February 2020).

The Caterer (2009) 'Muslim cocktail waitress wins damages over skimpy outfit'. Available at: www.thecaterer.com/archive/muslim-cocktail-waitress-wins-damages-over-skimpy-outfit (accessed 12 February 2020).

Cavico, F., Mufler, S. and Mujtaba, B. (2013) 'Appearance discrimination in employment: legal and ethical implications of "lookism" and "lookphobia"', *Equality, Diversity and Inclusion: An International Journal*, 32(1): 83–119.

Children's Society (2018) *The Good Childhood Report 2018*. London: The Children's Society.

Cho, J. (2017) *English Language Ideologies in Korea*. Cham: Springer International.

Chugh, S. and Hancock, P. (2009) 'Networks of aestheticization: the architecture, artefacts and embodiment of hairdressing salons', *Work, Employment and Society*, 23(3): 460–76.

Cockburn, C. (1983) *Brothers: Male Dominance and Technological Change*. London: Pluto.

Coffey, J., Farrugia, D., Adkins, L. and Threadgold, D. (2018) 'Gender, sexuality and risk in the practice of affective labour for young women in bar work', *Sociological Research Online*, 23(4): 728–43.

Corbett, W. (2007) 'The ugly truth about appearance discrimination and the beauty of our employment discrimination law', *Duke Journal of Gender Law and Policy*, 14(1): 153–78.

Corbett, W. (2011) 'Hotness discrimination: appearance discrimination as a mirror for reflecting on the body of employment discrimination law', *Catholic University Law Review*, 60(3): 615–60.

Cosmetic, Toiletry & Perfumery Association (CPTA) (2017) *CTPA Annual Report 2017*. Available at: www.ctpa.org.uk/storage/annualreports/2017/index.html (accessed 12 February 2020).

Cox, P. and Hobley, A. (2014) *Shopgirls*. London: Arrow.

Crang, P. and Martin, R. (1991) 'Mrs Thatcher's vision of the "new Britain" and other sides of the "Cambridge phenomenon"', *Environment and Planning D: Society and Space*, 9(1): 91–116.

Craven, V., Lawley, S. and J. Baker (2013) 'Performance, gender and sexualized work: beyond legislation? A case study of work in a recruitment company', *Equality, Diversity and Inclusion: An International Journal*, 32(5): 475–90.

Crenshaw, K. (1989) 'Demarginalising the intersection of race and sex: A black feminist critique of anti-discrimination doctrine', *University of Chicago Legal Forum*, 1989(1): 139–67.

Crichton, T. (2004) 'Scotland with style ... the new face of Glasgow', *Sunday Herald*, 7 March, p. 7.

Critchlow, H. (2019) *The Science of Fate*. London: Hodder & Stoughton.

Crompton, R. (2010) 'Class and employment', *Work, Employment and Society*, 24(1): 9–26.

Crossley, N. (2001) *The Social Body*. London: Sage.

Cullen, A.M. (2008) 'The Demand for Aesthetic Skills in Interactive Service Work: The Implications of This Demand Upon Unemployed Job Seekers' Access to This Work'. PhD thesis, University of Strathclyde, Glasgow.

Cullen, A.M. (2011) 'Unemployed jobs seekers' access to interactive service work', *Employee Relations*, 33(1): 64–80.

Curtis, P. (2008) 'State urged to help deprived children to communicate', *Guardian*, 2 December, p.12.

Curtis, S. and Lucas, R. (2001) 'A coincidence of needs? Employers and full-time students', *Employee Relations*, 23(1): 38–54.

Cutcher, L. and Achtel, P. (2017) '"Doing the brand": aesthetic labour as situated, relational performance in fashion retail', *Work, Employment and Society*, 31(4): 675–91.

Dahl, D. (2014) 'Looking neat on the street: aesthetic labour in public parking patrol', *Nordic Journal of Working Life Studies*, 3(2): 59–78.

Daily Record (2008) 'Scots wha say', 25 September, p. 23.

Daily Record (2011) 'Accent does matter', 11 June, p. 26.

Daniel, K., Johnson, L. and Miller, K (1996) 'Dimensions of uniform perceptions among service providers', *Journal of Services Marketing*, 10(2): 42–56.

Darr, A. (2004) 'The interdependence of social and technical skills in the sales of emergent technology', in C. Warhurst, E. Keep and I. Grugulis (eds), *The Skills that Matter*. Basingstoke: Palgrave, pp. 55–71.

Davies, C. (2011) 'Full make-up at all times: how Harrods "ladies code" drove out sale assistant', *Guardian*, 2 July, p. 10.

Davies, P. (1990) *Your Total Image*. London: Piatkus.

Davies, R. and Weaver, M. (2018) 'Elite men only club shuts amid furore over groping scandal', *Guardian*, 25 January, pp. 1, 8–9.

Davison, J. (1998) 'Streets paved with style', *The Herald*, 21 January, p. 14.

Dean, D. (2005) 'Recruiting a self: women performers and aesthetic labour', *Work, Employment and Society*, 19(4): 761–74.

Dear, P. (2009) 'Does "Glaswegian" need translation?'. Available at: http://news.bbc.co.uk/2/hi/uk_news/magazine/8308288.stm (accessed 12 February 2020).

Department for Business, Energy and Industrial Strategy (DBEIS) (2019) *Trade Union Membership Statistics 2018*. Available at: https://assets.publishing.service.gov.uk/government/uploads

system/uploads/attachment_data/file/805268/trade-union-membership-2018-statistical-bulletin.pdf (accessed 2 February 2020).

Disney (2016) *The Disney Look*. Available at: https://disneycasting.net/downloads/wdpr/Disney_Look_Book.pdf (accessed 2 February 2020).

Donald, C. (2008) 'Greater success in store', *Sunday Herald*, 15 September, p. 11.

Donkin, R. (2010) *The Future of Work*. Basingstoke: Palgrave Macmillan.

Dunbar, R. (2012) 'Love is in the air: time to sniff out the perfect partner', *Observer*, 15 April, p. 23.

Dunn, C. (2018) 'Bowing incorrectly: aesthetic labor and expert knowledge in Japanese business etiquette training', in H. Cook and J. Shibamoto-Smith (eds), *Japanese at Work: Politeness, Power and Personae in Japanese Workplace Discourse*. Cham: Springer, pp. 15–36.

Dutton, E., Warhurst, C., Lloyd, C., James, S. and Commander, J. and Nickson, D. (2008) 'Just like the elves in Harry Potter: room attendants in UK hotels', in C. Lloyd, G. Mason and K. Mayhew (eds), *Low Paid Work in the United Kingdom*. New York: Russell Sage Foundation, pp. 97–130.

Dutton, H. and King, J. (1981) *Ten Per Cent and No Surrender*. Cambridge: Cambridge University Press.

Ectoff, N. (2000) *Survival of the Prettiest: The Science of Beauty*. London: Abacus.

Edwards, M. (2005) 'Employer and employee branding: HR or PR?', in S. Bach (ed.), *Managing Human Resources: Personnel Management in Transition* (4th edn). London: Blackwell, pp. 266–86.

Edwards, R. (1979) *Contested Terrain: The Transformation of the Workplace in the Twentieth Century*. London: Heinemann.

Ehrenreich, B. (2001) *Nickel and Dimed*. New York: Metropolitan.

Eikhof, D. and Warhurst, C. (2013) 'The promised land? Why social inequalities are systemic in the creative industries', *Employee Relations*, 35(5): 495–508.

Ellen, B. (2019) 'Dressing attendants as Mile-High Barbies is just a last blast of sexism', *Observer*, 21 April, p. 21.

Elliott, A. (2008) 'Saving face', *The Weekend Australian Magazine*, 10–11 May, pp. 32–4.

Engels, F. (1971[1845]) *The Condition of the Working Class in England* (2nd edn), translated by W.O. Henderson and W.H. Chaloner. Oxford: Blackwell.

Entwistle, J. (2002) 'The aesthetic economy', *Journal of Consumer Culture*, 2(3): 317–39.

Entwistle, J. and Wissinger, E. (2006) 'Keeping up appearances: aesthetic labour in the fashion modelling industries of London and New York', *The Sociological Review*, 54(4): 774–94.

Erickson, K. (2004) 'Performing service in American restaurants', *Space and Culture*, 7(1): 76–89.

European Commission (EC) (2010) *Europe 2020: A Strategy for Smart, Sustainable and Inclusive Growth*. Brussels: Publications Office of the European Union.

Eustace, E. (2012) 'Speaking allowed? Workplace regulation of regional dialect', *Work, Employment and Society*, 26(2): 331–48.

Everett, L. (2008) *Drop Dead Brilliant: Dazzle in the Workplace with Confidence and Panache!* New York: McGraw-Hill.

Experian (2016) 'Experian identifies which UK retail centres are best placed to survive and thrive'. Available at: www.experian.co.uk/marketing-services/news-retailscape-uk-retail-centres-best-placed-to-thrive.html (accessed 12 February 2020).

Fast, J. (1971) *Body Language*. London: Pan.

Fawcett Society (2018) *#MeToo One Year On – What's Changed?* Available at: www.fawcettsociety.org.uk/Handlers/Download.ashx?IDMF=8709c721-6d67-4d1f-8e30-11347c56a7c5 (accessed 12 February 2020).

Featherstone, M., Hepworth, M. and Turner, B. (eds) (1991) *The Body: Social Process and Cultural Theory*. London: Sage.

Felstead, A., Gallie, D., Green, F. and Zhou, Y. (2007) *Skills at Work 1986–2006*. ESRC Centre on Skills, Knowledge and Organizational Performance (SKOPE), Universities of Oxford and Cardiff.

Fine, G. (2009) *Kitchens*. Berkeley: University of California Press.

Finkelstein, L., Frautschy Demuth, R. and Sweeney, D. (2007) 'Bias against overweight job applicants: further explorations of when and why', *Human Resource Management*, 46(2): 208–22.

Fleming, N. (2008) 'Men seek perfect body through surgery'. Available at: www.telegraph.co.uk/news/uknews/1577523/Men-seek-a-perfect-body-through-surgery.html (accessed 12 February 2020).

Florida, R. (2004) *The Rise of the Creative Class*. New York: Basic Books.

Ford, H. (1991) *Ford on Management*. Oxford: Basil Blackwell.

Forte, S. (2002) 'Can I show you up?', *Financial Times*, Weekend Section, 26 and 27 January, p. 15.

Foster, C. (2004) 'Gendered retailing: a study of customer perceptions of front-line staff in the DIY sector', *International Journal of Retail and Distribution Management*, 32(9): 442–47.

Foster, C. and Resnick, S. (2013) 'Service worker appearance and the retail service encounter: the influence of gender and age', *Service Industries Journal*, 33(2): 236–47.

Foucault, M. (1979) *Discipline and Punish*. Harmondsworth: Penguin.

Foucault, M. (1981) *The History of Sexuality, Vol.1*. Harmondsworth: Penguin.

Fox, K. (2004) *Watching the English*. London: Hodder.

Freeland, C. (2001) *But Is It Art?* Oxford: Oxford University Press.

Freeman, H. (2001) 'Only the young and stylish need apply', *Guardian G2*, 13 February, p. 10.

Freeman, H. (2005) 'Who would hire you?', *Guardian Work*, 4 June. Available at: www.guardian.co.uk/money/2005/jun/04/careers.graduation1 (accessed 12 February 2020).

Frey, H. (2015) '"Borgata babes" case: the weighty matter of appearance standards', *Widener Law Review*, 21(1): 95–116.

Gabbatt, A. (2011) 'Pressure on men to maintain their looks', *Guardian*, 11 June, p. 14.

Gagliardi, P. (1996) 'Exploring the aesthetic side of organizational life', in S.R. Clegg, C. Hardy and W. Nord (eds), *Handbook of Organizational Studies*. London: Sage, pp. 565–80.

Gallie, D. (2007) 'Production regimes, employment regimes and the quality of work', in D. Gallie (ed.), *Employment Regimes and the Quality of Work*. Oxford: Oxford University Press, pp. 1–33.

Gallo, C. (2016) 'The JW Marriott brand partners with ballet dancers to gain a competitive edge'. Available at: www.forbes.com/sites/carminegallo/2016/09/30/the-jw-marriott-brand-partners-with-ballet-dancers-to-gain-a-competitive-edge/#2812690d590a (accessed 12 February 2020).

Gardner, D. (1999) 'Z marks the spot for shopping gold', *Sunday Herald*, 23 May, p. 6.

Gatta, M. (2011) 'In the "blink" of an eye – American high-end small retail businesses and the public workforce system', in I. Grugulis and O. Bozkurt (eds), *Retail Work*. Basingstoke: Palgrave MacMillan, pp. 49–67.

Giddens, A. (1991) *Modernity and Self-Identity*. Cambridge: Polity.

Gillingham, J. (2009) 'The beginnings of English imperialism', in J. Mudoon (ed.), *The North Atlantic Frontier of Medieval Europe*. Farnham: Ashgate, pp. 71–88.

Gimlin, D. (2000) 'Cosmetic surgery: beauty as commodity', *Qualitative Sociology*, 23(1): 77–99.

Gimlin, D. (2006) 'The absent body project: cosmetic surgery as a response to bodily dys-appearance', *Sociology*, 40(4): 699–716.

Glasgow City Council (2016) *Glasgow Economic Strategy 2016–2023*. Available at: www.glasgow.gov.uk/CHttpHandler.ashx?id=36137&p=0 (accessed 12 February 2020).

Goffman, E. (1959) *Presentation of Self in Everyday Life*. New York: Anchor.

Goffman, E. (1963) *Behavior in Public Places*. New York: Free Press.

Gold, T. (2011) 'L'Oréal's pulled adverts: this ideal of female beauty is an abomination', *Guardian*, 29 July. Available at: www.theguardian.com/commentisfree/2011/jul/29/loreal-adverts-pulled-by-asa-beauty-tanya-gold (accessed 12 February 2020).

Good, L. and Cooper, R. (2016) '"But it's your job to be friendly": employees coping with and contesting sexual harassment from customers in the service sector', *Gender, Work and Organization*, 23(5): 447–69.

Government Equalities Office (2018) *Dress Codes and Sex Discrimination – What You Need to Know*. Available at: https://assets.publishing.service.gov.uk/government/uploads/system/uploads/attachment_data/file/709535/dress-code-guidance-may2018-2.pdf (accessed 12 February 2020).

Grene, N. (2010) 'Introduction', in G.B. Shaw, *Pygmalion*. Camberwell: Penguin.

Groom, N. (2006) *The Union Jack*. London: Atlantic.

Grosz, E. (1994) *Volatile Bodies: Toward a Corporeal Feminism.* Bloomington: Indiana University Press.

Grugulis, I. and Lloyd, C. (2010) 'Skill and the labour process: the conditions and consequences of change', in P. Thompson and C. Smith (eds), *Working Life.* London: Palgrave Macmillan, pp. 91–112.

Gruys, K. (2012) '"Does this make me look fat?": aesthetic labor and fat talk as emotional labor in a women's plus-size clothing store', *Social Problems*, 59(4): 481–500.

Gubbins, T. (2016) 'Even scantily clad servers couldn't make it happen for this Dallas restaurant'. Available at: http://dallas.culturemap.com/news/restaurants-bars/08-10-16-tallywackers-underwear-clad-servers-closes/ (accessed 12 February 2020).

Gumin, M. (2012) 'Ugly on the inside: an argument for a narrow interpretation of employer defences to appearance discrimination', *Minnesota Law Review*, 96(5): 1769–94.

Gurney, C.M. and Hines, F. (1999) 'Rattle and Hum – Gendered Accounts of Noise as a Pollutant: An Aural Sociology of Work and Home', paper presented at the British Sociological Conference, Glasgow.

Habia (2017) *Habia Industry Overview for the Hair and Beauty Industry.* Available at: www.habia.org/industry-overview/ (accessed 12 February 2020).

Hakim, C. (2010) 'Erotic capital', *European Sociological Review*, 26(5): 499–518.

Hakim, C. (2011) *Honey Money: The Power of Erotic Capital.* London: Penguin.

Hall, E. (1993) 'Smiling, deferring and flirting: doing gender and giving "good service"', *Work and Occupations*, 20(4): 452–71.

Hall, R. and van den Broek, D. (2012) 'Aestheticizing retail workers: orientations of aesthetic labour in Australian fashion retail', *Economic and Industrial Democracy*, 33(1): 85–102.

Hamermesh, D. (2011) *Beauty Pays: Why Attractive People Are More Successful.* Princeton: Princeton University Press.

Hamermesh, D. and Biddle, J. (1994) 'Beauty and the labour market', *American Economic Review*, 84(5): 1174–94.

Hanks, W.F. (2005) 'Pierre Bourdieu and the practices of language', *Annual Review of Anthropology*, 34: 67–83.

Harker, R., Mahar, C. and Wilkes, C. (1990) *An Introduction to the Work of Pierre Bourdieu.* London: Macmillan.

Harper, B. (2000) 'Beauty, stature and the labour market', *Oxford Bulletin of Economics and Statistics*, 62(s1): 771–800.

Harquail, C. (2005) 'Employees as animate artefacts: employee branding by "wearing the brand"', in A. Rafaeli and M.G. Pratt (eds), *Artifacts and Organizations.* Marwah, NJ: Lawrence Erlbaum, pp. 161–80.

Harrison, J. (2019) 'Glasgow is voted one of top 10 world cities', *Herald*, 14 March, p. 5.

Harvey, G., Vachhani, S. and Williams, K. (2014) 'Working out: aesthetic labour, affect and the fitness industry personal trainer', *Leisure Studies*, 33(5): 454–70.

Haslam, D. (2000) *Manchester, England*. London: Fourth Estate.

Hattenstone, S. (2013) 'Rafe's progress', *Guardian*, weekend magazine, 19 February, pp. 16–21.

Haunschild, A. and Eikhof, D.R. (2009) 'From HRM to employment rules and lifestyles: theory development through qualitative case study research into the creative industries', *Zeitschrift für Personalforschung – German Journal of Human Resource Research*, 23(2): 107–24.

Hawkes, H. (2016) 'Can cosmetic surgery give you a professional lift?'. Available at: www.intheblack.com/articles/2016/05/01/can-cosmetic-surgery-give-you-a-professional-lift (accessed 12 February 2020).

Hay, O. and Middlemiss, S. (2003) 'Fashion victims, dress to conform to the norm, or else? Comparative analysis of legal protection against employers' appearance codes in the United Kingdom and the United States', *International Journal of Discrimination and Law*, 6(1): 69–102.

He, L. (2018) 'China's cosmetic surgery boom doesn't look pretty when it comes to profits', *South China Morning Post*, 20 July. Available at: www.scmp.com/business/markets/article/2090105/chinas-cosmetic-surgery-boom-doesnt-look-pretty-when-it-comes (accessed 12 February 2020).

Health and Safety Executive (HSE) (2010) *Stress Related and Psychological Disorders*. London: HSE.

Heilbroner, R. (1995) *The Worldly Philosophers*. London: Penguin.

Helmefalk, M. and Berndt, A. (2018) 'Shedding light on the use of single and multisensory cues and their effect on consumer behaviours', *International Journal of Retail and Distribution Management*, 46(11/12): 1077–91.

Henderson, C. (1999) 'Style city seeks designer workforce', *Sunday Herald*, 7 November, p. 4.

Hochschild, A. (1983) *The Managed Heart*. Berkeley: University of California Press.

Hofmann, D., Burke, M. and Zohar, D. (2017) '100 years of occupational safety research: from basic protections and work analysis to a multilevel view of workplace safety and risk', *Journal of Applied Psychology*, 102(3): 375–88.

Holland, P. (1987) 'When a woman reads the news', in H. Baehr and G. Dyer (eds), *Boxed In: Women and Television*. London: Pandora, pp. 130–50.

Holley, P. (2015) 'There's finally a Hooters-style restaurant featuring men. It's called Tallywackers', *Washington Post*, 2 June. Available at: www.washingtonpost.com/news/morning-mix/wp/2015/06/02/theres-finally-a-hooters-style-restaurant-for-women-its-called-tallywackers/?noredirect=on&utm_term=.515f6945ebfe (accessed 2 February 2020).

Honey, J. (1989) *Does Accent Matter?* London: Faber and Faber.

Hopfl, H. (2000) '"*Suaviter in modo, fortiter in re*": appearance, reality and the early Jesuits', in S. Linstead and H. Hopfl (eds), *The Aesthetics of Organization*.London: Sage, pp. 197–211.

House of Commons (2017a) *High Heels and Workplace Dress Codes*. Available at: https://publications.parliament.uk/pa/cm201617/cmselect/cmpetitions/291/291.pdf (accessed 12 February 2020).

House of Commons (2017b) *High Heels and Workplace Dress Codes: Government Response to the First Joint Report of the Petitions Committee and the Women and Equalities Committee of Session 2016–17*. Available at: https://publications.parliament.uk/pa/cm201617/cmselect/cmpetitions/1147/1147.pdf (accessed 12 February 2020).

House of Commons Library (2019) *Service Industries: Key Economic Indicators*. London: House of Commons.

Howarth, M. (2000) 'You're too grubby to get a job', *The Scottish Sun*, 7 June, pp. 1–2.

Hracs, B. and Leslie, D. (2014) 'Aesthetic labour in creative industries: the case of independent musicians in Toronto, Canada', *Area*, 46(1), 66–73.

HSBC (2002) 'HSBC launches new advertising campaign'. www.hsbcusa.com/ourcompany/bankarchives/bk2002/news_hbarch031102.html.

Huczynski, A. (1996) *Influencing Within Organizations*. Hemel Hempstead: Prentice Hall.

Huczynski, A. (2004) *Influencing Within Organizations* (2nd edn). London: Routledge.

Hudson, A. (2018) 'How much is too much for a man to spend on grooming?', *Metro*, 18 August. Available at: https://metro.co.uk/2018/08/18/how-much-is-too-much-for-a-man-to-spend-on-grooming-7852774/ (accessed 6 April 2020).

Huebner, L. (2008) '"It is part of the job": waitresses and nurses define sexual harassment', *Sociological Viewpoints*, Fall: 75–90.

Huggins, M. (2015) 'Not "fit" for hire: the United States and France on weight discrimination in employment', *Fordham International Law Journal*, 38(3): 888–951.

Hurley, J., Fernández-Macías, E., Antón, J.I., Muñoz de Bustillo Llorente, R. Anxo, D., Franz, C. Kümmerling, A., Oesch, D., Murphy, E., Grimshaw, D., Rafferty, A., Gimpelson, V. Kapeliushnikov, R., Soon Hwang, S., Warhurst, C., Wright, S., Whelan, S., Teicher, J. Yang, D., Jie, C., Xiaobo, Q., Dwyer, R., Wright E.O. and Kambayashi, R. (2015) *Upgrading or Polarisation? Long-term and Global Shifts in the Employment Structure*. Dublin Eurofound.

Huzell, H. and Larsson, P. (2012) 'Aesthetic and athletic employees: the negative outcome of employers assuming responsibility for sickness benefits', *Economic and Industrial Democracy*, 33(1): 103–23.

Income Data Services (IDS) (2001) *Corporate Clothing and Dress Codes*, IDS Studies, Spring London: IDS.

Industrial Relations Law Bulletin (1993) 'Dress and appearance at work', *Industrial Relations Law Bulletin*, March, 2–13.

Industrial Relations Services (IRS) (2000) 'Dressed to impress', *IRS Employment Trends*, No 695, pp. 4–16.

Industrial Relations Services (IRS) (2003) 'Suits you, sir: policies on clothing and appearance', *IRS Employment Trends*, No. 783, pp. 8–17.

Industrial Relations Services (IRS) (2005) 'Style police: more employers tighten up on appearance', *IRS Employment Review*, No. 816, pp. 8–15.

Inge, S. (2018) 'Female academics told image more important than quality of work', *Times Higher Education*, 25 January, p. 9.

International Society of Aesthetic Plastic Surgery (2018) 'Latest international survey shows global rise in cosmetic surgery'. Available at: www.isaps.org/wp-content/uploads/2018/10/2017-Global-Survey-Press-Release-Demand-for-Cosmetic-Surgery-Procedures-Around-The-World-Continues-To-Skyrocket_2_RW.pdf (accessed 12 February 2020).

Invest Glasgow (2018a) *Hotel Prospectus*. Available at: http://investglasgow.com/wp-content/uploads/2018/03/GLASGOW_HOTEL_PROSPECTUS.pdf (accessed 12 February 2020).

Invest Glasgow (2018b) *Retail Prospectus*. Available at: http://investglasgow.com/wp-content/uploads/2018/03/GLASGOW_RETAIL_PROSPECTUS.pdf (accessed 12 February 2020).

Jackson, M., Goldthorpe, J. and Mills, C. (2002) 'Education, Employers and Class Mobility', paper presented at the International Sociological Association Research Committee 28 on Social Stratification and Mobility, 10–13 April, Oxford.

James, J. (1999) *Bodytalk*. London: Industrial Society.

James, S., Warhurst, C., Tholen, G. and Commander, J. (2013) 'What we know and what we need to know about graduate skills', *Work, Employment and Society*, 27(6): 952–63.

Jeffes, S. (1998) *Appearance is Everything*. Pittsburgh, PA: Sterling House.

Jenkins, R. (2002) *Pierre Bourdieu*. London: Routledge.

Johnston, A. and Sandberg, A. (2008) 'Controlling service work: an ambiguous accomplishment between employees, management and customers', *Journal of Consumer Culture*, 8(3): 389–417.

Johnston, G., Sanscartier, M. and Johnston, M. (2019) 'Retail therapy: making meaning out of menial labour', *Journal of Sociology*, 55(3): 446–62.

Johnston, R. (2008) 'Pure dead brilliant', *i-on Glasgow*, August, pp. 46–7.

Johnstone, A. (1997) 'An engaging new line in sales talk', *Herald*, 14 August, p. 13.

Jones, G. (2010) *Beauty Imagined: A History of the Global Beauty Industry*. Oxford: Oxford University Press.

Jones, O. (2011) *Chavs: The Demonization of the Working Class*. London: Verso.

Jung, H. (2015) 'Abercrombie and Fitch will no longer hire people based on sexy looks'. Available at: www.cosmopolitan.com/style-beauty/news/a39534/abercrombie-fitch-overhauls-policies/ (accessed 20 February 2020).

Kalleberg, A.L., Fuller, S. and Pullman, A. (2020) 'Job quality in the United States and Canada' in C. Warhurst, C. Mathieu and R. Dwyer (eds), *The Oxford Handbook of Job Quality*. Oxford: Oxford University Press.

Karlsson, J. (2012) 'Looking good and sounding right: aesthetic labour', *Economic and Industrial Democracy*, 33(1): 51–64.

Karpf, A. (2011) 'Surgery won't fix Ed's voice', *Guardian*, 30 July, p. 33.

Kasperkevie, J. (2015) 'Abercrombie & Fitch employees embrace death of sexualized dress code'. Available at: www.theguardian.com/business/2015/apr/26/abercrombie-fitch-ditches-sexualised-marketing-policy (accessed 8 April 2020).

Kaufman, B.E. (2004) *Theoretical Perspectives on Work and the Employment Relationship.* Princeton, NJ: Industrial Relations Research Association.

Kemp, K. (2008) 'St James carbuncle to be replaced by Continental-style retail quarter', *Sunday Herald*, 2 November, p. 83.

Kenner, M. (2018) 'Employers could face action for telling women what to wear'. Available at: www.peoplemanagement.co.uk/news/articles/employers-face-action-telling-women-wear (accessed 8 April 2020).

Kerner, I. (2012) 'Questions of intersectionality: reflections on the current debate in German gender studies', *European Journal of Women's Studies*, 19(2): 203–218.

Key Note (2008) *Cosmetic Surgery Market Report 2008.* Hampton: Key Note.

Kim, J., Ju, H. and Johnson, K. (2009) 'Sales associate appearance: links to consumers' emotions, store image and purchases', *Journal of Retailing and Consumer Services*, 16(5): 407–23.

Kinchin, P. (1998) *Taking Tea with Mackintosh.* Fullbridge: Pomegranate.

King, R., Winchester, D. and Sherwyn, D. (2006) '"You (don't) look marvellous": considerations for employers regulating employee appearance', *Cornell Hotel and Restaurant Administration Quarterly*, 47(4): 359–68.

Knox, A. (2013) 'Temping at the Top: "High End" Temporary Work Agency Employment', paper presented at the 27th Conference of the Association of Industrial Relations Academics of Australia and New Zealand (AIRAANZ), Freemantle.

Koller, V. (2007) '"The world's local bank": glocalization as a strategy in corporate branding discourse, *Social Semiotics*, 17(1): 111–31.

Korczynski, M. (2002) *Human Resource Management in the Service Sector.* Basingstoke: Palgrave

Korczynski, M. and Ott, U. (2004) 'When production and consumption meet', *Journal of Management Studies*, 41(4): 575–99.

Kristof, A. (1996) 'Person–organization fit: an integrative review of its conceptualizations, measurement, and implications', *Personnel Psychology*, 49(1): 1–49.

Laabs, J. (1995) 'Does image matter?', *Personnel Journal*, December, 48–61.

Labour Research Department (LRD) (2016) 'Heads not heels should rule when drawing up dress codes', *Workplace Report*, July, pp. 15–17.

Labour Research Department (2019) 'Duty to prevent sexual harassment demanded', *Labour Research*, August, p. 24.

Lambert, T. (n.d.) *A Brief History of Preston.* Available at: www.localhistories.org (accessed 12 February 2020).

Lee, S. (2015) 'Beauty pays but does investment in beauty pay?', *IZA World of Labour*, 198: 1–9.

Lennon, M. (2014) 'Glasgow the brand: whose story is it anyway?', in T. Brabazon (ed.) *City Imaging: Regeneration, Renewal and Decay.* London: Springer, pp. 13–24.

Lindsay, C. and McQuaid, R. (2004) 'Avoiding the "McJobs": unemployed job seekers and attitudes to service work', *Work, Employment and Society*, 18(2): 297–319.

The List (2004) *The Guide to Scotland's Cities*. Edinburgh: The List Ltd.

Little, S. (2004) *...isms: Understanding Art*. New York: Universal.

Loe, M. (1996) 'Working for men at the intersection of power, gender and sexuality', *Sociological Enquiry*, 66(4): 399–421.

Lowe, M. and Crewe, L. (1996) 'Shop work: image, customer care and the restructuring of retail employment', in N. Wrigley and M. Lowe (eds), *Retailing, Consumption and Capital: Towards the New Retail Geography*. Harlow: Longman, pp. 196–207.

Lucas, R. (1997) 'Youth, gender and part-time work – students in the labour process', *Work, Employment and Society*, 11(4): 595–614.

Lusher, A. (2001) 'Solicitor wants right to wear wig and gown in court', *Sunday Telegraph*, 11 February, p. 21.

Lyle, J. (1990) *Body Language: Read the Hidden Codes and Maximize Your Potential*. London: BCA.

Macdonald, C.L. and Merrill, D. (2009) 'Intersectionality in the emotional proletariat: a new lens on employment discrimination in service work', in M. Korczynski and C.L. Macdonald (eds), *Service Work: Critical Perspectives*. Abingdon: Taylor & Francis, pp. 113–33.

Maconie, S. (2009) *Adventures on the High Teas: In Search of Middle England*. London: Ebury.

Madera, J., Guchait, P. and Dawson, M. (2018) 'Managers' reactions to customer vs co-worker sexual harassment', *International Journal of Contemporary Hospitality Management*, 30(2): 1211–27

Magnini, V., Baker, M. and Karande, K. (2013) 'The frontline provider's appearance: a driver of guest perceptions', *Cornell Hospitality Quarterly*, 54(4): 396–405.

Maitra, S. and Maitra, S. (2018) 'Producing the aesthetic self: an analysis of aesthetic skill and labour in the organized retail industries in India', *Journal of South Asian Development*, 13(3): 337–57.

Malvern, J. (2009) 'Abercrombie & Fitch told to pay disabled worker Riam Dean £9,000', *The Times*, 14 August. Available at: www.timesonline.co.uk/tol/news/uk/article6795327 (accessed 12 February 2020).

Mangan, L. (2014) 'Let's hear it for the cheerleader suing her team', *Guardian*, G2, 17 February, p. 3.

Marriage, M. (2018) 'Men only: inside the charity fundraiser where hostesses are put on show', *Financial Times*, 23 January. Available at: www.ft.com/content/075d679e-0033-11e8-9650-9c0ad2d7c5b5 (accessed 2 February 2020).

Martin, E. and McCabe, S. (2007) 'Part-time work and postgraduate students: developing the skills for employment?', *Journal of Hospitality, Leisure, Sport and Tourism Education*, 6(2): 29–40.

Marx, K. (1946[1887]) *Capital: A Critical Analysis of Capitalist Production*. London: Allen and Unwin.

McDowell, L. (2009) *Working Bodies: Interactive Service Employment and Workplace Identities*. Chichester: Wiley.

McDowell, L., Batnitzky, A. and Dyer, S. (2007) 'Division, segmentation, and interpellation: the embodied labours of migrant workers in a Greater London hotel', *Economic Geography*, 83(1): 1–25.

McGinley, A. (2006) 'Harassment of sex(y) workers: applying Title VII to sexualized industries', *Yale Journal of Law and Feminism*, 18(1): 65–108.

McGinley, A. (2007a) 'Babes and beefcake: exclusive hiring arrangements and sexy dress codes', *Duke Journal of Gender, Law and Policy*, 14(1): 257–83.

McGinley, A. (2007b) 'Harassing "girls" at the Hard Rock: masculinities in sexualized environments', *University of Illinois Law Review*, 4. 1229–78.

McIntyre Petersson, M. (2014) 'Commodifying passion: the fashion of aesthetic labour', *Journal of Cultural Economy*, **7**(1): 79–94.

McRae, H. (2001) 'Look good, talk well and smell less: all keys to success', *Independent*, 14 February, p. 2.

Mears, A. (2012) 'Book review of *Beauty Pays: Why Attractive People Are More Successful*', *Contemporary Sociology*, 41(6): 814–15.

Mears, A. and Connell, C. (2016) 'The paradoxical value of deviant cases: towards a gendered theory of display work', *Signs: Journal of Women in Culture and Society*, 41(2). 333–59.

Mellahi, K. and Harris, L. (2016) 'Response rates in business and management research an overview of current practice and suggestions for future direction', *British Journal of Management*, 27(2): 426–37.

Metro (2002) 'Guess which accent is rated the most honest?, 5 June, p. 9.

Michael, A. (2000) *Best Impressions in Hospitality*. Albany, NY: Delmar.

Middlemiss, S. (2018) 'Not what to wear? Employers' liability for dress codes?', *Internationa Journal of Discrimination and the Law*, 18(1): 40–51.

Mills, A. (2006) *Sex, Strategy and the Stratosphere: Airlines and the Gendering of Organizationa Culture*. Basingstoke: Palgrave Macmillan.

Mills, C.W. (1951) *White Collar*. New York: Oxford University Press.

Mills. C.W. (2000[1959]) *The Sociological Imagination*. Oxford: Oxford University Press.

Misra, J. and Walters, K. (2016) 'All fun and cool clothes? Youth workers' consumer iden tity in clothing retail', *Work and Occupations*, 43(3): 294–325.

Mitra, B., Webb, M. and Wolfe, C. (2014) 'Audience responses to the physical appear ance of television newsreaders', *Participations: Journal of Audience and Reception Studies* 11(2): 45–57.

Moffitt, L. and Szymanski, D. (2011) 'Experiencing sexually objectifying environments: a qualitative study', *The Counselling Psychologist*, 39(1): 67–101.

Moore, H. (2014) 'Controversial Abercrombie & Fitch CEO Michael Jefferies to retire', *The Guardian*. Available at: www.theguardian.com/business/2014/dec/09/controversial-abercrombie-fitch-ceo-michael-jeffries-to-retire (accessed 7 April 2020).

Morgan, D. (2002) 'You too can have a body like mine' in S. Jackson and S. Scott (eds) Gender: A sociological reader, London: Routledge, pp. 406–22.

Morrish, J. (1999) 'The accent that dare not speak its name', *Independent on Sunday*, 21 March, p. 20.

Morrison, M., Gan, S., Dubelaar, C. and Oppewal, H. (2011) 'In-store music and aroma influences on shopper behaviour and satisfaction', *Journal of Business Research*, 64(6): 558–64.

Moshakis, A. (2019) 'The evolution of man', *Observer Magazine*, 17 March, pp. 20–5.

Moss, P. and Tilly, C. (2001) *Stories Employers Tell*. New York: Russell Sage Foundation.

Muñoz de Bustillo, R., Fernández-Macías, E., Antón J.I. and Esteve, F. (2011) *Measuring More Than Money*. Cheltenham: Edward Elgar.

Nath, V. (2011) 'Aesthetic and emotional labour through stigma: national identity management and racial abuse in offshored Indian call centres', *Work, Employment and Society*, 25(4): 709–25.

Nath, V., Bach, S., and Lockwood, G. (2016) *Dress Codes and Appearance at Work: Body Supplements, Body Modification and Aesthetic Labour*. London: ACAS Research Paper 07/16.

Neate, R. (2018) 'Presidents Club scandal: hostess agent promises "never again"', *Guardian*, 31 July. Available at: www.theguardian.com/uk-news/2018/jul/31/agent-for-hostesses-at-notorious-presidents-club-event-makes-ehrc-pledge (accessed 12 February 2020).

Nelson, K. and Bowen, J. (2000) 'The effect of employee uniforms on employee satisfaction', *Cornell, Hotel and Restaurant Administration Quarterly*, 41(2): 86–95.

Newton-Francis, M. and Young, G. (2015) 'Not winging it at Hooters: conventions for producing a cultural object of sexual fantasy', *Poetics*, 52: 1–17.

Nickson, D. and Baum, T. (2017) 'Young at heart, but what about my body? Age and aesthetic labour in the hospitality and retail industries', in E. Parry and J. McCarthy (eds), *The Palgrave Handbook of Age Diversity and Work*. Basingstoke: Palgrave Macmillan, pp. 539–59.

Nickson, D., Timming, A., Re, D. and Perrett, D. (2016) 'Subtle increases in BMI within a healthy weight range still reduce women's employment chances in the service sector', *PLoS ONE*, 11, 9, e0159659, 1–14.

Nickson, D., Warhurst, C., Commander, J., Hurrell, S. and Cullen, A.M. (2012) 'Soft skills and employability: evidence from UK Retail', *Economic and Industrial Democracy*, 33(1): 62–81.

Nickson, D., Warhurst, C., Cullen, A.M. and Watt, A. (2003) 'Bringing in the excluded? Aesthetic labour, skills and training in the new economy', *Journal of Education and Work*, 16(2): 185–203.

Nickson, D., Warhurst, C. and Dutton, E. (2005) 'The importance of attitude and appearance in the service encounter in retail and hospitality', *Managing Service Quality*, 15(2): 195–208.

Nickson, D., Warhurst, C., Witz, A. and Cullen, A.M. (2001) 'The importance of being aesthetic: work, employment and service organization', in A. Sturdy, I. Grugulis, and H. Wilmott (eds), *Customer Service: Empowerment and Entrapment*. Basingstoke: Palgrave, pp. 170–90.

Nienhüser, W. and Warhurst, C. (2018) 'Comparative employment relations: definitional, disciplinary and development issues', in C. Brewster and W. Mayrhofer (eds), *Handbook of Research in Comparative Human Resource Management* (2nd edn). Aldershot: Edward Elgar, pp. 200–22.

Nieuwesteeg, T. (2015) 'Diners, drive-ins and dicks'. Available at: https://melmagazine.com/en-us/story/diners-drive-ins-and-dicks (accessed 12 February 2020).

Nisbet, J. (2006) 'Plastic surgery saved our jobs', *Daily Mail*, 12 April, pp. 22–3.

Nixon, D. (2009) '"I can't put a smiley face on": working-class masculinity, emotional labour and service work in the "New Economy"', *Gender, Work and Organization*, 16(3) 300–22.

Nordstrom, K. and Ridderstrale, J. (2002) *Funky Business*. London: Financial Times Prentice Hall.

Novaresse, A. (1997) 'Language barrier?', *Scotsman*, 31 January, p. 12.

Observer Magazine (2018) 'This much I know: Diane Abbott', 28 January, p. 9.

Odum, S. (2016) 'Is it time to ditch the dress code?', *People Management*, November pp. 44–6.

Ogbonna, E. (1992) 'Organizational culture and human resource management', in P. Blyton and P. Turnbull (eds), *Reassessing Human Resource Management*. London: Sage pp. 74–96.

OK! Magazine (2011) 'I blew my chance of being a Von Trapp', 8 November, no.801 pp. 79–81.

O'Kelly, L. (2017) 'Q & A: Clive Myrie', *Observer New Review*, 3 December, p. 4.

Olins, W. (1991) *Corporate Identity*. London: Thames and Hudson.

Oppenheim, M. (2019) 'Norwegian Air tells female staff they must carry doctor's note at all times if they want to wear flat shoes', *The Independent*, 18 April. Available at: www.independent.co.uk/travel/news-and-advice/norweigan-air-female-staff-flat-shoes-doctors-note-heels-a8872321.html (accessed 12 February 2020).

Otis, E. (2012) *Markets and Bodies: Women, Service Work, and the Making of Inequality in China*. Stanford, CA: Stanford University Press.

Otis, E. (2016) 'China's beauty proletariat: the body politics of hegemony in a Walmart cosmetics department', *Positions*, 24(1): 156–77.

Ottensmeyer, E. (1996) 'Too strong to stop, too sweet to lose: aesthetics as a way to know organizations', *Organization* 3(2): 189–94.

Overell, S. (2006) *Paradigm Trades: The Iconic Jobs of the Early 21st Century*. London: Work Foundation.

Ozanne, M., Tews, M. and Mattila, A. (2019) 'Are tattoos still a taboo? The effect of employee tattoos on customers' service failure perceptions', *International Journal of Contemporary Hospitality Management*, 31(2): 874–88.

Packer, A. (2002) 'Has she got news ...', *Sunday Express*, S magazine, 25–31 August, pp. 14–16.

Pagliarini, T. (2014) 'It can't get that ugly; why employers should be able to take aesthetics into consideration', *Roger Williams University Law Review*, 19(1): 277–315.

Parmentier, M.A., Fischer, E. and Reuber, A.R. (2013) 'Positioning person brands in established organizational fields', *Journal of the Academy of Marketing Science*, 41(3): 373–87.

People Management (2019) 'Smells like team spirit', *People Management*, March, p. 7.

Pettinger, L. (2002) 'Aesthetic Labour and Retail Work: Why Dorothy Perkins Doesn't Work at French Connection', paper presented at the 20th Annual International Labour Process Conference, 2–4 April, Glasgow.

Pettinger, L. (2004) 'Brand culture and branded workers: service work and aesthetic labour in fashion retail', *Consumption, Markets and Culture*, 7(2): 165–84.

Pettinger, L. (2005) 'Gendered work meets gendered goods: selling and service in clothing retail', *Gender, Work and Organization*, 12(5): 460–78.

Pidd, H. (2009) 'Disabled student sues Abercrombie & Fitch for discrimination', *Guardian*, 24 June. Available at: www.guardian.co.uk/money/2009/jun/24/abercrombie-fitch-tribunal-riam-dean (accessed 12 February 2020).

Porter, M.E. (1980) *Competitive Strategy: Techniques for Analyzing Industries and Competitors*. New York: Free Press.

Poster, W.R. (2007) 'Who's on the line? Indian call center agents pose as Americans for US-outsourced firms', *Industrial Relations*, 46(2): 271–304.

Postrel, V. (2004) *The Substance of Style*. New York: HarperCollins.

Pounders, K., Babin, B. and Close, A. (2015) 'All the same to me: outcomes of aesthetic labour performed by frontline service providers', *Journal of the Academy of Marketing Science*, 43(6): 670–93.

Poutvaara, P. (2017) 'How do candidates' looks effect their election chances?', *IZA World of Labor*, 370: 1–11.

Preston, P. (2008) 'Serious sexism on TV news', *Observer*, Business & Media, 31 August, p. 10.

Pyrillis, R. (2010) 'Body of work', *Workforce Management*, November, pp. 20–22, 24, 26, 28.

Quach, S., Jebarajakirthy, C. and Thaichon, P. (2017) 'Aesthetic labour and visible diversity: the role in retailing service encounters', *Journal of Retailing and Consumer Services*, 38(September): 34–43.

Quilantan, V. (2015) 'Tallywackers is like Hooters, but with dicks'. Available at: www.vice.com/en_uk/article/mvxvn3/tallywackers-is-like-hooters-but-with-dicks-456 (accessed 2 February 2020).

Quinn, B. (2008) 'Aesthetic labour, rocky horrors, and the 007 dynamic', *International Journal of Tourism and Hospitality Research*, 2(1): 77–85.

Rackham, A. (2018) 'Kylie Jenner and the celebrity surgery effect', 10 July. Available at: www.bbc.co.uk/news/entertainment-arts-44767897 (accessed 2 February 2020).

Rafaeli, A. (1993) 'Dress and behaviour of customer contact employees: a framework for analysis', *Services Marketing and Management*, 2: 175–211.

Rafaeli, A. and Pratt, M. (1993) 'Tailored meanings: on the meaning and impact of organizational dress', *Academy of Management Review*, 18(1): 32–55.

Raffler-Engel, W. (1983) *Non-Verbal Behaviour in the Career Interview*. Amsterdam: John Benjamins.

Ramjattan, V. (2019) 'Raciolinguistics and the aesthetic labourer', *Journal of Industrial Relations*, 61(5): 726–38.

Rasmusson, S. (2011) '"We're real here": Hooters girls, big tips and provocative research methods', *Cultural Studies and Critical Methodologies*, 11(6): 574–85.

Rayner, G. (2008) 'Beijing 2008 Olympics: China gets ready to smile for the cameras', *The Telegraph*, 11 July. Available at: www.telegraph.co.uk/news/features/3637262/Beijing-2008-Olympics-China-gets-ready-to-smile-for-the-cameras.html (accessed 12 February 2020).

Reid, A. (2003) 'Understanding teachers' work: is there still a place for labour process theory?', *British Journal of Sociology of Education*, 24(5): 559–73.

Reidy, J. (2010) *Hard Sell*. Kansas City: Andrews McMeel.

Ren, X. (2017) 'Exploiting women's aesthetic labour to fly high in the Chinese airline industry', *Gender in Management*, 32(6): 386–403.

Rhode, D. (2010) *The Beauty Bias: The Injustice of Appearance in Life and Law*. Oxford: Oxford University Press.

Rhodes, C. (2018) *Retail Sector in the UK*. London: House of Commons Library.

Ricard-Wolf, A. (2005) 'Bodysplash statt Bier', *Managermagazin*, 4: 210–14.

Richardson, H. (2011) 'Free parenting classes to run in England'. Available at: www.bbc.co.uk/news/education-15312216 (accessed on 7 April 2020).

Riegel, B. (2013) *Up in the Air*. New York: Simon and Schuster.

Ritzer, G. (2000) *Sociological Theory*. New York: McGraw-Hill.

Robbins, T. (2006) 'Prêt a dormer from £1 a night', *Observer*, Escape, 27 August, p. 5.

Roberts, S. (2011) '"The lost boys": an overlooked detail in retail', in I. Grugulis and O. Bozkurt (eds), *Retail Work*. Basingstoke: Palgrave Macmillan, pp. 128–48.

Roberts, S. (2013) 'Boys will be boys...won't they? Change and continuities in contemporary young working class masculinities', *Sociology*, 47(4): 671–86.

Ross, A. (2009) *Nice Work If You Can Get It.* New York: New York University Press.

Rowe, S. (2013) 'Hooters: 30 years old and no sign of growing up', *Daily Telegraph*, 4 October. Available at: www.telegraph.co.uk/men/thinking-man/10353858/Hooters-30-years-old-and-no-sign-of-growing-up.html (accessed 12 February 2020).

Rudgard, O. (2018) 'Presidents Club dinner: treatment of female staff "fell short of what would be expected in the 21st century", says watchdog', *Daily Telegraph*, 13 July. Available at: www.telegraph.co.uk/news/2018/07/12/presidents-club-dinner-treatment-female-staff-fell-short-would/ (accessed 12 February 2020).

Rule, J. (1991) *The Labouring Classes in Early Industrial England 1750–1850.* London: Longman.

Saner, E. (2012) 'Abercrombie & Fitch: for beautiful people only', *Guardian*, 28 April. Available at: www.theguardian.com/fashion/2012/apr/28/abercrombie-fitch-savile-row (accessed 2 February 2020).

Scarpetta, S. (2014) 'What an inclusive recovery needs is more, and better, jobs', OECD Observer. Available at: http://oecdobserver.org/news/fullstory.php/aid/4521/What_an_inclusive_recovery_needs_is_more,_and_better,_jobs__.html (accessed 12 February 2020).

Schaubroeck, J. and Jones, J.R. (2000) 'Antecedents of workplace emotional labor dimensions and moderators of their effects on physical symptoms', *Journal of Organizational Behavior*, 21(2): 163–83.

Schmitt, B. and Simonson, A. (1997) *Marketing Aesthetics.* New York: The Free Press.

Schneider, B. and Bowen, D.E. (1995) *Winning the Service Game.* Watertown, MA: Harvard Business School Press.

Schor, J. (2000) *Do Americans Shop Too Much?* Boston, MA: Beacon.

Schuler, R. and Jackson, S. (1987) 'Linking competitive strategy with human resource management', *The Academy of Management Executive*, 1(3): 207–19.

Scotsman (2008) 'Style mile to raise profile of city centre', 11 June, p. 7.

Sedivy, J. and Carlson, G. (2011) *Sold on Language.* London: Wiley.

Shaw, G.B. (2010 [1916]) *Pygmalion.* Camberwell: Penguin.

Shilling, C. (1996) *The Body and Social Theory.* London: Sage.

Shilling, C. (2007) 'Sociology and the body: classical traditions and new agendas', *Sociological Review*, 55(S1): 1–18.

Sierminska, E. (2015) 'Does it pay to be beautiful?', *IZA World of Labour*, 161(June): 1–10.

Silverman, G. (2017) 'A death in Alabama exposes the American factory dream', *Financial Times*, 5 February. Available at: www.ft.com/content/54d05c3e-e9fa-11e6-893c-082c54a7f539 (accessed 2 February 2020).

Simorangkir, D. (2013) 'Lookism in Indonesia's public relations industry', *Women Studies International Forum*, 40(September/October): 111–20.

Slavishak, E. (2010) '"Made by the work": a century of laboring bodies in the United States', in L.J. Moore and M. Kosut (eds), *The Body Reader*. New York: New York University Press, pp. 147–63.

Soderlund, M. and Julander, C. (2009) 'Physical attractiveness of the new service worker in the moment of truth and its effect on customer satisfaction', *Journal of Retailing and Consumer Services*, 16(3): 216–26.

Solomon, M. (1985) 'Packaging the service provider', *Service Industries Journal*, 5(1): 64–72.

Solomon, M. (1986) 'Dressed for effect', *Psychology Today*, April: 20–8.

Spillane, M. (2000) *Branding Yourself: How to Look, Sound and Behave Your Way to Success*. London: Pan.

Sprague, K. (2018) 'Express yourself: Walmart introduces relaxed dress guidelines in stores'. Available at: https://blog.walmart.com/business/20180530/express-yourself-walmart-introduces-relaxed-dress-guidelines-in-stores (accessed 12 February 2020).

Stephen, R. and Zweigenhaft , R.L. (2001) 'The effect on tipping of a waitress touching male and female customers', *Journal of Social Psychology*, 126(1): 141–42.

Stinchcombe, A. (1959) 'Bureaucratic and craft administration of production: a comparative study', *Administrative Science Quarterly*, 4(2): 168–87.

Sulaiman, T. (2005) 'City boys pay handsomely to look good', *The Times*, 7 November. Available at: www.timesonline.co.uk/tol/news/uk/article587439.ece (accessed 12 February 2020).

Swanger, N. (2006) 'Visible body modification (VBM): evidence from human resource managers and recruiters and the effects on employment', *International Journal of Hospitality Management*, 25(1): 154–58.

Sweet, M. (1997) 'A dash of Armani with your soup?', *Independent on Sunday*, 9 March, p. 3

Szymanski, D. and Feltman, C. (2015) 'Linking sexually objectifying work environment among waitresses to psychological and job related outcomes', *Psychology of Women Quarterly*, 39(3): 390–404.

Talbot, M. (2015) 'Abercrombie's legal defeat – and its cultural failure'. Available at: www newyorker.com/news/daily-comment/abercrombie-fitch-samantha-elauf-discrimination supreme-court (accessed 12 February 2020).

Taylor, F.W. (1947[1911]) *The Principles of Scientific Management*. New York: Norton.

Taylor, P. and Anderson, P. (2008) *Contact Centres in Scotland – The 2008 Audit*. Report for Scottish Enterprise/Scottish Development International, University of Strathclyde.

Taylor, P. and Bain, P. (1999) '"An assembly line in the head": work and employee relations in the call centre', *Industrial Relations Journal*, 30(2): 101–17.

Taylor, P. and Bain, P. (2005) 'India calling to the faraway towns: the call centre labour process and globalization', *Work, Employment and Society*, 19(2): 262–81.

Taylor, P. and Connelly, L. (2009) 'Before the disaster: health, safety and working conditions at a plastics factory', *Work, Employment and Society*, 23(1): 160–8.

Taylor, S. (1998) 'Emotional labour and the new workplace', in P. Thompson and C. Warhurst (eds), *Workplaces of the Future*. London: Macmillan, pp. 84–103.

Terkel, S. (1972) *Working*. New York: Avon Books.

Thompson, P. (1983) *The Nature of Work: An Introduction to Debates in the Labour Process*. Basingstoke: Macmillan.

Thompson, P. and Smith, C. (2001) 'Follow the redbrick road: reflections on pathways in and out of the labor process debate', *International Studies of Management and Organization*, 30(4): 40–67.

Thompson, P. and Smith, C. (eds) (2010) *Working Life*. Basingstoke: Palgrave Macmillan.

Thompson, P. and Vincent, S. (2010) 'Labour process theory and critical realism', in P. Thompson and C. Smith (eds), *Working Life*. Basingstoke: Palgrave Macmillan, pp. 47–70.

Thompson, P. and Warhurst, C. (1998) 'Hands, hearts and minds: changing work and workers at the end of the century', in P. Thompson and C. Warhurst (eds), *Workplaces of the Future*, London: Macmillan, pp. 1–24.

Thornton, P. (1999) 'Scent of cut grass to soothe air travellers', *Independent*, 27 January. Available at: www.independent.co.uk/news/scent-of-cut-grass-to-soothe-air-travellers-1076486.html (accessed 12 February 2020).

Tietje, L. and Cresap, S. (2005) 'Is lookism unjust? The ethics of aesthetics and public policy implications', *Journal of Libertarian Studies*, 19(2): 31–50.

Times Higher Education (THE) (2008) 'Top 10 academic bestsellers: Blackwell, London WC2', 6 November, p. 49.

Timming, A. (2015) 'Visible tattoos in the service sector: a new challenge to recruitment and selection', *Work, Employment and Society*, 29(1): 60–78.

Timming, A. (2017a) 'Body art as branded labour: at the intersection of employee selection and relationship marketing', *Human Relations*, 70(9): 1041–63.

Timming, A. (2017b) 'The effect of foreign accent on employability: a study of the aural dimensions of aesthetic labour in customer-facing and non-customer facing jobs', *Work, Employment and Society*, 31(3): 409–28.

Timming, A., Nickson, D., Re, D. and Perrett, D. (2017) 'What do you think of my ink? Assessing the effects of body art on employment chances', *Human Resource Management*, 56(1): 133–49.

Topham, G. (2019) 'Virgin Atlantic drops mandatory makeup for female cabin crew', *Guardian*, 4 March. Available at: www.theguardian.com/business/2019/mar/04/virgin-atlantic-drops-mandatory-makeup-for-female-cabin-crew (accessed 2 February 2020).

Topping, A. (2018) 'Sexual harassment rampant in hospitality industry, survey finds', *Guardian*, 24 January. Available at: www.theguardian.com/world/2018/jan/24/sexual-harassment-rampant-hospitality-industry-unite-survey-finds (accessed 2 February 2020).

Trades Union Congress (TUC) (2018) *Not Part of the Job: Young Workers' Experiences of Third Party Harassment.* Available at: www.tuc.org.uk/sites/default/files/NotPartoftheJob.pdf (accessed 2 February 2020).

Tran, M. (2011) 'Utter perfection', *Guardian*, Work section, 2 April, p. 3.

Tsaur, S. and Tang, W. (2013) 'The burden of aesthetic labour on front line employees in the hospitality industry', *International Journal of Hospitality Management*, 35(December), 19–27.

Tsaur, S., Luoh, H. and Syue, S. (2015) 'Positive emotions and behavioural intentions of customers in full service restaurants: does aesthetic labour matter?', *International Journal of Hospitality Management*, 51(October): 115–26.

Turner, B. (1996) *The Body and Society*. London: Sage.

Turok, I. and Bailey, N. (2004) 'Glasgow's recent trajectory: partial recovery and its consequences', in D. Newlands, M. Damson and J. McCarthy (eds), *Divided Scotland? The Nature, Causes and Consequences of Economic Disparities Within Scotland*. Farnham. Ashgate, pp. 35–59.

Turok, I., Bailey, N., Atkinson, R., Bramley, G., Docherty, I., Gibb, K., Goodlad, R., Hastings, A., Kintrea, K., Kirk, K., Leibovitz, J., Lever, B., Morgan, J., Paddisin, R. and Sterling, R. (2003) *Twin Track Cities?*, Department of Urban Studies, University of Glasgow/School of Planning and Housing, Heriot-Watt University.

Tyler, M. and Taylor, S. (1998) 'The exchange of aesthetics: women's work and "The Gift" *Gender, Work and Organization*, 5(3): 165–71.

UK Hospitality (2018) *The Economic Contribution of the British Hospitality Industry*. Available at www.ukhospitality.org.uk/page/EconomicContributionoftheUKHospitalityIndustry2018 (accessed 12 February 2020).

UNITE HERE Local 1 (2016) *Hands Off Pants On. Sexual Harassment in Chicago's Hospitality Industry*. Available at: www.handsoffpantson.org/ (accessed 12 February 2020).

van den Berg, M. and Arts, J. (2019) 'The aesthetics of work-readiness: aesthetic judgements and pedagogies for conditional welfare and Post-Fordist labour markets', *Work Employment and Society*, 33(2): 298–313.

Van Maanen, J. (1990) 'The smile factory: work at Disneyland', in P. Frost, L. Moore and M. Louis (eds), *Reframing Organizational Culture*. Newbury Park, CA: Sage, pp. 58–76.

Veblen, T. (1994[1899]) *The Theory of the Leisure Class*. New York: Penguin.

Vernon, P. (2005) 'Best bar none', *Observer*, Escape section, 27 February, pp. 2–3.

Viprey, M. (2002) 'New anti-discrimination law adopted'. Available at: www.eurofound europa.eu/publications/article/2002/new-anti-discrimination-law-adopted (accessed February 2020).

Walls, S. (2007) 'Are You Being Served? Gendered Aesthetics Among Retail Workers', PhD thesis, Durham University. *Available at:* http://etheses.dur.ac.uk/2446/ (accessed April 2020).

Walter, N. (2010) *Living Dolls*. London: Virago.

Walters, K. (2016) 'Mall models: how Abercrombie & Fitch sexualizes its retail workers', *Sexualization, Media, and Society*, 2(2): 1–5.

Walters, K. (2018) '"They'll go with the lighter": tri-racial aesthetic labor in clothing retail', *Sociology of Race and Ethnicity*, 4(1): 128–41.

Walters, S. (2008) 'Osborne's speech lessons … to sound less posh', *Daily Mail*. Available at: www.dailymail.co.uk/news/article-1086207/Osbornes-speech-lessons--sound-posh. html (accessed 13 February 2020).

Wang, L. (2016) 'When the customer is king: employment discrimination as customer service', *Virginia Journal of Social Policy and the Law*, 23(3): 249–92.

Wang, Y. and Lang, C. (2019) 'Service employee dress: effects on employee-customer interactions and customer-brand relationship at full service restaurants', *Journal of Retail and Consumer Services*, 50(September): 1–9.

Ward, D. (2000) 'Scousers put the accent on success', *Guardian*, 22 September, p. 6.

Warhurst, C. (1997) 'Political economy and the social organization of economic activity: a synthesis of neo-institutional and labour process analyses', *Competition and Change*, 2(2): 213–46.

Warhurst, C. (1998) 'Recognizing the possible: the organization and control of a socialist labour process', *Administrative Science Quarterly*, 43(2): 470–97.

Warhurst, C., Hall, R. and van den Broek, D. (2020) 'Legislating against Lookism in Australia' in A. Broadbridge and S. Saunders (eds), *Appearance in the Workplace: Impact on Career Development*.

Warhurst, C. and Nickson, D. (2001) *Looking Good, Sounding Right: Style Counselling and the Aesthetics of the New Economy*. London: Industrial Society.

Warhurst, C. and Nickson, D. (2007a) 'Employee experience of aesthetic labour in retail and hospitality', *Work, Employment and Society*, 21(1): 103–20.

Warhurst, C. and Nickson, D. (2007b) 'A new labour aristocracy? Aesthetic labour and routine interactive service', *Work, Employment and Society*, 21(4): 785–98.

Warhurst, C. and Nickson, D. (2009) '"Who's got the look?": emotional, aesthetic and sexualized labour in interactive services', *Gender, Work and Organization*, 16(3): 385–404.

Warhurst, C., Nickson, D., Witz, A. and Cullen, A. M. (2000) 'Aesthetic labour in interactive service work: some case study evidence from the 'New' Glasgow', *Service Industries Journal*, 20(3): 1–18.

Warhurst, C., Thompson, P. and Nickson, D. (2009) 'Labour process theory: putting the materialism back into the meaning of services', in M. Korczynski and C. Macdonald (eds), *Service Work: Critical Perspectives*. London: Routledge, pp. 91–112.

Warhurst, C., Tilly, C. and Gatta, M. (2017) 'A new social construction of skill', in C. Warhurst, K. Mayhew, D. Finegold and J. Buchanan (eds), *Oxford Handbook of Skills and Training*. Oxford: Oxford University Press, pp. 72–91.

Warhurst, C., van den Broek, D., Hall, D. and Nickson, D. (2009) 'Lookism: the new frontier of employment discrimination', *Journal of Industrial Relations*, 51(1) 131–36.

Warhurst C., van den Broek, D., Nickson, D. and Hall, R. (2012) 'Great expectations: gender, looks and lookism at work', *International Journal of Work, Organization and Emotion*, 5(1): 72–90.

Waring, P. (2011) 'Keeping up appearances: aesthetic labour and discrimination law', *Journal of Industrial Relations*, 53(2): 193–207.

Waters, H. and Graf, M. (2018) *America's Obesity Crisis: The Health and Economic Costs of Excess Weight*. Available at: https://assets1b.milkeninstitute.org/assets/Publication/ResearchReport/PDF/Mi-Americas-Obesity-Crisis-WEB.pdf (accessed 13 February 2020).

Watts, G. (2000) 'It's not what you say … it's the way that you say it', *Sunday Herald*, 15 October, p. 26.

Waudby, B. and Poulston, J. (2017) 'Sexualization and harassment in hospitality workplaces: who is responsible?', *International Journal of Culture, Tourism and Hospitality Research*, 11(4): 483-99.

Weaver, M. and France-Presse, A. (2019) 'Women submit petition against high heels rule in Japanese workplaces', *Guardian*, 4 June, p. 4.

Weggeman, M., Lammers, I. and Akkermans, H. (2007) 'Aesthetics from a design perspective', *Journal of Organizational Change Management*, 20(3): 346–58.

Weinswig, D. (2017) 'Global male grooming market', Coresight Research. Available at: https://coresight.com/research/deep-dive-global-male-grooming-market/ (accessed 6 April 2020)

Weller, S. (2007) 'Discrimination, labour markets and the labour market prospects of older workers: what can a legal case teach us?', *Work, Employment and Society*, 21(3): 417–37

Wellington, C. and Bryson, J. (2001) 'At face value? Image consultancy, emotional labour and professional work', *Sociology*, 35(4): 933–46.

Wengrow, D. (2001) 'The evolution of simplicity: aesthetic labour and social change in the Neolithic Near East', *Archeology and Aesthetics*, 33(2): 168–88.

Westwood, A. (2004) *Me, Myself and Work*. London: Work Foundation.

Westwood, A. and Nathan, M. (2002) *Manchester: Ideopolis? Developing a Knowledge Capital* London: Work Foundation.

White, D. and Nugent, E. (1999) 'Wanted: hard workers (but not if you're ugly)', *Daily Record*, 10 November, p. 16.

White, E. and Lane, D. (2008) 'Just one look', *Caterer and Hotelkeeper*, 3 April, pp. 39–40.

Whitehead, K. (2016) 'Empowering or embarrassing? Hooters on defensive ahead o Hong Kong launch', *South China Morning Post*, 22 June. Available at: www.scmp.com lifestyle/food-drink/article/1978489/empowering-or-embarrassing-hooters-defensive ahead-hong-kong (accessed 13 February 2020).

Williams, C. and Connell, C. (2010), '"Looking good and sounding right": aesthetic labour and social inequality in the retail industry', *Work and Occupations*, 37(3): 349–77.

Williams, R. (1990) *Keywords*. London: Fontana.

Willis, D. (2011) '10 of the best budget hotels in London', *Guardian Travel*, 6 May. Available at: www.guardian.co.uk/travel/2011/may/06/top-10-budget-hotels-london (accessed 13 February 2020).

Willis, P. (1977) *Learning to Labour*. Westmead: Saxon House.

Willment, N. (2019) 'Geographies of aesthetic labour and the creative work of grime DJs', *Geography Compass*, 13(5): e12439, 1–11.

Wilson, E. (2016) 'Matching up: producing proximal service in a Los Angeles restaurant', *Research in the Sociology of Work*, 29: 99–124.

Wilson, E. (2018a) 'Stuck behind the kitchen doors? Assessing the work prospects of latter-generation Latino workers in a Los Angeles restaurant', *Ethnic and Racial Studies*, 41(2): 210–28.

Wilson, E. (2018b) 'Bridging the service divide: dual labour niches and embedded opportunities in restaurant work', *RSF: The Russell Sage Foundation Journal of Social Sciences*, 4(1): 115–27.

Windolf, P. and Wood, S. (1988) *Recruitment and Selection in the Labour Market: A Comparative Study of Britain and West Germany*. Aldershot: Avebury.

Wiseman, E. (2018) 'They told me I was too fat', *Observer Magazine*, 28 January, pp. 12–15.

Wissinger, E. (2012) 'Managing the semiotics of skin tone: race and aesthetic labour in the fashion modelling industry', *Economic and Industrial Democracy*, 33(1): 125–43.

Witz, A., Warhurst, C. and Nickson, D. (2003) 'The labour of aesthetics and the aesthetics of organization', *Organization*, 10(1): 33–54.

Wolff, C. (2015) *Dress Code Survey 2015*, XpertHR.

Wolkowitz, C. (2002) 'The social relations of body work', *Work, Employment and Society*, 16(3): 497–510.

Wolkowitz, C. (2006) *Bodies at Work*. London: Sage.

Wolkowitz, C. and Warhurst, C. (2010) 'Embodying labour', in P. Thompson and C. Smith (eds), *Working Life*. London: Palgrave Macmillan, pp. 223–43.

Wright, D. (2005) 'Commodifying respectability: distinctions at work in the bookshop', *Journal of Consumer Culture*, 5(3): 295–314.

Wu, L., King, C., Lu, L. and Guchait, P. (2019) 'Hospitality aesthetic labour management: consumers' and prospective employees' perspectives of hospitality brands', *International Journal of Hospitality Management*, https://doi.org/10.1016/j.ijhm.2019.102373.

Yagil, D. (2008) 'When the customer is wrong: a review of research on aggression and sexual harassment in service encounters', *Aggression and Violent Behavior*, 13(2): 141–52.

Yeung, R. (2014) *Answering Tough Interview Questions for Dummies* (2nd edn). Chichester: Wiley.

Younge, G. (1997) ''Ow to talk yourself out of a job', *Guardian*, 2 January, p. 5.

Zeitlin, M. (2015) 'Abercrombie says farewell to its shirtless men and sexy vibes'. Available at: www.buzzfeednews.com/article/matthewzeitlin/abercrombie-says-goodbye-to-its-shirt-less-men (accessed 7 April 2020).

Zhang, T. (2016) 'From China to the big top: Chinese acrobats and the politics of aesthetic labour 1950–2010', *International Labour and Working Class History*, 89(Spring): 40–63.

INDEX

Note: Page numbers in *italic* type refer to figures and tables.

s